S0-ACK-824

Democracy for the Few

Democracy for the Few

Michael Parenti
THE JAMES ALLEN COLLEGIATE CENTER
STATE UNIVERSITY OF NEW YORK AT ALBANY

St. Martin's Press
NEW YORK

CARL A. RUDISILL LIBRARY
LENOIR RHYNE COLLEGE

320.973
P21d
91641
Jan. 1975

Library of Congress Catalog Card Number: 74-75043
Copyright © 1974 by St. Martin's Press, Inc.
All Rights Reserved.
Manufactured in the United States of America.
For information, write: St. Martin's Press, Inc.,
175 Fifth Avenue, New York, N.Y. 10010

AFFILIATED PUBLISHERS: Macmillan Limited, London—
also at Bombay, Calcutta, Madras and Melbourne.

Original artwork by Warren Linn

To Samuel Hendel and Clara Hendel

Acknowledgments

I wish to thank Peter Bachrach, Philip Meranto and Peter Schwab for reading early portions of the manuscript and giving me the necessary criticisms and encouragements. My thanks also go to Catherine MacKinnon and Richard Warner for making valuable critiques of the entire final draft, and to Douglas Rosenberg for helpful discussions on several questions treated here. An expression of appreciation is owed to Lyman Jay Gould, Garrison Nelson and Alan Wertheimer for generously providing me with ideas and information drawn from their own ongoing research. I might add that Jay Gould's guidance proved downright essential in the writing of the chapter on the Supreme Court, although he is not responsible for and might not agree with every word in it.

At St. Martin's Press, Barry Rossinoff provided that blend of tactful but firm criticism and support which is the mark of a gifted editor. Thomas Broadbent, Judy Green and the production staff at St. Martin's also have my appreciation for their assistance. Most of all, Cheryl Smalley lived through this entire effort with me, providing information from her own field experiences, helping me track down research sources, spending long hours discussing the ideas of this book, and reading and working over each page. She deserves a special expression of gratitude as that indispensable other without whom the feat could not have been accomplished.

Finally I would like to mention one of the very nicest and best teams in the academic world: Clara and Samuel Hendel. Their friendship and support, extending back over many years, have helped me in ways that go beyond the confines of scholarship. In return they have my lasting appreciation and the dedication of this book.

Contents

Democracy for the Few

The Study of Politics

1

THIS BOOK EXPLORES HOW THE AMER-
ican political system operates. American government as portrayed in most textbooks bears
little resemblance to American government
as practiced by the men who rule this country.
What most of us are taught in secondary school
might be summarized as follows:

(a) The United States was founded by
men dedicated to building a nation for the
good of all its citizens. A Constitution was
fashioned to divide authority and check potential abuses of power. Over the generations it
has proven to be a "living document" which,
through reinterpretation and amendment, has
served us well.

(b) The nation's political leaders, the
President and the Congress, are for the most
part responsive to the popular will. The
people's desires are registered through periodic elections, political parties and a free
press. Decisions are made by small groups of
persons within the various circles of government, but these decision-makers are kept in
check by each other's power and by their need
to satisfy the electorate in order to remain in
office. The people do not rule but they select
those who do. Thus government decisions are
grounded in majority rule—subject to the restraints imposed by the Constitution for the
protection of minority rights.

(c) The United States is a nation of many
different social, economic, ethnic and regional
groups, which make varied and competing
demands on public officeholders. The role of
government is to act as a mediator of these

1

conflicting demands, attempting to formulate policies that offer the greatest good for the greatest number while trying not to hurt any particular interest too much. Most decisions are compromises that seldom satisfy all interested parties but usually allow for a working consensus. In this way everyone can have a say and no particular interest chronically dominates.

(d) These institutional arrangements have given us a government of laws and not of men, one which is far from perfect but which allows for a high degree of popular participation and a slow but steady advance toward a better life for all.

Allowing for some sophisticated amplifications, this interpretation remains the version many students are exposed to in college.

Up from Innocence

Recently, however, many of us have begun to question whether the American political system works as described above. With the persistence of poverty, urban decay, unemployment, inflation, overseas military interventions, gargantuan defense budgets, transportation crises, environmental devastation, deficient but increasingly expensive health care, poor consumer and worker protection, increasing taxes, a growing national debt, widespread crime in the streets and in high public places—with the persistence and sometimes worsening of these social problems, many of us find it increasingly difficult to believe that "every day, in every way, we get better and better," as some people would have it. The suspicion arises that the interests of many or even most people are not served by the political process.

The central theme here is that our government represents the privileged few rather than the needy many and that elections, political parties and the right to speak out are seldom effective measures against the influences of corporate wealth. The laws of our polity operate chiefly with undemocratic effect—first, because they are written principally to protect the haves against the claims of the have-nots and, second, because even if equitable in appearance, they usually are enforced in highly discriminatory ways. Furthermore, it will be argued that this democracy for the few is not a product of the venality of officeholders as such but a reflection of how the resources of power are distributed within the entire politico-economic system. The chapters ahead treat such topics as America's dominant value system, the structure of the corporate economy, the outputs of public policy, the role of the mass media, the uses of law and the order it imposes and the functions and effects of voting, elections, political parties, pressure groups, the Constitution, Congress, the presidency, the courts and the federal bureaucracy.

At no time is it pretended that what is offered here represents all that could be said about these subjects. I have purposely omitted discussion of aspects that contribute little to our understanding of why political reality is what it is. Many subject areas have been treated only in passing, if at all, because of the limits of space and because any attempt to cover every possible aspect of a subject leaves us saying too little about too much. The selection of topics here is guided by my understanding of what are the important questions: Who governs in the United States? Who gets what, when and how? Who pays and in what ways?

The Inescapability of Politics

The "political system," as the term is used in the pages ahead, refers to the executive, legislative and judicial institutions of government along with the political parties, elections, laws, lobbyists and private-interest groups that affect public policy. One of the conclusions of this book is that the distinction between what is "public" and what is "private" is often an artificial one. Public agencies are heavily penetrated with the influences of private-interest groups. And there are private groups, like some defense companies, that depend completely on the public treasure for their funding, contracts, profits and survival.

The political decisions made by government are called "policy" decisions. One characteristic of policy decisions is that they are seldom, if ever, neutral. They almost always benefit some interests more than others, and they entail social costs that are rarely equally distributed. The shaping of a budget, the passage of a piece of legislation and the development of an administrative program are all policy decisions, all *political* decisions, and there is no way to execute them with neutral effects. If the wants and demands of all persons could be automatically and universally satisfied, there would be no need for discrimination and selectivity, no need to set priorities and give some interests precedence over others—indeed, no need for policies or politics as the words have just been used.

Political things are not just those bearing directly upon the decision-making process but also those that relate to the dynamics of power, group interest and class interest. The way prisons and mental institutions are run, for instance, is not only an administrative matter but a political one, involving the application of a particular ideology about normality, authority and social control and involving both the protection of certain interests and values and the suppression of others.[1]

"Politics" can be used in something other than the interest-group sense. Among radicals, for instance, "politics" signifies not only the competition among groups within the present system but also the struggle to change the entire politico-economic structure, not only the desire to achieve predefined ends but the struggle to redefine ends. For the radical, politics is a process of confrontation and education designed to change consciousness by exposing the injustices of the capitalist system and posing alternatives to it.[2]

Politics under the existing system covers every kind of issue from abortion practices to school prayers, but the bulk of public policy is concerned with economic matters. The most important document the government produces each year is the budget. Probably the two most important functions of government are taxing and spending. Certainly they are necessary conditions for everything else it does, whether it be delivering the mail or making war. The very structure of our government reflects the close involvement the state has with the economy: thus one finds the Departments of Commerce, Labor, Agriculture, Interior, Transportation and Treasury, and the Federal Trade Commission, the National Labor Relations Board, the Interstate Commerce Commission, the Federal Communications Commission, the Securities and Exchange Commission, etc. Most of the committees in Congress can be identified according to their economic functions, the most important having to do with taxing and appropriations.

1. See the section in Chapter Eight entitled "Psycho-controls for Law and Order."

2. However, radicals will frequently engage in political struggles for immediate goals—for instance, supporting the lettuce and grape boycotts led by the United Farm Workers. They do this because they are interested in alleviating the plight of oppressed people even if only in marginal ways. Also they want to strengthen the position of the underdog for further challenges and demonstrate to people that there are ways of fighting back. Even when running their own candidates, most radicals see the campaign primarily as a way of alerting voters to the evasive and deceptive qualities of the major candidates and creating a dialogue that goes beyond mainstream politics.

If so much of this study of American government seems concerned with politico-economic matters, it is because that's what government is mostly about. Nor should this relationship between politics and economics be surprising. Economics is concerned with the allocation of scarce resources and outputs among competing ends, involving conflicts between social classes and groups within classes. Much of politics is a carry-over of this same struggle. Both economics and politics deal with questions affecting the material survival, prosperity and well-being of millions of people; both deal with the first conditions of social life itself.

One of the central propositions of this book is that there exists a close relationship between political power and economic wealth. By *power* I mean the ability to get what one wants, either by having one's interests prevail in conflicts with others or by preventing others from raising conflicting demands at all. Power presumes the ability to control the actions and choices of others either through favor, fear, fraud or force and to manipulate the political environment in ways that serve one's own interests. Power belongs to those who possess the resources which enable them to control the choices and behavior of others. Among the resources of power one might list such things as jobs, organization, manpower, publicity, media communication, social legitimacy, expertise, essential goods and services and—the ingredient that often determines the availability of these resources—money.

Many political scientists have managed to skirt the whole question of the relationship between power and wealth, treating the corporate giants, if at all, as if they were but one of a number of interest groups. Most often this evasion is accomplished by labeling any approach which links class, wealth and capitalism to politics as "Marxist." To be sure, Marx saw such a relationship, but so did more conservative theorists like Hobbes, Locke, John Harrington, Adam Smith and, in America, Hamilton, Adams, Madison, Otis, Webster. Indeed, just about every theorist and practitioner of politics in the seventeenth, eighteenth and early nineteenth centuries saw the linkage between political organization and economic interest, and between state and class, as not only real but *desirable* and of primary importance to the well-being of the polity. "Those who own the land shall govern it," declared John Jay. A permanent check over the populace should be exercised by "the rich and the well-born," urged Alexander Hamilton.

The difference between Marx and most of the theorists before him is that he was one of the first in the modern era to see the relationship between property and power as *un*desirable, and this was the unforgiveable sin. Marx wrote during the mid-to-late-nineteenth century, when large numbers of people were becoming increasingly critical of the abuses of industrial capitalism and when those who owned the wealth of society preferred to direct attention away from the whole question. The desire to ignore the relationship between private wealth and public power and confine one's attention to more "respectable" and safer subjects persists within academic circles today. In this book we will try to confront that relationship.[3]

Repelled by the deception, venality and violence in the political world, some people have chosen to devote their attention to more private and less tainted pursuits. Yet politics remains very much a part of their lives, whether they want it that way or not. The government plays a crucial role in determining the condition of our communities—housing, education, medical care, work, recreation, transportation and natural environment. As a protector of privilege and purveyor of power, the state can bestow favors on a select few while sending many off to fight wars halfway around the world.

In ostrich-like fashion the reader might go "do his own thing," pretending that he has removed himself from the world of politics and power, but even his modes of escape will be shaped in part by the political influences that bear upon him. He can leave political life alone but it will not leave him alone. He can escape its noise and its pretensions but not some of its worst effects. One ignores the doings of the state only at one's own risk—and at the risk of one's fellow citizens, many of whom are less fortunately situated and more adversely affected by what the government does and does not do.

Rather than evade or smooth over controversial questions in the pages ahead, I will pursue certain of them. Rather than try to avoid a point of view, I will attempt to formulate one that might bring people to think critically about what they read here and elsewhere. The intent is not to provoke controversy for its own

3. See William Appleman Williams, *The Great Evasion* (Chicago: Quadrangle Books, 1964) for an analysis of the way that Marxist thought has been stigmatized or ignored by American intellectuals and those who pay their salaries. See also Sidney Fine, *Laissez-Faire and the General-Welfare State* (Ann Arbor: University of Michigan Press, 1964) for a description of capitalist, anti-Marxist orthodoxy in the United States in the late nineteenth century and its control over those in business, law, economics, university teaching and religion.

sake but to offer a realistic analysis of what is happening in American society, even at the risk of courting some heretical notions about the political life of our nation.

Wealth and Want in the United States

2

IF POLITICS IS CONCERNED WITH WHO gets what, we might begin by considering who's already got what. How are social benefits, wealth and economic power distributed in the United States? The answer to this question will tell us something about both the justice of the capitalist politico-economic system and the relative power and efficacy of various interests within it.[1]

The Distribution of Want

Many Americans are of the opinion that our country is a land of wealth and well-being. But when we turn from the self-congratulatory pronouncements of politicians and businessmen and scrutinize the facts, we discover there is not much cause for celebration. The life expectancy of men in the United States is lower than in eighteen other countries. The infant mortality rate in the United States is worse than in thirteen other countries. In eleven countries, women have a better chance to live through childbirth than in the United

1. By *capitalism* I mean that system of production and ownership found in most Western countries and Japan which manifests two essential conditions: (1) the means of production, specifically the factories, mills, mines, utilities, offices, banks, etc., are under private ownership; (2) their primary function is to make money for those who own them. Terms like *corporate capitalism, corporatism, corporate system* and *monopoly capitalism* refer herein to modern-day capitalism; they point out that economic power is embodied in a relatively small number of large corporations.

States.[2] Millions of Americans live in crowded, dilapidated, poorly ventilated, ill-heated and hazardous domiciles. Millions more who identify themselves as middle class live in overpriced, poorly constructed, heavily mortgaged homes or in high-rent apartments that consume the better part of their incomes while providing living quarters that are far from satisfactory. Millions are immobilized by low income and inadequate or nonexistent public transportation facilities; millions have no access to recreational areas.

Almost all Americans, including better-income, middle-class people, are insufficiently protected by private health insurance against prolonged illness and hospitalization. There is an estimated shortage of 100,000 physicians, 85,000 nurses and a million health service technicians. Educational opportunities are limited according to one's ability to pay rather than one's ability to learn. The children of the sharecropper, the seasonally employed, the migrant worker, the unwed mother, the ghetto poor, the unemployed, and the disabled have little chance for getting an advanced education.

The problem of pollution continues unabated: our rivers are turned into open sewers by the millions of tons of raw industrial waste dumped into them, our air made foul by industry and automobiles, our forests and wildlife destroyed and our roadsides uglified by commercial enterprise. At the same time, our cities are showing serious signs of decay and social demoralization. Perhaps symptomatic of our social malaise is the high incidence of violent crime and heroin addiction, especially among the more economically deprived classes.

Almost 80 million Americans live in conditions of need on incomes that have been estimated as below minimum adequacy by the Department of Labor. Of these about half are designated as living in acute poverty and want. Of the 40 million who are very poor, only 5.4 million get either food stamps or free food. Of 6 million school children from rock-bottom poverty families, most attend substandard, overcrowded schools and fewer than 2 million receive either free or reduced-price school lunches.[3] The majority of the poor are Whites, a fact which is not surprising in a country with a White population of more than 85 percent. Yet the

2. Samuel Shapiro et al., *Infant, Prenatal, Maternal and Childhood Mortality in the United States* (Cambridge, Mass.: Harvard University Press, 1968) and Erwin Knoll, "The Coming Struggle for National Health Insurance," *Progressive*, December 1969, p. 30.

3. See *Hunger, U.S.A.*, a report by the Citizens' Board of Inquiry into Hunger and Malnutrition in the United States (Boston: Beacon Press, 1968).

non-White racial minorities are represented in disproportionate numbers. If Black people compose only about 12 percent of the population, they make up something closer to 45 percent of those below the officially designated poverty level. (Statistics like these are usually distorted in a way that underestimates the number of poor, and of Black poor in particular, being based on a national census that drastically undercounts transients, homeless people and those living in crowded urban ghettos. In April 1973 the Census Bureau reported that the 1970 census had missed counting an estimated 5.3 million people, a disproportionate number being poor and Black.)

Some Americans believe that poverty is a relative category and that those described as "poor" in the United States would be considered fairly well-off in Third World nations. In his early study of poverty, Michael Harrington opined that the poor in this country were "not impoverished in the same sense as those [in] poor nations where millions cling to hunger as a defense against starvation. This country has escaped such extremes."[4] More recent studies show that the United States has not escaped such extremes. Hunger and infant mortality are as prevalent in certain counties of America as in places like Turkey or Pakistan. The Citizens' Board of Inquiry into Hunger and Malnutrition discovered in 1968 that as many as half of the very poor suffer from acute conditions of malnutrition and hunger. These conditions were not confined to any one area like the Mississippi delta but could be found in Texas, Wisconsin, New Hampshire, Maine, Iowa, New York, Illinois, Massachusetts, California, Alaska, Appalachia, in rural areas, in small towns and in every large city.

Some 12 million Americans do not get enough to eat, according to a report made in 1973 by a Senate select committee. The Citizens' Board found that large numbers of infants died within the first two years of life because of starvation. Malnourished mothers failed to lactate and could not nurse their infants. Protein deficiencies in early infancy caused permanent brain damage and vulnerability to serious diseases. "Mother after mother in region after region reported that the cupboard was bare, sometimes at the beginning and throughout the month, sometimes only in the last week of the month."[5] Teachers reported that children came to school too hungry to learn and sometimes in such pain that they had to be taken home. Younger

4. Michael Harrington, *The Other America: Poverty in the United States* (Baltimore: Penguin Books, 1963), p. 9.
5. *Hunger, U.S.A.*, p. 9.

children regularly went to bed hungry, never knowing the taste of milk.

Children who live in chronic hunger, according to Dr. Robert Coles, "become tired, petulant, suspicious and finally apathetic." Malnourished four- and five-year-olds, he noted, experience the aches of the body as more than just a physical fact of life. They interpret such misery as a judgment made by the outside world upon them and their families, a judgment that causes them to reflect upon their own worth.

They ask themselves and others what they have done to be kept from the food they want or what they have done to deserve the pain they seem to feel. . . .

All one has to do is ask some of these children in Appalachia who have gone north to Chicago and Detroit to draw pictures and see the way they will sometimes put food in the pictures. . . . All one has to do is ask them what they want, to confirm the desires for food and for some kind of medical care for the illnesses that plague them.[6]

The well-known Field Foundation report by a team of doctors investigating rural poverty in 1967 is worth quoting at length:

In child after child we saw: evidence of vitamin and mineral deficiencies; serious untreated skin infestation and ulcerations; eye and ear diseases, also unattended bone diseases secondary to poor food intake; the prevalence of bacterial and parasitic disease as well as severe anemia, with resulting loss of energy and ability to live a normally active life; diseases of the heart and lungs—requiring surgery—which have gone undiagnosed and untreated; epileptic and other neurological disorders; severe kidney ailments, that in other children would warrant immediate hospitalization; and finally, in boys and girls in every county we visited, obvious evidence of severe malnutrition with injury to the body's tissues—its muscles, bones, and skin as well as an associated psychological state of fatigue, listlessness, and exhaustion.

We saw children afflicted with chronic diarrhea, chronic sores, chronic leg and arm (untreated) injuries and deformities. We saw homes without running water . . . with germ-bearing mosquitoes and flies everywhere around. We saw homes with children who are lucky to eat one meal a day—and that one inadequate so far as vitamins, minerals, or protein is concerned. We saw children who don't get to drink milk, don't get to eat fruit, green vegetables, or meat. They live on starches—grits, bread, Kool Aid. Their parents may be declared ineligible for commodities, ineligible for the food stamp program, even though they have literally nothing. We saw children fed communally—that is, by neigh-

6. Quoted in *ibid*., pp. 31–32.

bors who give scraps of food to children whose own parents have nothing to give them.[7]

In the United States today, people living in shacks on the outskirts of cities like New Orleans scavenge the dumps, eating and surviving on the garbage they find. In some communities people band together to share the little food they have. Many, despite prolonged illness and destitution, cannot get on welfare after repeated attempts. Government food programs and private charities reach only a small portion of the poor, and often not those most in need.

Poverty is a widespread condition among the elderly. One study showed that as many as 50 percent of persons sixty-five or older live on diets that fail to provide adequate protective nutrients; many of the aged "subsist on liquid foods that provide inadequate sustenance."[8] One out of every two spend their retirement in lonely, grinding poverty, unable to feed themselves properly, unable to afford needed medical and home nursing care, and unable to find decent housing or transportation that would allow them to maintain normal social relations.

Many of us have been taught that "America belongs to the people," but in fact almost all Americans are tenants, debtors, and hired hands in their own country, working for someone else, paying rent to someone else, or paying high interest rates on mortgages, loans and installment purchases to someone else. In these relationships the advantage is on the side of the employer, the landlord, the manufacturer and the bank. The boss hires us because he can make a profit from our labor; the landlord rents to us so that he can make an income on the rental; the manufacturer sells to us because he can make more wealth on his product than he put into it; and the bank or loan company extends credit so that it can get back substantially more than it lends.[9]

If Americans enjoy all "the good things that money can buy,"

7. Quoted in *ibid.*, p. 13.
8. *Ibid.*, p. 9 and p. 24.
9. A basic distinction one might make is between those who own and control the wealth, production and institutions of the society—the "owning class" or "propertied interests"—and those who do not own corporate property and who are dependent on the owning class for their employment. By this distinction, the "working class" includes not only blue-collar workers in factories and mills and on construction sites but also accountants, clerks, professors and anyone else who has a job or is trying to get one. The distinction is blurred somewhat by the range of wealth *within* both the owning and the working class. Thus while "owners" includes both the leaders of giant corporations and the struggling proprietors of small grocery stores, the latter hardly qualify as part of the *corporate* owning class

they also are burdened with many of the things they cannot afford to buy, being bombarded each year by multibillion-dollar advertising campaigns to induce them to purchase more and more of the great mountains of commodities produced by the profit-oriented consumer market. And each year they go deeper into debt. In 1945 the installment debt owed by Americans on their automobiles, television sets, clothing, furniture, fixtures and other such goods and services amounted to $2.5 billion. A decade later, in 1955, it had reached $29 billion. In 1967 the installment debt stood at $75 billion. By the early 1970s estimates were well over $100 billion. According to one conservative publication, mounting debts "are threatening a financial crackup in more and more families. . . . Excessive debt is engulfing thousands of families."[10] The interest rates charged on most sales often bring more profit to the producer than the price mark-up, thus constituting a kind of legal usury. As consumers, Americans are also victimized by shoddy products, deceptive packaging, swindling deals, and numerous other unscrupulous practices.

The history of the great "affluence" in the United States since World War II, then, is a history of people becoming increasingly entrapped as wage earners, tenants and debtors in a high-production, high-consumption, high-profit system.

Who Owns America?

About one half of one percent of the population—the part constituting the "super rich" in Lundberg's terms—controls the greater part of the corporate wealth of this country. The four top families are the Du Ponts, the Rockefellers, the Mellons and the Fords. Approximately 1.6 percent of the population own 80 percent of all stock, 100 percent of all state and municipal bonds, and 88.5 percent of corporate bonds.[11] (The concentration of

as that term is used here. In contrast, among the non-owning class are engineers, scientists, business agents, top salesmen and others who in income, life-style and perspective tend to be identified as "middle class" and apart from "ordinary workers." Then there are some movie stars, a few sports heroes, some lawyers and many doctors who earn such lavish incomes that they invest their surplus wealth and become in part, or eventually in whole, members of the owning class.

10. *U.S. News and World Report*, June 22, 1970. See also David Caplovitz, *The Poor Pay More* (New York: Free Press, 1967) for a study of how the poor are victimized as consumers and debtors.

11. Ferdinand Lundberg, *The Rich and the Super Rich* (New York: Lyle Stuart, 1968), pp. 144 ff. Also Robert Lampman, *The Share of Top Wealth-Holders in National Wealth* (Princeton, N.J.: Princeton University Press, 1962).

wealth is equally striking in other capitalist nations like Great Britain, France, West Germany and Japan.) In just about every major industry, be it oil, steel, aluminum or automotive, three or four giant companies do at least 80 percent of the business. In 1960 four corporations accounted for approximately 22 percent of all industrial research done in the United States, and some two hundred corporations for about 80 percent of all resources used in manufacturing.[12] The view that the wealth of America is in the possession of a broadly based "middle-class ownership" is not borne out by the available statistics.

While various sectors of industry are brought under centralized financial control, the public still thinks of the economy as consisting of a wide array of distinct and independent productive units. Thus we often refer to "farmers" as an interest apart from businessmen and bankers, at a time when the Bank of America has a multimillion-dollar stake in California farmlands; the Southern Pacific Railroad is a shipper to "agribusiness" and an owner of vast land acreage; Cal Pak, the world's largest canner of fruits and vegetables, operates at every level from the field to the supermarket with annual sales of over $400 million; and Hunt Foods and Industries, also with sales of over $400 million, has holdings in steel, matches and glass containers.

A notion enjoying popularity today is that the "owning class" is an obsolete concept because control of wealth has passed into the hands of corporation managers who themselves own but a small segment of the assets they command, while the corporation's actual owners, the stockholders, exercise little of the economic or political power their wealth would normally confer and have little say about the management of their own holdings. Since Berle and Means first conjured up the vision of the giant firms as developing "into a purely neutral technocracy," controlled by disinterested managers who allocated resources "on the basis of public policy rather than private cupidity,"[13] many observers have come to treat this fantasy as a reality.

Supposedly the separation of ownership from management has created a benign, service-minded corporation. In fact, the separation of ownership and management is far from complete: of the five hundred largest corporations in the United States,

12. John Kenneth Galbraith, *The New Industrial State* (New York: Houghton Mifflin, 1967), pp. 74–75.
13. A. A. Berle, Jr., and Gardner C. Means, *The Modern Corporation and Private Property* (New York: Harcourt, Brace, 1932), p. 356.

controlling ownership of some 30 percent rests in the hands of one individual or of the members of a single family. Furthermore, many of the "smaller" companies are controlled by the wealthy class in America, including "more than 25,000 family-owned or closely held corporations with assets of more than $1 million which have grown and prospered. . . ."[14] The decline of family capitalism, as Domhoff reminds us, has not led to widespread ownership among the general public. *The diffusion of stock ownership has not cut across class lines to any marked degree but has occurred within the upper class itself.* In an earlier day three families might have owned companies A, B and C respectively, whereas today all three families have large holdings in all three companies, thereby giving "the upper class an even greater community of interest than they had in the past when they were bitterly involved in protecting their standing by maintaining their individual companies."[15]

In those firms not under family control, the supposedly public-minded managers are themselves large investors in corporate America. "The managerial class is the largest single group in the stockholding population," notes Kolko, "and a greater proportion of this class owns stock than any other."[16] Managers award themselves stupendous salaries, stock options, bonuses and other benefits. The managerial elite of the top corporations are almost always wealthy men. One need only think of names like Thomas Watson, George Humphrey, David Packard, Charles Wilson and Robert McNamara (the last four also having been presidential cabinet appointees). As president of General Motors, Wilson owned GM stock worth $2.5 million; as Ford president, McNamara owned Ford stock worth $1.6 million and held Ford stock options valued at $270,000. The interest that managers have in the corporation's profits is a direct one. Far from being technocrats whose first dedication is to advance the public welfare, they represent the more active and powerful element of a self-interested owning class.[17] Their power does not rest in their individual holdings but in their corporate positions.

14. F. G. Clark and S. Ramonaczy, *Where the Money Comes From* (New York: Van Nostrand, 1961), p. 42; quoted in G. William Domhoff, *Who Rules America?* (Englewood Cliffs, N.J.: Prentice-Hall, 1967), p. 38.

15. Domhoff, *Who Rules America?*, p. 40.

16. Gabriel Kolko, *Wealth and Power in America* (New York: Praeger, 1962), p. 67.

17. For lucid discussions of these points see Ralph Miliband, *The State in Capitalist Society* (New York: Basic Books, 1969), pp. 28–36, and Paul Baran and Paul Sweezy, *Monopoly Capital* (New York: Monthly Review Press, 1968).

"Not great fortunes, but great corporations are the important units of wealth, to which individuals of property are variously attached," C. Wright Mills reminds us. "The corporation is the source of, and the basis of, the continued power and privilege of wealth."[18]

More than half of all corporate stock in America is held not by individuals but by other corporate entities. "This means," Andrew Hacker notes, "that when a vote is taken at an annual meeting, the ballots of the myriad Smiths and Joneses and Browns are joined by those of Merrill Lynch and Metropolitan Life and Ford Foundation. Individual stockholders support existing management out of habit or inertia, while institutional stockholders do so as a matter of considered policy."[19]

The Pursuit of Corporate Profit

In their book *Monopoly Capital*, Baran and Sweezy write: "The primary objectives of corporate policy—which are at the same time and inevitably the personal objectives of the corporate managers—are . . . strength, rate of growth and size. . . . Profits provide the internal funds for expansion. Profits are the sinew and muscle of strength. . . . As such they become the immediate, unique, unifying, quantitative aim of corporate success."[20] The function of the corporation, as corporation leaders themselves announce in their more candid moments, is not to perform public services or engage in philanthropy but to make money.

The social uses of the product, its effects upon communal life, personal safety, human well-being and the natural environment, win consideration in capitalist production, if at all, only to the extent that they do not violate the pecuniary interests of the producer.

This relentless pursuit of profit results from something more than just the greed of businessmen. It is an unavoidable fact of capitalist life that enterprises must expand in order to survive. To stand still amidst growth is to decline, not only relatively but absolutely. Robert Theobald concludes that business firms

18. C. Wright Mills, *The Power Elite* (New York: Oxford University Press, 1956), p. 116.
19. Andrew Hacker, *The End of the American Era* (New York: Atheneum, 1970), p. 41.
20. Baran and Sweezy, *Monopoly Capital*, pp. 39–40.

WARREN LINN

have a special interest in the fastest possible rate of growth, which may not be compatible in the long run with the interests of society. . . . The corporation's profits depend essentially on economic growth and . . . any slowing down in the rate of increase in production tends to cut into the profits of the firm. The corporation must therefore press for policies that will cause the most rapid rate of growth.[21]

One explanation as to why so many of our nation's socioeconomic problems remain unsolved or actually worsen is that most of the resources of our society are devoted to other things, to the production of goods and services for a private market. Those who insist that private enterprise can answer our needs seem to overlook the fact that private enterprise has no such interest, at least not in those areas where no profit is to be had. The poor may *need* shoes but they offer no market for shoes; there is a market only when need (or want) is coupled with *buying power* to become *demand.* The shoe manufacturer responds to market demand—that is, to a situation in which he can make money—and not to human need no matter how dire it be. When asked by the Citizens' Board what they were doing about the widespread hunger in the United States, numerous food manufacturers responded that the hungry poor were not their responsibility. As one company noted: "If we saw evidence of profitability, we might look into this."[22]

Some defenders of the established system contend that the pursuit of profit is ultimately beneficial to all since the productivity and inventiveness of the corporations create mass prosperity. This argument overlooks several things: first, high productivity frequently *detracts* from the common prosperity even while making fortunes for the few, and it not only fails to answer to certain social needs but may create new ones. The coal mining companies in Appalachia, for example, not only failed to mitigate the miseries of the people in that area; they *created* many miseries, swindling the Appalachians out of their land, underpaying them for their labor, forcing them to work under inhumane conditions, destroying their countryside and refusing to pay for any of the social costs resulting from corporate exploits.

The value of productivity rests in the social purposes to which it is directed. Is the purpose to plunder the environment,

21. Robert Theobald, *The Challenge of Abundance* (New York: American Library, 1962), p. 111.
22. *Hunger, U.S.A.*, p. 46.

fabricate endless consumer desires, pander to snobbism and acquisitiveness and grab as big a profit as one can by squeezing as much compulsive toil as possible out of workers while paying them as little as possible? Or is productivity geared to the basic needs of the populace and the collective needs of the community, including the care and preservation of the environment, and is it organized to maximize the capabilities, responsibilities and inventiveness of its workers? Capitalist productivity-for-profit seldom gives consideration to the latter set of values. What is called productivity, as measured by *quantitative* indices, may actually represent a decline in the *quality* of life—hence the relationship between the increasing quantity of automobiles and the decreasing quality of the air we breathe. Such measurements of "prosperity" offer, at best, a most haphazard accounting of many qualities of social life.

The apologists for corporate capitalism argue that the accumulation of great private fortunes is a necessary condition for economic growth—at least in a private economy—for only the wealthy can provide the huge sums needed for the capitalization of new enterprises. Yet a closer look at many important industries, from railroads to atomic energy, would suggest that much of the funding has come from the public treasury—that is, from the taxpayer—and that most of the growth capital has come from increased sales to the public—from the pockets of consumers. It is one thing to say that large-scale production requires capital accumulation but something else to presume that the only or prime source of accumulation is the purses of the rich.

In areas of private research giant corporations leave a good deal of the pioneering work to smaller businesses and individual entrepreneurs, holding back their own resources until money is to be made. Referring to electric appliances one General Electric vice-president noted: "I know of no original product invention, not even electric shavers or heating pads, made by any of the giant laboratories or corporations. . . . The record of the giants is one of moving in, buying out and absorbing the small creators."[23]

Apologists for the present system insist that big production units are more efficient than smaller ones; hence, to criticize corporations for their bigness is to oppose efficiency and progress. In fact, it is highly questionable whether the huge modern firm represents the most efficient form of production. In many instances, production units tend to become less efficient and

23. Quoted in Baran and Sweezy, *Monopoly Capital*, p. 49.

more bureaucratized with size, and after a certain point in growth there is a diminishing return in productivity. Moreover, the bigness of most modern companies is not an outgrowth of industrial productivity but a manifestation of capital accumulation in often unrelated fields.

Bigness, then, is less representative of an increasing technological efficiency than of an increasing greed. When the same giant corporation has holdings in mining, manufacturing, housing, insurance, utilities, amusement parks, publishing and communications, it becomes clear that giantism is not the result of a technological necessity that supposedly brings greater efficiency but the outcome of capital concentration. The search is not for more efficient production but for new areas of investment. Thus firms like ITT, Gulf Oil, and General Motors are today buying up great tracts of land throughout America, aware that land values have almost doubled in one decade. With control over the land, corporations are able to profit greatly in the development of residential areas.

It is said that the accumulation of great fortunes entails the taking of great risks, and these risks must be rewarded. Yet in a capitalist culture there is a tendency to overdramatize the tribulations endured by our "captains of industry" and overlook the very real hardships suffered throughout the years by the anonymous millions in rural and urban areas who have had to live under the effects of entrepreneurial decisions. During hard times, the very rich, enjoying vast reserves, suffer no deprivations to speak of in their personal lives, and in business affairs they often are able to turn the adversity of others into gain for themselves. In the depression of 1875, Morgan, Rockefeller, Gould, Carnegie, Vanderbilt, Frick and others found ample opportunity to press their advantages without stint, gathering control over the broken holdings of smaller competitors. Today, during good times and bad, giant firms rarely go bankrupt. As the steel companies have shown, they can be inefficient and still make profits. While operating at less than full capacity, at a time of high unemployment and price squeeze, U.S. Steel still showed a profit increase of 62 percent in the first quarter of 1973. For the various giants, their position in the industry and their share of the market may change slightly over the years, "but mergers and reorganizations keep the assets and production facilities intact."[24] Even if it is assumed that great profits must be

24. Hacker, *The End of the American Era*, p. 44.

the reward for great risks, in truth there is seldom much risk.

If the public welfare is at most a secondary consideration in the management of business affairs, the same may be said of the well-being of industrial production itself. One need only recall how railroads, shipping lines, mines and factories have been bought and sold like so many game pieces for the sole purpose of extracting as much profit as possible, often with little regard for maintaining the functional capacity of the firms themselves. Describing the doings of the tycoon Jay Gould, one historian noted that whenever Gould acquired a railroad "the effects of his management never wore off entirely. . . . There was never any effort to build up a strong, soundly managed group of roads. . . . The one dominant note was speculation. . . . The roads that he touched never quite recovered from his lack of knowledge and interest in sound railroading."[25] What was true then still holds today: the long-term survival, social use and functional capacity of an office, factory, farm, mine, railroad, bus line or newspaper are of less concern to the investor than the margin of profit to be had. If railroads and aeronautic firms sometimes totter on the edge of ruin, to be rescued only by generous infusions of government funds, it is usually after stockholders have collected millions in high profits.

The power of the business class is not total, "but as near as it may be said of any human power in modern times, the large businessman controls the exigencies of life under which the community lives."[26] The giant corporations wield a stupendous influence over American life. They command scarce and vital resources, the rate of technological development, the availability of livelihoods; they fix the structure of prices and set the terms and tempo of production; they decide which labor markets to explore and which to abandon; they determine the quality of goods and services and the standards of consumption and employment; they distribute their productive outputs according to principles applied mostly by themselves—dividing income among labor, management, suppliers and those political and social causes they deem worthy of support; they transform the physical and ecological environment itself, preempting the

25. R. E. Riegal, *The Story of the Western Railroads* (New York: Macmillan, 1926), cited in Matthew Josephson, *The Robber Barons* (New York: Harcourt, Brace, 1934), p. 203. Josephson offers a similar observation about Daniel Drew, p. 19.

26. Thorstein Veblen, *The Theory of Business Enterprise* (New York: New American Library Edition, n.d.), p. 8. Originally published in 1904.

natural resources of land, minerals, water and air; they command enormous surpluses while millions live in acute want. And they exercise trustee power over religious, recreational, medical and charitable institutions and over much of the content of the media and the educational system. Describing the power and scope of Standard Oil Company of New Jersey, David Horowitz writes:

It has a budget exceeding $15 billion, or double the Gross National Product of Cuba. More powerful than many sovereign states, it has 150,000 agents, organizers and hired hands operating 250 suborganizations in more than 50 countries. It is part of an international syndicate which controls the economic lifeblood of half a dozen strategic countries in the underdeveloped world. In itself it is a major political force in the key electoral states of New York, Pennsylvania, New Jersey and Texas, and it has close links with other syndicate members that are major political forces in California, Ohio, Louisiana, Indiana and elsewhere. Its agents and their associates occupied the cabinet post of Secretary of State in the Administrations of Eisenhower, Kennedy and Johnson, and at the same time had influence in the CIA and other foreign-policy-making organizations of government at the highest levels. It has its own intelligence and paramilitary networks, and a fleet of ships larger than the Greek Navy. It is not a secret organization, but it is run by a self-perpetuating oligarchy whose decisions and operations are secret. And these affect directly and significantly, the level of activity of the whole U.S. economy.[27]

Assessing the size and scope of large corporations, Theobald concludes that "in fact the actual 'political' role of business is wider than that which has been held proper for *governments* under Western [political] theory."[28]

27. David Horowitz, "Social Science or Ideology?" *Social Policy*, 1, September–October 1970, p. 30.
28. Theobald, *The Challenge of Abundance*, p. 110. Italics in the original.

The American Way

3

BEFORE INVESTIGATING THE AMERI-
can political system, we might ask: What
kind of a nation is the United States? What are
its predominant values and modes of social
organization? Although our society is composed of over 200 million persons of varying
occupational, regional, ethnic and religious
backgrounds, there are certain generalizations
one can make about its values and institutions—keeping in mind that, like most generalizations, these allow for exceptions. The
characteristics discussed in this chapter might
be considered some of the more important
facets of American society.

Who's on Top?

A remarkable but often overlooked feature of
American society is that almost all its industrial, communicational, transportational, educational, recreational and cultural institutions
are controlled by well-to-do businessmen. Industry is ruled largely by wealthy individuals
or, more commonly, by boards of directors
composed of successful businessmen. These
corporate boards meet periodically to make
the decisions on production, investment, mar-
keting and personnel.[1] In almost no instance
do the workers, the people who contribute the
labor and skills essential for production, have

1. See Richard Barber, *The American Corporation* (New
York: Dutton, 1970); Richard C. Edwards, Michael Reich
and Thomas E. Weisskopf, *The Capitalist System*
(Englewood Cliffs, N.J.: Prentice-Hall, 1972); and Paul
Baran and Paul Sweezy, *Monopoly Capital* (New York:
Monthly Review Press, 1968).

any decision-making powers over methods, purposes, products and profits.

Business control extends into areas beyond the business world. Most universities and colleges, publishing houses, newspapers, television and radio stations, professional sports teams, foundations, churches, private museums and hospitals are organized as corporations and ruled by self-perpetuating, self-appointed boards of trustees (or directors or regents) composed primarily of wealthy middle-aged businessmen of conventional wisdom and conservative opinion. These boards are accountable to no one for their decisions; they can and often do exercise final and absolute judgment over all institutional matters.[2]

Consider the university: most institutions of higher education are public or private corporations (e.g., the Harvard Corporation, the Yale Corporation) ruled by boards of trustees with ultimate authority over all matters of capital funding and budget; curriculum, scholarships and tuition; departmental organization; hiring, firing and promotion of faculty and staff; degree awards and student fees. Most of the tasks related to these activities have been delegated downward to administrators and even to faculty and students; but the power can be easily recalled by the trustees, and in times of controversy it usually is.[3] These trustees (one of whom is usually the university president) are not elected by students, faculty or staff workers, although an occasional student or professor may be allowed to sit on the board, usually in a nonvoting capacity. The board members are granted legal control of the property and charter of the institution not because they have claim to any academic experience but because as successful bankers, industrialists, insurance men, realtors and heirs to family wealth, they supposedly have proven themselves to be the responsible and proper leaders of the community.[4]

This, then, is a feature of real significance in any understand-

2. My *Power and the Powerless* (forthcoming) has a more detailed discussion of power within social institutions.

3. See James Ridgeway, *The Closed Corporation* (New York: Random House, 1969) for a study of the university that differs from the "ivy-covered" image we usually have of it.

4. Even if it were true that their guidance and advice might be needed on financial matters, it is never explained why trustees should have ultimate power. They could function as advisers or consultants without being accorded executive authority over all matters. The argument is made that trustees take the financial risks for the university and should therefore have the authority. In fact, they usually take on no personal financial risks or liabilities as trustees. If anything, they are more likely to profit personally from their positions on the board, frequently awarding university contracts to their own private firms or the firms of business associates.

ing of political power in America: *almost all the social institutions and material resources that exist in this society are controlled by nonelective, self-perpetuating groups of self-willed corporate businessmen who are accountable to no one but themselves.*

The rest of us make our way through these institutions as employees and clients of one sort or another. The positions we occupy within them depend in some degree upon our ability to meet the standards set by the ruling oligarchs. The method of rule exercised over us is administrative, hierarchical and non-democratic. In most of the private institutions, and many of the public ones, which determine so many of our opportunities and experiences as citizens, students, workers, professionals, consumers, tenants, etc., we have no vote, no portion of the ownership and no legal decision-making power.

Labor unions provide some collective voice for employees and sometimes help limit the abuses of management. But contrary to popular belief, in most political and economic struggles unions seldom can match the material resources that corporations command. Furthermore, fewer than one in four American workers are unionized and many have no legal right to strike. Most union leaders tend to be easily reconciled and bought off by management. Having developed some kind of working relationship with management, they are more inclined to see the corporation's side of things and trim their own demands, less willing to press for strong contract terms or strike, than their own rank and file. They emphasize labor's common stakes with management and stress the necessity of maintaining high productivity; they do little about layoffs and speedups, and they share the owners' desire to keep workers in a compliant frame of mind.

Most union leaders have about as much commitment to institutional democracy as do corporate rulers. They allow their membership little voice in running the union, and in many cases they turn the union organization into a personal bureaucratic empire, misusing funds, padding payrolls and voting munificent salaries for themselves and their cohorts. Union leaders are often described as potentates who preside over vast armies of workers. They are indeed powerful in relation to their own rank and file, but with management they tend to be tame junior partners.[5]

5. For some of the many accounts recently published on the complicity of union leaders with management and their betrayal of their own rank and file, see Don Stillman, "Murder and the Mines," *New Politics*, 9, Winter 1972, pp. 22–29;

Thus, in our "democracy," the individual's opportunities for self-governance seem to be limited to those few moments spent in the polling booth—assuming that voting is an act of self-government.[6] Many Americans do not seem terribly upset by this situation. They believe as they were taught, that they are a free people. This belief is held even by many who refuse to take controversial stands for fear of jeopardizing their jobs and their careers.

The power of business does not stand naked before the public; rather it is enshrouded in a mystique of its own making. In the minds of many, the "free-enterprise system" has become indelibly associated with the symbols of Nation, Democracy, Family, Church, Prosperity and Progress.

Today convictions about the virtues of private enterprise and the evils of socialism and communism are widely disseminated among Americans of all classes. Yet we should remember that such beliefs did not emerge full-blown from nowhere, nor do they circulate like disembodied spirits. Rather they have been propagated over a period of several generations by the conditioning agencies of a capitalist society, including the media, the professions, the schools, the churches, the politicians and the policy-makers.[7]

Criticisms of "free enterprise" often are equated with un-Americanism. Capitalism is treated as a necessary condition for political freedom, contraposed as the sole alternative to "communist tyranny." The study of private enterprise by the National Association of Manufacturers observes: "Two . . . things have been of outstanding and dominating importance in our development: our system of representative democracy and our system of individual enterprise. . . . Inevitably and irrevocably the two go

Membership Party of Local 6, "Our Union Elections Are a Fraud," *ibid.*, pp. 30–39; Joseph Nabach, "The Telephone Strike: Frozen Militancy," *ibid.*, pp. 40–46; Burton Hall, "ILGWU and the Labor Department: Just a Perfect Friendship," *New Politics*, 9, Spring 1970, pp. 15–23; Paul Schrade, "Growing Bureaucratization of the UAW," *New Politics*, 10, Winter 1973, pp. 13–21; Burt Hall, "Painter's Union: Troubles of an Ex-Reformer," *ibid.*, pp. 22–29.

6. See Chapters Nine and Ten for a critical discussion of voting and elections as exercises in self-rule.

7. See William Preston, Jr., *Aliens and Dissenters* (Cambridge, Mass.: Harvard University Press, 1963); William Appleman Williams, *The Great Evasion* (Chicago: Quadrangle Books, 1964); Michael Parenti, *The Anti-Communist Impulse* (New York: Random House, 1969); Francis X. Sutton et al., *The American Business Creed* (New York: Schocken Books, 1962); Sidney Fine, *Laissez-Faire and the General-Welfare State* (Ann Arbor: University of Michigan Press, 1964).

hand in hand."[8] The private-enterprise system, it is taught, creates equality of opportunity, rewards those who show ability and initiative, justly relegates the parasitic and slothful to the bottom of the ladder, provides a national prosperity that is the envy of other lands, safeguards (through unspecified means) personal civil liberties and political freedom, promises continued progress in the endless proliferation of goods and services and has made America the great, free and beautiful nation it is.

Getting More and Getting Ahead

In the United States many billions of dollars are spent each year to induce people to consume as much as they can and—through installment plans—more than they can afford. The inducements seem to work: Americans are a people dedicated to the piling up of goods, services and income. One American describes his compatriots as "people already weighted down with possessions acting as if every object they did not own were bread withheld from a hungry mouth."[9] This consumerism is not just a habit but *a way of life*, a measure of one's accomplishment and a proof of one's worth, both for the "middle American" with his big color-television set, power lawnmower and shiny Buick and for the well-educated and well-paid professional with his comfortable home, gourmet foods, and expensive antiques.

Material success is also the key determinant of one's life chances. When human services are not based on need but on ability to pay, money becomes a matter of life and death. To be poor is to run a higher risk of death, illness, insufficient medical care, malnutrition, personal insecurity, police brutality, unemployment, job exploitation, etc., and to have a lesser opportunity for recreation, education, comfort, mobility, leisure, travel, etc.

For many people life is defined as a series of private goals to be attained through personal means, rather than as collective efforts in pursuit of rewards that might be *communally* distributed and enjoyed. One should endeavor to "get ahead." Ahead of what? Of others and of one's own present status. This "individualism" is not to be mistaken for freedom to choose moral, political and cultural alternatives of one's own making.

8. Quoted in Sutton et al., *The American Business Creed*, pp. 25–26.
9. Philip Slater, *The Pursuit of Loneliness: American Culture at the Breaking Point* (Boston: Beacon Press, 1970), p. xiii.

Each person is expected to operate independently and "individually" *but in more or less similar ways and similar directions.* Everyone competes against everyone else but for the same goals and with the same values in mind. "Individualism" in the United States refers to *privatization* and the absence of communal forms of production, consumption and recreation. You are an individualist in that you are expected to get what you can for yourself, by yourself, and not to be too troubled by the needs and problems faced by others. This attitude, considered criminal in many human societies, is labeled approvingly as "ambition" in our own and is treated as a quality of great social value.

Whether or not this "individualism" allows one to have control over one's own life is another story. The decisions about the quality of the food we eat, the goods we buy and the air we breathe, the prices we pay, the way work tasks are divided and jobs defined, the kinds of transportation, recreation and entertainment we are offered, the opinions and values we are exposed to in local and national newspapers, in magazines and on television and radio, the kind of treatment accorded us in our schools, clinics and hospitals—the controlling decisions concerning the palpable realities of our lives—are made by people other than ourselves. Yet Americans continue to think of themselves as self-reliant individualists. What they seem to be referring to is the privatism and atomization of their social relations and the relative absence of collective, cooperative endeavor.

Competitive privatism brings a good deal of loneliness and isolation and few occasions for meaningful community experiences with other human beings. This may explain why, during times of natural disaster such as floods and storms, when people engage in collective emergency tasks, some admit to the "great feeling" of working together and being drawn close to each other in a functional and urgent undertaking. (In some of the more rural areas of America, remnants of such friendliness and cooperation can still be found.) The emphasis on privatized acquisitiveness influences most of our social relations. Philip Slater argues that Americans constantly attempt to minimize or deny human interdependence. We seek a private home, a private country place, a private means of transportation, a private laundry, private recreation, private lessons, a private garden, etc. Even within the family, each member seeks a separate room and a separate telephone, television and car when it is economically possible to do so. "We seek more and more privacy," Slater notes, "and feel more and more alienated and lonely when we get it."[10]

The lack of community does not prevent Americans from making identifications with larger collective entities such as a school, a town or, most passionately, the nation. But even this identification is expressed in terms that are competitive with other schools, towns or nations. In sports, for instance, it is said that the important thing is not who wins but how the game is played; yet, in truth, whole schools and whole cities are gripped by joyful frenzy when their teams win a championship. The really important thing is the winning.[11]

The need to be "on top," to be first and foremost, extends with special intensity to the nation. We are instructed to love America because it is "the greatest country in the world," the presumption being that if it were not so great it would not be so lovable. America is great because of its laudable intentions and practices—and its military might. Greatness, then, is a matter not only of virtue but of strength. The superpatriots are usually the most militaristic. Love of country becomes associated with huge military budgets and armed intervention throughout the world, because as part of our greatness we need to keep the world safe from those revolutionaries who advocate a different kind of social order. The presumption that the United States has a right to police the entire globe rests on the belief that our intentions are honorable, our interests selfless and the outcomes of our actions salutary for other peoples.

In their personal and national egoisms Americans are hardly unique; but the United States is unique in the magnitude of its powers and the effects its actions have on other peoples. For many generations Americans have envisioned mankind developing as an extension of the American experience and enjoying the inspirational example of our political institutions. Our goal has been a world of "law and order" with a decided advantage going to those who define the order and enforce the law—a world respectful of mankind's best interests. That these interests also happen to be identical with the best interests of the United States is no cause for embarrassment, it being understood that

10. *Ibid.*, p. 7.
11. A writer recently returned from China informed me that competitive team sports are deliberately underplayed by the Chinese. Newspaper reports on games focus on the skills and good sportsmanship of the players and report scores only at the end of the story. In the United States the score of the game is headlined. "Who won?" is the only thing some Americans want to know.

less fortunate peoples, if not misled by revolutionaries and if given occasional succor from the happiest, richest, most successful nation in the world, will eventually learn productive ways, develop orderly liberal institutions like our own and achieve the blessings of peace, prosperity and property. Give or take some cultural variations, they will emerge as did America, from the howling wilderness to the machine-fed garden.

This global vision is still with us, but so is the nightmare that always lurked behind it—the fear that others might turn their backs on the American-defined world order and construct competing social systems which propagate values (especially those relating to the use and distribution of wealth) that might somehow undermine our American Way of Life, plunder our treasure and oust us from our position of preeminence. "America," President Nixon warned, "must never become a second-rate power." Only in supremacy do we seem able to find security. The haves always live in fear that the have-nots will try to equalize things. President Johnson summed it up before a Junior Chamber of Commerce audience: "We own half the trucks in the world. We own almost half of the radios in the world. We own a third of all the electricity. . . ." But the rest of the world wants it for themselves, he added. "Now I would like to see them enjoy the blessings that we enjoy. But don't you help them exchange places with us, because I don't want to be where they are." For many Americans, Johnson was touching the vulgar heart of the matter: Keep others from taking what we have.[12]

The Fear of Equality

From their earliest grade school days Americans are taught privatized, competitive methods of accomplishment. One's peers are potentially one's enemies; their successes can cause us envy and anxiety, and their failures bring secret feelings of relief. The ability or desire to work collectively with others of the same social group or class is much retarded. Competitive efforts are primarily directed against those of the same class or those below, a condition that suits the interests of those at the top. Among the strongest critics of workers who get better wages through collective bargaining and collective action are workers who do not and who complain, like management itself, that their more fortunate

12. See the discussion in Parenti, *The Anti-Communist Impulse*, pp. 301–302.

brethren are never satisfied and are going "to kill the goose that lays the golden egg." Any unusual success enjoyed by a friend, co-worker or professional colleague can evoke more jealousy in us than the successes enjoyed by a multimillionaire on the far-off upper rungs of the social ladder.

Many feel even more competitive toward those defined as their social *inferiors:* the poor, Blacks and other racial minorities and women. To be outdone by one's peers is bad enough, but for the status-conscious, status-seeking White male, who defines his self-worth and his manliness in terms of his presumed racial, sexual and class superiority, to be outdone by a woman, a Black or someone of humbler occupation and class is insufferable. *Rather than welcoming equality, many Americans fear and detest it and have a profound commitment to inequality.*

People who have invested much psychic energy and years of toil in maintaining or furthering their positions within the social hierarchy become profoundly committed to the hierarchy's preservation. Even those perched on modest rungs of the ladder —the millions of small proprietors, lower-paid semiprofessionals and white-collar workers, often described as "middle Americans," who could have much to gain from a more egalitarian social order—fear that they might be overtaken by those below, making all their toil and sacrifice count for naught.[13]

The hostility they may feel for the welfare poor does not encompass—at least not with the same intensity—the welfare rich, those at the top who receive billions of dollars from the government in the form of subsidies, tax write-offs and other services.[14] The middle Americans might utter a passing criticism of corporations and millionaires who do not pay taxes, but their greatest passion is reserved for the poor. The millions in tax write-offs given to oil tycoons like H. L. Hunt cause less resentment than the pennies given to the indigent family in Appalachia or Watts. If anything, the advantages enjoyed by the wealthy are seen as "earned" by their intelligence and resourcefulness and therefore deserved. Proximity to the poor is to be avoided by every effort, while wealth is something to be attained someday by oneself or one's children—something, in any case, to be admired. Hence the road upward should be kept open with no artificial impediments imposed by the government on those who

13. See Robert Lane, *Political Ideology* (New York: Free Press, 1962), pp. 57–81.

14. For a discussion of the welfare rich, see Chapter Six.

can advance, while the road behind should not be provided with conveyances for those who wish to catch up effortlessly.

To be sure, middle Americans have their doubts about the rat race, but they cannot lightly discard the years of effort and sacrifice they have invested in it and shift to another set of values. As Slater notes: "Suburbanites who philosophize over their back fence with complete sincerity about their dog-eat-dog-world, and what-is-it-all-for, and you-can't-take-it-with-you, and success-doesn't-make-you-happy-it-just-gives-you-ulcers-and-a-heart-condition—would be enraged should their children pay serious attention to such a viewpoint."[15]

The American's competitiveness is fortified by a *scarcity psychology* that bears little relation to how much he has. There is always more to want and more to get. And with increasing acquisitions there is always more to hang on to and more to lose. Thus the highly paid professional is burdened by a scarcity psychology and feels the pressure of "moreness" as much as the lowly paid blue-collar worker. Economically deprived groups like urban ghetto dwellers, sharecroppers, welfare recipients, female employees, low-income workers, racial minorities and poor people in general are seen as a nuisance and a threat because, like the rest of us, they want more, and more for them is less for us. The scarcity psychology, then, leaves us with the feeling that the poor and the racial minorities (our potential competitors) should be kept in their place and away from what we have and want.

A belief in the inferiority of deprived groups is quite functional for those possessed by a scarcity psychology. Racism, sexism and class bigotry help us to exclude large numbers of people, limiting the field of competitors and justifying in our minds the inequities these groups are made to endure. Having designated them as moral inferiors, we become easily convinced that the hardships they suffer are due to their own deficiencies (lazy poor, dumb Blacks, dirty Mexicans, silly women, etc.). "Those people don't *want* to better themselves," is the comment often made by individuals who then become quite hostile when lower-status groups do take actions intended to better themselves. The belief that other groups are lacking in natural abilities does not seem to free us of the anxiety that they might catch up and even surpass us.

15. Slater, *The Pursuit of Loneliness*, pp. 6–7.

Stereotyped images of lower-status people are propagated in movies, on television, in grade-school textbooks and in everyday life attitudes. In popular fiction and the mass media the world is portrayed as a predominantly middle-class place; working-class people are seldom presented except as uncouth, unintelligent and generally undesirable. A TV series like "All in the Family," while supposedly exposing bigotry, practices a bigotry of its own by stereotyping the working-class lead character as a loud-mouthed ignoramus and bully, poking fun at his mispronunciations, life-style and physical appearance. Class chauvinism is one of the most widely spread forms of prejudice in American society and one of the least investigated and least challenged. As one of the characters in Kurt Vonnegut's *Slaughterhouse-Five* observes:

America is the wealthiest nation on Earth, but its people are mainly poor, and poor Americans are urged to hate themselves. To quote the American humorist Kim Hubbard, "It ain't no disgrace to be poor, but it might as well be." It is in fact a crime for an American to be poor. . . . Every other nation has folk traditions of men who were poor but extremely wise and virtuous, and therefore more estimable than anyone with power and gold. No such tales are told by the American poor. They mock themselves and glorify their betters. The meanest eating or drinking establishment, owned by a man who is himself poor, is very likely to have a sign on its wall asking this cruel question: "If you're so smart, why ain't you rich?". . .

Americans . . . who have no money blame and blame and blame themselves. This inward blame has been a treasure for the rich and powerful, who have had to do less for their poor, publicly and privately, than any other ruling class since, say, Napoleonic times.[16]

If material success is a measure of one's worth, then the poor are not worth much and society's resources should not be squandered on them. If rich and poor get pretty much what they deserve, then it is self-evident that the poor are not very deserving. When farm workers earn only $2,000 a year, as one prosperous, middle-class White male remarked to me, "Then that's all they must be worth." The competitive, individuated, acquisitive society has little room for compassion and collective social betterment; those who dream of getting ahead and making it to the top have little time for those below.

16. Kurt Vonnegut, Jr., *Slaughterhouse-Five* (New York: Delta, 1969), pp. 111–112.

Conservatives, Liberals and Radicals

Not all Americans think alike, of course. Within the present spectrum one can detect various shades of political opinion which might roughly be categorized as conservative, liberal and radical. A *conservative* might be described as someone who allies himself wholeheartedly to the ideology of free enterprise and the interests of business and the well-to-do. He is convinced that the status quo is to be protected and reforms are to be resisted, except in rare instances. To be sure, the conservative believes there are some real social problems, but these will either take care of themselves or be taken care of over a long period of time in slow and cautious ways or, as with poverty, will always be with us. The conservative generally resists policies that impress him as moving toward an equalization of life chances, income and class. He puts his stock in individual self-advancement, a sound business market, authority, hierarchy, a strong police force, gut patriotism and American military strength. He believes that people are poor usually because, as Richard Nixon notes, they are given to a "welfare ethic rather than a work ethic." Nixon is fairly representative of American conservatism.

A *liberal*, like a conservative, accepts the basic structure and value system of the capitalist system but believes that pressing social problems exist and should be rectified by a redirection of government spending and by better regulatory policies. The liberal does not usually see these problems as being interrelated and endemic to the present system. Since he assumes that the ills of the politico-economic system have nothing to do with the fundamental essence of capitalism, he believes that the fault must be with the personages who have gained power. If the right men finally win office, and with the right combination of will, public awareness and political push, the system will be able to take care of its many crises. Some liberals are not overly fond of capitalism, but they like socialism even less. Most of them have thought little about socialism and read little about it outside the capitalist press, but this does not prevent them from having some firm feelings against it. Socialism, in their minds, conjures up stereotyped images of "drabness' and "regimentation," of people waiting in line for shoddy goods wrapped in dull gray packages, of Stalinist purges and labor camps, and of horrific scenes from fictional works like George Orwell's *1984* and Arthur Koestler's *Darkness at Noon.* The liberal's concern seems to be that freedom would be lost or diminished under socialism. (Most liberals firmly believe they are free under the present politico-economic system.) They are also worried about the diminution of their own class and professional privileges and the loss of status they might suffer with the democratization and equalization that is promised in a socialist society. In this respect, they often closely resemble conservatives.

In matters of foreign policy, liberals generally have shown themselves as willing as conservatives to contain the spread of socialism in other lands and make the world safe for American corporate investments and markets. Liberals want to cut the military budget because it is bloated and wasteful, and, especially since Vietnam, many liberals have come to think that we should not get involved in suppressing social revolutionary movements in other countries. But whatever their feelings about revolution abroad, most liberals have little tolerance for revolutionary struggle in the United States, especially of the kind that might involve violent or otherwise disruptive confrontations. The readiness of liberal governors to call out the National Guard against ghetto Blacks and the readiness of liberal college presidents to call in police squads against campus rebellions indicate that when the challenge gets close enough to *their* interests, liberal institutional leaders respond not much differently than conservative ones.

A *radical* is someone who wants to replace the capitalist system with a socialist system of public and communal ownership and who sees capitalism as the major cause of imperialism, racism and sexism. At times the word *radical* has been given a broader application; it has been used to describe almost any person engaged in antiwar activities or other protest politics. In this book, radicals are distinguished from liberal reformers in their belief that our social problems cannot be solved within the very system that is creating them. Radicals do not believe that *every* human problem at *every* level of existence is caused by capitalism but that many of the most important ones are and that capitalism propagates a kind of culture and social organization that destroys human potentials and guarantees the perpetuation of poverty, racism, pollution and exploitative social relations at home and abroad. Radicals even argue that much of the unhappiness suffered in what are considered purely "interpersonal" experiences relates to the false values and anxieties of an acquisitive, competitive capitalist society.

Radicals believe that American corporate and military expansionism abroad is not the result of "wrong thinking" but the natural outgrowth of profit-oriented capitalism. To the radical, American foreign policy is not beset by folly and irrationality but has been quite successful in maintaining the status quo and the interests of multinational corporations, crushing social change in countries like Indonesia, Guatemala, the Dominican Republic, Iran, Greece, Chile, Brazil, the Philippines, etc., and establishing an American financial and military presence throughout most of the world.

Conservatives, liberals and radicals all profess a dedication to "democracy," but all tend to mean different things by the term. As used in this book, *democracy* refers to a system of rule in which decision-makers are held accountable and responsible to the constituency that is affected by their judgments rather than allowed to operate irresponsibly and arbitrarily. Those who are ruled exercise a measure of control by picking their rulers and by subjecting them to open criticism and the periodic checks of free elections.

Many people think that if you are free to say what you like, you are living in a democracy. But freedom of speech is not the sum total of democracy, only one of its necessary conditions. A government is not a democracy that leaves us free to *say* what we want but leaves others free to *do* what they want with our country, our resources, our taxes and our lives. Democracy is not a seminar but a system of power, like any other form of governance. Free speech, like freedom of assembly and freedom of political organization, is meaningful only if it serves as a check on those in power and helps keep them responsible to those over whom power is exercised.

Nor are elections and political party competitions a sure test of democracy. Some two-party or multiparty systems are so thoroughly controlled by like-minded elites that they discourage broad participation and offer policies that serve establishment interests no matter who is elected. In contrast, a one-party system, especially in a newly emerging, social revolutionary system, might actually provide *more* democracy—that is, more popular participation, more meaningful policy debate within the party than occurs between the parties in the other system, and more accountability and responsiveness to the people.

In the chapters ahead, we will take a critical look at our own two-party system and measure it not according to its undoubted ability to hold elections but according to its ability to serve democratic ends. It will be argued later on that whether a political system is democratic or not depends not only on its procedures but on the *substantive* outputs—that is, the actual material benefits and costs of policy and the kind of social justice or injustice that is propagated. By this view, a government that pursues policies which by design or neglect are so inequitable as to deny people the very conditions of life is not democratic no matter how many competitive elections it holds.

What the Founding Fathers Did

4

TO HELP US UNDERSTAND THE AMERican political system, we might give some attention to its formal structure, the rules under which it operates and the interests that established it. We will begin with the Constitution and the men who wrote it.

It is commonly taught that entrepreneurs of earlier times adhered to the doctrine of laissez-faire. Supposedly they preferred a government that kept its activities to a minimum and its hands off commercial affairs. In actuality, the more intelligent capitalist theorists and practitioners of the eighteenth and nineteenth centuries were not against a strong state but against state restrictions on commercial enterprise. It was never their desire to remove civil authority from economic affairs but to make sure that its intervention worked *for* rather than against the interests of property. If they were for laissez-faire, it was in a highly selective way: they did not want government limiting their trade, controlling their prices or restricting their markets, but not for a moment did they want a weak government as such. Rather they sought one that was actively on their side; they frequently advocated an *extension* rather than a diminution of governmental activities.

"Civil authority," wrote Adam Smith in 1776, "so far as it is instituted for the security of property, is in reality instituted for the defense of the rich against the poor, or of those who have some property against those who have none at all."[1] Smith, who is above suspicion in his dedication to capitalism, argued that as wealth increased in scope, a government would have to perform more extensive services on behalf of the wealthy. "The necessity of civil government," he wrote, "grows up with the acquisition of valuable property."[2] He expected government to "facilitate commerce in general" by maintaining the necessary auxiliaries of trade, transportation and communication and providing for the armed protection of goods, ships and storage facilities for commerce "carried on with barbarous and uncivilized nations."[3]

"The Public Good and Private Rights"

Adam Smith's views of the importance of government were shared by most men of substance in the late eighteenth century. In America similar sentiments were expressed by the propertied class. Describing the period between Revolution and Constitution, Merrill Jensen writes that the dominant political tone was set by the commercial and financial interests. Far from wanting to keep a distance between themselves and the state, they were very much involved in shaping its activities.

Their power was born of place, position, and fortune. They were located at or near the seats of government and they were in direct contact with legislatures and government officers. They influenced and often dominated the local newspapers which voiced the ideas and interests of commerce and identified them with the good of the whole people, the state, and the nation. The published writings of the leaders of the period are almost without exception those of merchants, of their lawyers, or of politicians sympathetic with them.[4]

Most of these men were to agree with James Madison when he wrote in *Federalist* No. 10 that "the most common and durable source of factions has been the various and unequal distribution of property. Those who hold and those who are without property have ever formed distinct interests in society."

1. Adam Smith, *An Inquiry Into the Nature and Causes of the Wealth of Nations* (Chicago: Encyclopaedia Britannica, Inc., 1952), p. 311. A century before Smith, John Locke in his *Second Treatise of Civil Government* described one of the central purposes of government as protecting the interests of property. Needless to say, neither Smith nor Locke was a Marxist.
2. Smith, *Wealth of Nations*, p. 309.
3. *Ibid.*, pp. 315 ff.
4. Merrill Jensen, *The New Nation* (New York: Random House, 1950), p. 178.

And most of them, when the time came, did not hesitate to construct a strong central government that would insure their victory in the struggle between these "distinct interests."

The American Constitution was framed by financially successful planters, merchants, lawyers, bankers and creditors, many of them linked by ties of family and acquaintance and by years of service in the Congress, the military or diplomacy. They congregated in Philadelphia in 1787 for the professed purpose of revising the Articles of Confederation and strengthening the powers of the central government. They were impelled by a desire to build a nation and by the explicit and often repeated intent of doing something about the increasingly insurgent spirit evidenced among poorer people.

The rebellious populace of that day has been portrayed by many historians and textbook writers as consisting of irresponsible spendthrifts who never paid their debts and who believed in nothing more than timid state governments and inflated paper money. Little has been said about the actual plight of the common people, the great bulk of whom lived at a subsistence level. While concentrations of landed and commercial wealth were growing among the few, the poorer farmers were burdened by the low prices offered for their crops by traders and merchants, the high costs for merchandised goods and regressive taxes. They often bought land at inflated prices, only to see its value collapse and to find themselves unable to meet their mortgage obligations. Their labor and their crops usually were theirs in name only. To survive, they frequently had to borrow money at high interest rates. To meet their debts they mortgaged their future crops and went still deeper into debt. Large numbers were caught in that cycle of rural indebtedness which is the common fate of agrarian peoples in many countries to this day. The underpaid and underemployed artisans and workers (or "mechanics," as they were called) in the towns were not much better off.

Among the poor there grew the feeling that the revolution against the king of England had been fought for naught. When large numbers of debtors were jailed in Massachusetts early in 1787 and others were threatened with foreclosures on their farms, many of the poor began gathering at the county towns to prevent the courts from presiding over debtor cases. By the winter of 1787, farmers in western Massachusetts led by Daniel Shays had taken up arms. But their rebellion was forcibly put down by the state militia after a series of ragged skirmishes.

The specter of Shays' Rebellion hovered over the men who gathered in Philadelphia three months later. It confirmed their worst fears about the unreliable and irresponsible nature of the populace. They were determined that persons of birth and fortune should control the affairs of the nation and check the leveling impulses of that propertyless multitude which composed the "majority faction." "To secure the public good and private rights against the danger of such a faction," announced James Madison at the Philadelphia Convention, "and at the same time preserve the spirit and form of popular government is then the great object to which our inquiries are directed."

The Founding Fathers were of the opinion that things had become, in the words of one, "too democratic." They deemed the state legislatures too responsive to the people and not respectful enough of the needs of the prosperous. "The evils we experience flow from the excess of democracy," complained Elbridge Gerry of Massachusetts, who also noted that the people are "daily misled into the most baneful measures and opinions" and that he could readily see "the danger of the leveling spirit." "Symptoms of a leveling spirit, as we have understood, have sufficiently appeared in certain quarters to give notice of the future danger," warned Madison. "The people," said Roger Sherman, "should have as little to do as may be about the Government. They want information and are constantly liable to be misled." And Alexander Hamilton provided the memorable summation:

All communities divide themselves into the few and the many. The first are the rich and the well born, the other the mass of the people. The voice of the people has been said to be the voice of God; and however generally this maxim has been quoted and believed, it is not true in fact. The people are turbulent and changing; they seldom judge or determine right. Give therefore to the first class a distinct, permanent share in the government. They will check the unsteadiness of the second, and as they cannot receive any advantage by a change, they therefore will ever maintain good government.[5]

The Framers spent many weeks debating their differences, but these were the differences of merchants, slave owners and

5. The quotations by Gerry, Madison, Sherman and Hamilton are taken from Max Farrand (ed.), *Records of the Federal Convention* (New Haven: Yale University Press, 1927), vol. 1, *passim*. For further testimony by the Founding Fathers and other early leaders see John C. Miller, *Origins of the American Revolution* (Boston: Little, Brown, 1943), pp. 491 ff., and Andrew C. McLaughlin, *A Constitutional History of the United States* (New York: Appleton-Century, 1935), pp. 141–144.

manufacturers, a debate of haves versus haves in which each group sought certain safeguards within the new Constitution for its particular regional interests. Added to this were the inevitable disagreements that arise among men who are not certain what are the best means of achieving agreed-upon ends. One major question was how to erect a sturdy national government while preserving some kind of state representation. Questions of structure and authority occupied a good deal of the delegates' time: How much representation for the large and small states? How might the legislature be organized? How should the executive be selected? What length of tenure for the different officeholders? But certain questions of enormous significance, relating to the new government's ability to protect the interests of commerce and wealth, were agreed upon with surprisingly little debate. For on these issues there were no dirt farmers, dockworkers, indentured servants or poor artisans attending the Convention to proffer an opposing viewpoint. The debate between haves and have-nots never took place.

The portions of the Constitution which give the federal government the power to support commerce and protect property were decided upon after amiable deliberation and with remarkable dispatch considering their importance. Thus all of Article I, Section 8 was adopted within a few days.[6] This section delegated to Congress the power to (a) regulate commerce among the states and commerce with foreign nations and Indian tribes, (b) lay and collect taxes, duties and tariffs on imports but not on commercial exports, (c) establish a national currency and regulate its value, (d) "borrow Money on the credit of the United States"—a measure of special interest to creditors,[7] (e) fix the standard of weights and measures necessary for trade, (f) protect the value of securities and currency against counterfeiting, (g)

6. John Bach McMaster, "Framing the Constitution," in his *The Political Depravity of the Founding Fathers* (New York: Farrar, Straus, 1964), p. 137. Originally published in 1896. Farrand refers to the consensus for a strong national government that emerged after the small states had been given equal representation in the Senate. Much of the work that followed "was purely formal" albeit sometimes time-consuming. See Max Farrand, *The Framing of the Constitution of the United States* (New Haven: Yale University Press, 1913), pp. 134–135.

7. The original wording was "borrow money and emit bills." But the latter phrase was deleted after Gouverneur Morris warned that "The Monied interest will oppose the plan of Government if paper emissions be not prohibited." There was much strong feeling about this among creditors. In any case, it was assumed that the borrowing power would allow for "safe and proper" public notes should they be necessary. See Farrand, *The Framing of the Constitution*, p. 147.

establish "uniform Laws on the subject of Bankruptcies through-out the United States," (h) "pay the Debts and provide for the common Defence and general Welfare of the United States." Congress was to be limited to powers which either were specifically delegated to it by the Constitution or could be implied as "necessary and proper" for the performance of the delegated powers. Over the years, under this "implied power" clause, federal intervention in the private economy grew to an extraordinary magnitude and came to include activities unknown to and undreamed of by the Framers.

Among the delegates at the Convention were some who speculated in land and who expressed a concern about western holdings; accordingly, Congress was given the "Power to dispose of and make all needful Rules and Regulations respecting the Territory or other Property belonging to the United States. . . ." Some of the delegates were speculators or holders of highly inflated and nearly worthless Confederation securities. Under Article VI, all debts incurred by the Confederation were valid against the new government, a provision that allowed speculators to make generous profits when their securities matured and were honored at face value.[8]

In the interest of merchants and creditors, the states were prohibited from issuing paper money or imposing duties on imports and exports or interfering with the payment of debts by passing any "Law impairing the Obligation of Contracts." The Constitution guaranteed "Full Faith and Credit" in each state "to the Acts, Records, and judicial Proceedings" of other states, thus allowing creditors to pursue their debtors more effectively. The property interests of slave owners were looked after. To give the slave-owning states a greater influence, three fifths of the slave population were to be counted when calculating the representation deserved by each state in the lower house. The importation of slaves was allowed to continue until 1808. And under Article IV, slaves who fled from one state to another to escape bondage had to be delivered up to the original owner upon claim, a provision that was unanimously adopted at the Convention.

8. The classic study of the economic interests of the Founding Fathers is Charles A. Beard, *An Economic Interpretation of the Constitution* (New York: Macmillan, 1913). Critiques of Beard have been made by Robert E. Brown, *Charles Beard and the American Constitution* (Princeton, N.J.: Princeton University Press, 1956), and Forrest McDonald, *We the People—The Economic Origins of the Constitution* (Chicago: Chicago University Press, 1958).

The Framers believed the states acted with insufficient force against the agitations of the day, so Congress was given the task of "organizing, arming, and disciplining the Militia" and calling it forth, among other things, to "suppress Insurrections." The federal government guaranteed to every state in the Union a "Republican Form of Government" and protection against invasion and "against domestic Violence." Provision was also made for "the Erection of Forts, Magazines, Arsenals, dock-Yards and other needful Buildings," and for the maintenance of an army and navy for national defense and to police unsettled American territories. To protect overseas trade, Congress could take steps to "punish Piracies and Felonies committed on the high Seas, and Offences against the Law of Nations."

Containing the Spread of Democracy

In keeping with their desire to divest the majority of its alleged propensity toward self-aggrandizement, the Founding Fathers inserted "auxiliary precautions" *designed to fragment power without democratizing it.* By separating the executive, legislative and judiciary functions and then providing a system of checks and balances among the various branches, including staggered elections, executive veto, Senate confirmation of appointments and ratification of treaties, bicameralism, etc., they hoped to dilute the impact of popular sentiments. To the extent that it existed at all, the majoritarian principle was tightly locked into a system of minority vetoes, making swift and sweeping actions nearly impossible.

The propertyless majority, as Madison was to point out in *Federalist* No. 10, must not be allowed to concert in common cause against the established social order.[9] First, it was necessary to prevent a unity of public sentiment by enlarging the polity and then compartmentalizing it into geographically insulated political communities. The larger the nation, the greater the "variety

9. *Federalist* No. 10 can be found in any of the good editions of the *Federalist Papers.* It is one of the finest essays on American politics ever written by a theorist or practitioner. With clarity and economy of language it explains, as do few other short works, how a government may utilize the republican principle to co-opt the people and protect the propertied few from the propertyless many, and it confronts, if not solves, the essential question of how government may reconcile the tensions between liberty, authority and dominant class interest. In effect, the Tenth Federalist Paper maps out a method of preserving the politico-economic status quo which is relevant to this day.

of parties and interests" and the more difficult it would be for a majority to find itself and act in unison. As Madison argued, "A rage for paper money, for an abolition of debts, for an equal division of property, or for any other wicked project will be less apt to pervade the whole body of the Union than a particular member of it...." Thus an uprising of impoverished farmers may threaten Massachusetts at one time and Rhode Island at another, but a national government will be large and varied enough to contain each of these and insulate the rest of the nation from the contamination of rebellion.

Second, not only must the majority be prevented from finding horizontal cohesion, but its vertical force—that is, its upward thrust upon government—should be blunted by inter-jecting an essentially nonmajoritarian and indirect form of rep-resentation. Thus the Senators from each state were to be elected by their respective state legislatures. The chief executive was to be selected by an electoral college voted by the people but, as anticipated by the Framers, composed of political leaders and men of substance who would gather in their various states and choose a President of their own liking. Most probably, they would be unable to muster a majority for any one candidate, it was believed, and the final selection would be left to the House, with each state delegation therein having only one vote.[10] The Supreme Court was to be elected by no one, its Justices being appointed to life tenure by the President and confirmed by the Senate. In time, of course, the electoral college proved to be something of a rubber stamp, and the Seventeenth Amendment, adopted in 1913, provided for the direct election of the Senate.

The only portion of government that was initially "left to the people" in the Constitution was the House of Representatives. Many of the Framers would have preferred excluding the public entirely from direct representation: John Mercer observed that he found nothing in the proposed Constitution more objection-able than "the mode of election by the people. The people cannot know and judge of the characters of Candidates. The worst possible choice will be made." Others were concerned that the people would sell their votes to ambitious adventurists and demagogues, who would ride into office on a populist tide only to pillage the treasury and wreck havoc on all. "The time is not distant," warned Gouverneur Morris, "when this Country will

10. The delegates did anticipate that George Washington would be over-whelmingly elected the first President, but they believed that after that the electoral college would seldom be able to decide on one man.

abound with mechanics and manufacturers [industrial workers] who will receive their bread from their employers. Will such men be the secure and faithful Guardians of liberty? . . . Children do not vote. Why? Because they want prudence, because they have no will of their own. The ignorant and dependent can be as little trusted with the public interest."[11]

Several considerations mitigated the Framers' hostility toward the common people. First and most important, the delegates restrained themselves out of an anticipation that there were limits to what the states would accept. Second, some of the delegates feared not only the tyranny of the many but the machinations of the few. It was Madison who reminded his colleagues that in protecting themselves from the multitude, they must not reintroduce a "cabal" or a monarchy and thus err in the opposite direction. Third, a few of the Framers, notably men like George Mason and Benjamin Franklin, felt less hostility toward the democratic principle than did their colleagues. If they said nothing in support of extending the franchise, they did speak out against limiting it. Franklin lauded "the virtue and public spirit of our common people; of which they displayed a great deal during the war" and noted that when they were treated decently they were likely to be loyal and faithful citizens.

In any case, when the delegates agreed to having "the people" elect the lower house, they were referring to a somewhat select portion of the population. Property qualifications disfranchised the poorest in various states. Half the adult population was denied suffrage because they were women. About one fourth, both men and women, had no vote because they were held in bondage, and even among Blacks who had bought their freedom, in both the North and the South, none was allowed to vote until the passage of the Fourteenth Amendment after the Civil War.

Plotters or Patriots?

The question of whether the Founding Fathers were motivated by financial or national interest has been debated ever since Charles A. Beard published his *An Economic Interpretation of the Constitution* in 1913. It was Beard's view that the Founding

11. Farrand, *Records of the Federal Convention*, vol. 2, pp. 200 ff.

WARREN LINN

Fathers were guided by direct material and class interests, many of which are clearly reflected in the document they wrote. Arguing against Beard's thesis are those who believe that the Framers were concerned with higher things than just lining their purses and protecting their property. True, they were monied men who profited directly from the policies initiated under the new Constitution, but they were motivated by a concern for nation-building that went beyond their particular class interests, the argument goes.[12] To paraphrase Justice Holmes, these men invested their belief to make a nation; they did not make a nation because they had invested. "High-mindedness is not impossible to man," Holmes reminds us. And that is exactly the point: high-mindedness is one of man's most common attributes even when, or especially when, he is pursuing his personal and class interest. The fallacy in the position taken by those who deny the class-motivated perspective of the Framers is to presume that there is a dichotomy between the desire to build a strong nation and the desire to protect property and that the Framers could have been motivated by both. It presumes a felt antagonism between their sense of the public interest and their sense of their own class interest. In fact, like most other people, they believed that what was good for themselves was ultimately good for the entire society and that there was a compatibility between their universal values and their particular interests. Regardless of which comes first, the two usually go hand in hand, and to discover the existence of the "higher" sentiment does not eliminate the self-interested one.

All persons believe in their own virtue. The Founding Fathers never doubted the nobility of their effort and its importance for the generations to come. Just as they could feel dedicated to the principle of "liberty for all" and at the same time own slaves, or accept the existence of slavery, so could they serve both their nation and their estates. The point is not that the Framers were devoid of the grander sentiments of nation-building but that *there was nothing in that concept of nation and*

12. For some typical apologistic arguments on behalf of the Founding Fathers see Broadus Mitchell and Louise Pearson Mitchell, *A Biography of the Constitution of the United States* (New York: Oxford University Press, 1964), pp. 46–51, and David G. Smith, *The Convention and the Constitution* (New York: St. Martin's Press, 1965), Chapter Three. Smith argues that the Framers had not only economic motives but "larger" political objectives, as if the political had no relation to the economic or as if the political objectives were more impelling because they were directed toward a "national interest" rather than self-interest or a class interest.

state which worked against their class interest and a great deal that worked for it.

People tend to perceive things in accordance with the position they occupy in the ongoing social structure, and that position is largely determined by their class status. Even if we deny that the Framers were motivated by the kind of personal gain that moves corrupt and plundering politicians, we cannot thereby dismiss the existence of their class interest. The Founding Fathers may not have been concerned with getting their own hands in the till, although enough of them did; but they were preoccupied with defending the propertied few from the propertyless many—for the ultimate benefit of all, as they understood it. "The Constitution," as Staughton Lynd notes, "was the settlement of a revolution. What was at stake for Hamilton, Livingston, and their opponents, was more than speculative windfalls in securities: it was the question, what kind of society would emerge from the revolution when the dust had settled, and on which class the political center of gravity would come to rest."[13]

Finally, the apologists who argue that the Founding Fathers were motivated primarily by high-minded objectives rather consistently overlook the fact that during the Convention the delegates explicitly and repeatedly stated their intention to erect a government strong enough to protect the haves from the have-nots. They gave voice to the crassest class prejudices and never found it necessary to disguise the fact—as have latter-day apologists—that their uppermost concern was to diminish popular control and resist all tendencies toward class equalization (or "leveling" as it was called). Their opposition to democracy and their dedication to the propertied and monied interests were a matter of consciously avowed ideology. Their preoccupation was so pronounced that one delegate to the Convention did finally complain of hearing too much about how the purpose of government was to protect property. He wanted it noted that the ultimate objective of government was the ennoblement of mankind—a fine sentiment that evoked no opposition from his colleagues as they continued about their business.

13. Staughton Lynd, *Class Conflict, Slavery and the United States Constitution* (Indianapolis: Bobbs-Merrill, 1967), selection in Irwin Unger (ed.), *Beyond Liberalism: The New Left Views American History* (Waltham, Mass.: Xerox College Publishing, 1971), p. 17.

An Elitist Document

Whatever conjectures we might make about the motivations of the Framers, the more important task is to judge the end product of their efforts. And the Constitution they fashioned tells us a good deal about their objectives. It was and still is largely an elitist[14] document, more concerned with the securing of property interests than with personal liberties. Bills of attainder and ex post facto laws are expressly prohibited, and Article I, Section 9 assures us that "the Privilege of the Writ of Habeas Corpus shall not be suspended, unless when in Cases of Rebellion or Invasion the public Safety may require it," a restriction that still leaves authorities with a good measure of discretion. Other than these few provisions and similar ones imposed on the states, the Constitution that emerged from the Philadelphia Convention gave no attention to civil liberties. When Colonel Mason suggested to the Convention that a committee be formed to draft "a Bill of Rights," a task that could be accomplished "in a few hours," the representatives of the various states offered little discussion on the motion and voted unanimously against it. Guarantees of individual rights—including freedom of speech and religion; freedom to assemble peaceably and petition (i.e., urge, remonstrate and demonstrate) for redress of grievances; the right to keep and bear arms; freedom from unreasonable searches and seizures, from self-incrimination, double jeopardy, cruel and unusual punishment and excessive bail and fines; and the right to a fair and impartial trial and other forms of due process—were tacked on in the form of the first ten amendments (the Bill of Rights) only after the Constitution was ratified and the first Congress and President had been elected.

The twentieth-century concept of social justice, involving something more than formal and procedural liberties, is afforded no explicit place in our eighteenth-century Constitution. The Constitution says nothing about those conditions of life which

14. "Elitist" refers to interests or persons deemed to be socially select and superior and therefore deserving of positions of rule, at least according to those who apply the elitist description to themselves. "Elites" in the politico-economic system are those close to the loci of decision making who exercise a special initiative in public policy or who occupy top command positions within our political, social and economic institutions. These elites may not always work with perfect cohesion and sometimes they come into conflict with each other over policy particulars, but generally they share a common commitment to the ongoing social order.

have come to be treated by many people as essential human rights—for instance, freedom from hunger, the right to decent housing, good medical care and education regardless of ability to pay, the right to regular and gainful employment, safe working conditions, decent recreational facilities, a clean, nontoxic environment. Under the Constitution the right to equality is treated as a *procedural* right without a *substantive* content. Thus "equality of opportunity" means equality of opportunity to move ahead competitively and become unequal to others; it means an equal chance to get in the game and best others rather than an equal chance to enjoy an equal distribution and use of the resources needed for the maintenance of community life.

Some people, like the philosophy professor Sidney Hook, have argued that democracy is simply a system of rules for playing the game which allows some measure of mass participation and government accountability, and the Constitution is a kind of rule book. One should not try to impose particular public policies, class relations, economic philosophies or other substantive arrangements on this open-ended game. This position certainly does reduce democracy to a game. It overlooks the inextricable relationship between substance and procedure and presumes that procedural rules can exist in a meaningful way independently of substantive realities. But whether procedural rights are violated or actually enjoyed, whether one is treated by the law as pariah or prince, depends largely on material realities that extend beyond a written constitution or other formal guarantees of law. The law in its majestic equality, Anatole France once observed, prohibits rich and poor alike from stealing bread and sleeping under the bridges. And, it might be added, in so doing the law becomes something of a farce, a fiction that allows us to speak of "the rights of all persons" divorced from the class conditions that place rich and powerful corporations above the law and poor individuals below it. In the absence of certain substantive conditions, legalistic and procedural rights are of little value to millions who suffer the miseries of hunger and poverty and who have neither the time, money nor opportunity to make a reality of their formal rights.

Take the "right of every citizen to be heard." In its majestic equality the law allows both the rich and the poor to raise high their political voices: both are free to hire the best-placed lobbyists and Washington lawyers to pressure and manipulate public officeholders; both are free to shape public opinion through the use of a privately owned and privately financed press; and both rich and poor have the right to engage in multimillion-dollar election campaigns in order to pick the right persons for office or win office themselves. But again, this formal political equality is something of a fiction.[15] Of what good are the rules of the game for those millions who never get a chance to play?

15. See the discussion in Chapters Eight, Nine, Ten and Twelve.

The Growth
of Government

5

ALTHOUGH THE DECISIONS OF GOV-
ernment are made in the name of the entire
society, they rarely benefit everyone with
equal effect. No government represents all
its people. Some portion of the populace, frequently a majority, loses out on government
decisions. What is considered *national* policy
is usually the policy of dominant social groups,
and what is called *public* policy is not formulated by the public but by those sectors of the
public that are most strategically located
within the political system. The standard
textbook view is that American government
represents no particular set of interests and
manifests no class bias in the functions it
serves. The political system is said to involve an
interplay of many different groups, "a plurality
of interests." What government supposedly
does in this pluralistic interplay is act as a
regulator of social conflict, trying to limit the
advantages of the strong and minimize the
disadvantages of the weak.

In violation of that notion, I will argue that
the present political system may regulate but it
does not equalize, and that its overall effect is
to *advance* rather than redress the inequities
of capitalist society. The political system enjoys no special immunity to the way power
resources are distributed in the wider society.
It responds first and foremost, although not
exclusively, to the powers of the corporate
system, and in doing so it serves that system in
essential ways. "The business of government
is business," President Calvin Coolidge once

said. In this chapter we will explore the meaning of that observation, drawing from the history of the past century.

The Class Function of Government

The growth of business from local enterprises to large-scale manufacture during the nineteenth century was accompanied by a similar growth in governmental activity in the economy. While insisting that the free market worked justly for all, most businessmen showed little inclination to deliver their own interests to the stern judgments of an untrammeled, competitive economy; instead they resorted to such things as protective tariffs, public subsidies, price regulations, contract protections, patents, trademarks and other legal artifacts provided by civil authority. The purpose of government as defined by men of wealth was to provide the services that would make the market society work. During the period of industrial growth—from the early nineteenth century onward—the national government became the guardian and provider for commercial interests. Writing in his diary in 1866, Gideon Welles observed:

Congress accomplishes little that is good. . . . There is little statesmanship in the body, but a vast amount of party depravity. The granting of acts of incorporation, bounties, special privileges, favors, and profligate legislation of every description is shocking. Schemes for increasing the enormous taxation which already exists to benefit the iron and wool interests are occupying the session.[1]

When government intervened in the economy, it was almost invariably on the side of the strong against the weak. The unemployment, misery and hunger that beset great numbers of miners, farmers and laborers did little to enlist the efforts of public officials, but when rebellious workers seized the railroads, civil authorities were moved to energetic measures on behalf of corporate property. During the depression of 1873, many railroads became battlefields between strikers and militia. When militia units proved unreliable, federal troops were brought in. From that time, "the industrial barons made a habit of calling soldiers to their assistance; and armories were erected in

1. Quoted in Matthew Josephson, *The Politicos, 1865–1896* (New York: Harcourt, Brace, 1938), p. 52.

the principal cities as measures of convenience."[2] Short of having the regular army permanently garrisoned in industrialized areas, as was the desire of some corporate owners and state authorities, government officials took steps "to establish an effective antiradical National Guard."[3]

In most instances, the high-ranking officials who were quick to use force against workers were themselves men of property, like President Cleveland's Attorney General, Richard Olney, a millionaire owner of railroad securities, a man of "self-righteous, ruthless, and property-loving nature"[4] who used antitrust laws, court injunctions, mass arrests, labor spies, undercover provocateurs, deputy marshals and federal troops against workers and their unions. "A long step forward was being taken by which our national government authority and police apparatus were being applied to the defensive needs of large capitalist enterprises."[5] From the local magistrate to the President and the Supreme Court, the forces of law and order were utilized to crush the "conspiracy" of labor. The very laws they had found to be unworkable against the well-known monopolistic and collusive practices of business were now invoked "with remarkable promptness and effectiveness against the associations of laborers."[6]

At about this time, the federal government accumulated through tariffs and revenue taxes an enormous budget surplus, much of which it distributed to the wealthy in high-premium government bonds. The great sums "collected from the consuming population, and above all from the . . . poor wage earners and farmers, were used to pour into the pockets of the investing classes, especially in the East, a heavy unearned increment."[7] From 1888 to 1890 alone, some $45 million from the public treasury was paid in high premiums to big investors. At the same time, a billion acres of land in the public domain, *almost half of the present area of the United States*, was distributed to private hands. Josephson describes the government's attempts to privatize the public wealth:

2. Matthew Josephson, *The Robber Barons* (New York: Harcourt, Brace, 1934), p. 365.
3. William Preston, Jr., *Aliens and Dissenters* (Cambridge, Mass.: Harvard University Press, 1963), p. 24.
4. Josephson, *The Politicos*, p. 562.
5. *Ibid.*, p. 566.
6. Josephson, *The Robber Barons*, p. 367.
7. Allan Nevins, *Grover Cleveland: A Study in Courage* (New York: Dodd, Mead, 1932), p. 279, quoted in *ibid.*, p. 395.

In a hurried partition, for nominal sums or by cession, this benevolent government handed over to its friends or to astute first comers, . . . all those treasures of coal and oil, of copper and gold and iron, the land grants, the terminal sites, the perpetual rights of way—an act of largesse which is still one of the wonders of history. To the new railroad enterprises in addition, great money subsidies totaling many hundreds of millions were given. The Tariff Act of 1864 was in itself a sheltering wall of subsidies; and to aid further the new heavy industries and manufactures, an Immigration Act allowing contract labor to be imported freely was quickly enacted; a national banking system was perfected. . . . Having conferred these vast rights and controls, the . . . government would preserve them, as Conkling termed it, so as to "curb the many who would do to the few as they would not have the few do to them."[8]

The national platforms of the Democratic and Republican parties from the Civil War to the turn of the century, a period of great social ferment, dealt with the same questions that had been uppermost since 1789: tariffs, currency, banking and the disposal of public lands and resources. But for all its activities on behalf of business, the federal government did exercise a kind of laissez-faire in certain other areas: little attention was given to unemployment, poverty, education, the spread of urban slums, and the spoliation of natural resources. "The hatred of monopolies, the great animus of Jacksonian Democrats, now and then still blazed out in platform attacks on railway corporations, 'trusts,' and 'combines,' " note the historians Charles and Mary Beard, "but on the whole both parties passed over with slight recognition the basic changes that were taking place in American economy under their very eyes."[9]

The "Progressive" Era

By the turn of the century, government was to play a still more active role in helping the large interests rationalize their hold over the economy. Contrary to the view that the giant trusts controlled everything, price competition with smaller companies in 1900 was vigorous enough to cut seriously into profit rates in many industries, including iron and steel, copper, agricultural

8. Josephson, *The Robber Barons*, p. 52.
9. Charles A. Beard and Mary R. Beard, *A Basic History of the United States* (Garden City, N.Y.: Garden City Books, 1944), p. 327.

machinery, automobile and telephone.[10] Suffering from an inability to regulate prices, expand profits, limit competitors and free themselves from the "vexatious" laws of state and local governments, big corporations began demanding greater federal regulation of the economy. As the utilities magnate Samuel Insull said, it was better to "help shape the right kind of regulation than to have the wrong kind forced upon [us]."[11] The first major regulatory effort by the federal government under the Interstate Commerce Commission had been so helpful to the railroads as to make them enthusiastic advocates of regulation after 1887; their enthusiasm persists to this very day.[12]

During the 1900–1916 period, known as the Progressive Era, federal regulations in meat packing, food and drugs, banking, timber and mining were initiated at the insistence and with the guidance of the strongest corporations within these industries. In most instances, the effect of regulation was to raise prices and profits for the large producers.

Of the several White House occupants during the Progressive Era, Teddy Roosevelt might be considered most representative of the period. Hailed by many as a "trust-buster," Roosevelt actually was hostile toward unionists and contemptuous of reformers, whom he baptized as "muckrakers." Toward business he manifested bluster but virtually no bite: his major legislative proposals reflected the desires of corporation interests. Like other Presidents before and since, he enjoyed close relations with big businessmen, invited them into his administration, and showed active concern for their problems.

However much President Theodore Roosevelt might thunder against the "malefactors of great wealth" (much as his namesake, Franklin, attacked the "economic royalists" during the New Deal) these "robber barons" and industrialists knew the attacks were largely moral and ceremonial in character—and that anyway they could often control corrupt state and even national legislatures, as well as the judiciary.[13]

10. Gabriel Kolko marshals a great deal of evidence to support this conclusion; see his *The Triumph of Conservatism* (Chicago: Quadrangle Books, 1967), Chapters 1 and 2.
11. See James Weinstein, *The Corporate Ideal in the Liberal State* (Boston: Beacon Press, 1968), p. 87.
12. See Samuel P. Huntington, "The Marasmus of the ICC," *Yale Law Journal*, April 1952, reprinted in Francis Rourke (ed.), *Bureaucratic Power in National Politics* (Boston: Little, Brown, 1965), pp. 73–86.
13. Patrick Renshaw, *The Wobblies* (Garden City, N.Y.: Doubleday, 1968), p. 24.

What was true of Roosevelt held equally for Taft and Wilson, the other two Presidents of the Progressive Era. Neither of them "had a distinct consciousness of any fundamental conflict between their political goals and those of business."[14] In the quality of his appointees, his Latin American interventionism and his implementation of the Federal Reserve Act and the Federal Trade Commission Act, Woodrow Wilson, the "liberal Democrat," showed himself as responsive to business as any of the previous Republican White House occupants. As Gabriel Kolko concludes: "Progressivism was not the triumph of small business over the trusts, as has often been suggested, but the victory of big businesses in achieving the rationalization of the economy that only the federal government could provide."[15]

The advent of World War I further intensified relations between industry and government. During 1917, notes one historian, businessmen used government agencies to curtail civilian production and convert industry to war production. In addition, they commanded price, priority, allocation and other economic controls.[16] If large sectors of the economy were mobilized for the business of war, it was along lines proposed by those business interests enjoying privileged access to the councils of the warriors. During the war, the police and military were used without hesitation against workers who challenged the prerogatives of business and property. Strikes were now treated as seditious interference with war production. In many Western states, federal troops raided and ransacked headquarters of the Industrial Workers of the World and imprisoned large numbers of workers suspected of socialist sympathies. Nor did things improve during the postwar "Red scare"; the federal government resorted to mass arrests, deportations, political trials and congressional investigations in its efforts to suppress anticapitalist ideas.[17]

During the normalcy of the 1920s, prosperity was supposedly within everyone's grasp; stock speculations and other get-rich-quick schemes engaged the energies and hopes of many. Not since the Gilded Age of the robber barons had the more vulgar manifestations of capitalist culture enjoyed such an uncrit-

14. Kolko, *The Triumph of Conservatism*, p. 281.
15. *Ibid.*, pp. 283–284.
16. Paul A. C. Koistinen, "The 'Industrial-Military Complex' in Historical Perspective: The Inter War Years," *Journal of American History*, 56, March 1970, reprinted in Irwin Unger (ed.), *Beyond Liberalism: The New Left Views American History* (Waltham, Mass.: Xerox College Publishing, 1971), pp. 228–229.
17. See Preston, *Aliens and Dissenters, passim.*

ical reception. But there were millions of urban and rural lower-income people who remained untouched by the postwar prosperity, and with the depression of 1929, their ranks were soon joined by millions more.

The New Deal: Reform for Whom?

The New Deal era of the 1930s is commonly believed to have been a period of great transformation on behalf of "the forgotten man," but the definitive history of who got what during the 1930s has still to be written.[18]

From what we know, the central dedication of the Franklin Roosevelt administration was to *business recovery* rather than to *social reform*. The stock market crash and the subsequent depression demonstrated that attempts to rationalize the corporate economy through government subsidies, credits and regulations were inadequate. In response to the crisis, the government turned first to price and market regulatory methods of a kind frequently advocated by industry. Hence, much of the National Industrial Recovery Act allowing business to limit production and fix prices was little more than governmental enactment of a plan sponsored by the U.S. Chamber of Commerce. When an earlier version of the act was opposed by corporation spokesmen, the Roosevelt administration simply withdrew it and substituted the business version.[19] The Roosevelt administration then attempted to spur production by directly financing private investments: in nine years the Reconstruction Finance Corporation alone lent $15 billion to business.

As long as such measures were directed toward price and production recovery, they were popular with most of the business community, though of little help to lower-strata interests. As

18. The standard works on the period are often quite detailed yet lacking in any analysis of the class distributions of in-puts and out-puts. See, for instance, the vapid treatment by James McGregor Burns, *Roosevelt: The Lion and the Fox* (New York: Harcourt, Brace and World, 1956). At least one American historian does describe how the Roosevelt administration serviced the corporate class while reserving its best rhetoric for the common man: see Paul K. Conkin, *The New Deal* (New York: Crowell, 1967). A brief but good statement is Brad Wiley, "Historians and the New Deal" (unpublished paper). A fine treatment of welfare and relief policy under the New Deal can be found in Frances Fox Piven and Richard A. Cloward, *Regulating the Poor* (New York: Pantheon Books, 1971), Chapters 2 and 3.

19. Piven and Cloward, *Regulating the Poor*, p. 72. Also Basil Rauch, *The History of the New Deal, 1933–1938* (New York: Creative Age Press, 1944), pp. 70–71.

Piven and Cloward conclude: "Many New Deal programs rode roughshod over the most destitute."[20] Thus many tenant farmers and sharecroppers were evicted from their holdings when federal acreage rental programs took land out of cultivation.[21] And a number of New Deal programs, seeking to placate organized interests, permitted racial discrimination in wage and hiring practices.

In the area of social welfare the New Deal brought few triumphs to the common man. The local relief and charity arrangements of 1929, almost unchanged from colonial times,[22] were hopelessly inadequate. Faced with an unrest of unprecedented scope, the federal government instituted a massive relief program in the early 1930s which prevented widespread starvation and—more importantly from the perspective of the business community—limited the instances of violent protest and radicalization. But as the New Deal moved toward public works programs which threatened to compete with private enterprises and undermine low wage structures in various regions, businessmen withdrew their initial support and became openly hostile. While infuriating Roosevelt, who saw himself as trying to rescue the capitalist system, business opposition probably enhanced the administration's reformist image in the public mind and helped obscure the New Deal's gross insufficiencies.

The enormous disparity between the New Deal's popular image and its actual accomplishments in the area of relief and reform remains one of the unappreciated aspects of the Roosevelt era. To cite specifics: the Civilian Conservation Corps, restricted to men between 18 and 25, provided jobs at subsistence wages for 250,000 out of 15 million unemployed persons. At its peak, WPA reached about one in four unemployed, often with work of unstable duration and with wages generally scaled below the already inadequate ones of private industry. The Social Security Act of 1935 made retirement benefits payable *only in 1942 and thereafter,* covering only about half of the population and provid-

20. Piven and Cloward, *Regulating the Poor,* p. 76.
21. By February 1935, 733,000 farm families were on the relief rolls, a rise of 75 percent in sixteen months under the New Deal's AAA. The lot of the small farmer did not noticeably improve under Roosevelt and frequently worsened.
22. Charity measures in 1929 included the use of almshouses and indentured service. See Piven and Cloward, p. 48. Most of the charitable contributions made by the wealthy in the early depression period were, as Robert Hutchins asserts, "not for the relief of the unemployed but for the prevention of socialism." See his "In the Thirties, We Were Prisoners of Our Illusions, Are We Prisoners in the Sixties?" *New York Times Magazine,* September 8, 1968, p. 45.

ing no medical insurance and no protection against illness before retirement. Similarly, old-age and unemployment insurance applied only to those who had enjoyed sustained employment in select occupations. Implementation was left to the states, which were free to set whatever restrictive conditions they chose. In response to the housing crisis, the government expended its greatest efforts in stimulating private construction, aiding home buyers (mostly middle-class) and protecting mortgage bankers through the loan insurance program. By 1937 fewer than 25,000 housing units had been built from federal loans given to local, limited-dividend housing corporations.

The fate of the New Deal "land reform" efforts was typical of most of its assistance programs. In rural areas the government began buying up land and redistributing it to the destitute. Some ten thousand families were resettled in 152 projects, but even this limited effort was soon thwarted. Conservatives in Congress managed to stop land distribution, and the indigent farmers were required to buy the land with borrowed funds. Direct government loans were replaced by government guarantee of private loans, leaving poor Whites with little chance—and poor Blacks with even less chance—of favored treatment when it came to securing loans.[23]

Piven and Cloward argue that it was not the misery of millions which brought government aid—since misery had prevailed for several years before—but rather the continued threat of acute political unrest. That government programs were markedly inadequate for the tasks at hand seemed less important than that they achieved a high visibility and did much to dilute public discontent. Once the threat of political unrest and violence subsided and popular confidence was somewhat restored, *federal relief was cut back:* in 1936–1937 WPA rolls were reduced by more than half and the direct emergency relief program was slashed, leaving large numbers of families with neither work nor relief and thereby reducing many to a destitution worse than any they had known since the 1929 crash. "Large numbers of people were put off the rolls and thrust into a labor market still glutted with unemployed. But with stability restored, the continued suffering of these millions had little political force."[24]

At the same time, organized labor gained a new legitimacy,

23. See Ben H. Bagdikian, "A Forgotten New Deal Experiment in Land Reform," *I. F. Stone Weekly*, July 31, 1967, p. 3. See also Conkin, *The New Deal*, Chapter 3; Piven and Cloward, *Regulating the Poor*, Chapters 2 and 3.
24. Piven and Cloward, *Regulating the Poor*, p. 46.

but it was on terms that were highly functional to the corporate system and of little assistance to the great mass of unemployed and nonunionized workers. Labor leaders, including most of those who had earned reputations as "militants," were dedicated to maintaining the capitalist system. Thus in 1935 John L. Lewis warned that "the dangerous state of affairs" might lead to "class consciousness" and "revolution as well"; he pledged that his own union was "doing everything in their power to make the system work and thereby avoid it."[25] Men like Lewis, William Green and Sidney Hillman cooperated closely with management in introducing efficiency methods into production, limiting strikes and maintaining a "disciplined" labor force. The CIO's period of militancy came early and ended early; its dedication, as Hillman noted, was not to changing "the competitive system" but to trying "to make the system workable."[26] Hillman thought the industry-wide unionization of labor avoided the kind of jurisdictional strikes that plagued the older craft unions and more readily stabilized the working force under a leadership willing to cooperate with management. Many owners agreed, relying on CIO leaders to keep a "production-minded" control over the workers and thereby utilizing the good will of the union for management's purposes. One Baltimore manufacturer once complained to Hillman that a local union leader was unavailable "when we need him most." The manufacturer noted that he had been "trying to get more production for weeks" without success and asked Hillman to urge the local union leader to make more frequent appearances "because I feel that with his finesse he is able to get for us what we want, better than we can ourselves and it is urgent from many angles that we get our production."[27] To the very poor and the many millions of unemployed, the unions offered no help, giving little support to relief programs and little attention to the wider problems of economic change.

The Roosevelt administration's tax policies provide another instance of the disparity between image and performance. Contrary to common belief, the New Deal's taxation program was virtually a continuation of the program of the Hoover administration. If anything, the effect of most New Deal policies through the 1930s was to create a more regressive tax system: the various

25. Quoted in Ronald Radosh, "The Corporate Ideology of American Labor Leaders from Gompers to Hillman," *Studies on the Left*, 6, November–December 1966, reprinted in Unger, *Beyond Liberalism*, p. 226.
26. *Ibid.*, p. 224.
27. *Ibid.*, p. 222.

benefits under Social Security were paid for mostly by those who benefited; even relief payments were disguised subsidies to business, since the buying power they created was largely financed by future taxes on individual wages and consumer items. Big corporations had avoided many taxes during the depression by reducing debts, increasing liquid capital, and taking advantage of various loopholes in existing tax schedules.[28] When higher income taxes came with America's involvement in World War II, as a response to military spending, much of the increased load fell on the upper-income brackets, but the major tax burden was taken up by those of more modest means who had never before been subjected to income taxes. "Thus, the ironic fact is that the extension of the income tax to middle and low-income classes was the only original aspect of the New Deal tax policy."[29]

In sum, of the New Deal's "3 R's," relief, recovery and reform, it can be said that *relief* was markedly insufficient for meeting the suffering of the times and, in any case, was rather harshly curtailed after the 1936 electoral victory; that attempts at *recovery* focused on business concerns, and achieved little until the advent of war spending; and that *reform*, of the kind that might have ended the maldistributions and class abuses of the capitalist political economy, was rarely attempted. "The welfare legislation, large in hopes generated, often pitifully small in actual benefits, hardly represented a social revolution," concludes Conkin.[30]

Along with the absence of class reform there was no noticeable attempt at race reform. The New Deal's record on school desegregation, open housing, fair employment practices, voting rights, White lynch-mob violence and other such issues is nonexistent. The Resettlement Administration headed by Rexford Tugwell was probably the only New Deal agency to support equal benefits for Blacks. According to Conkin, the RA was one of the most honest and most class-conscious of New Deal agencies. Eventually antagonizing every vested interest, it was tied to the Department of Agriculture and then abolished by Congress.

By 1940, the last year of peace, the numbers of ill-clothed, ill-fed and ill-housed had shown no substantial decrease; unem-

28. Conkin, *The New Deal*, p. 67 and *passim*.
29. Gabriel Kolko, *Wealth and Power in America* (New York: Praeger, 1962), p. 31.
30. Conkin, *The New Deal*, pp. 65–66.

ployment was nearly as high as in 1933, and the national income was still lower than in 1929. Looking back to the 1930s, former New Dealer Robert M. Hutchins offers some criticisms that are strikingly at odds with the popular notion of that period.

It does not seem possible that there was ever another decade like the thirties, distinguished by the air of stupification, not to say petrification, that hung over us. We were and remained prisoners of our illusions. We rejected the evidence of our senses. We declined to think. When we acted, we did so because we were forced to; the actions we took were against our better judgment, and our judgment did not change during the decade. . . .

We entered the thirties with . . . no suspicion that there could be anything wrong with such a system or that it could ever come to an end. . . .

After eight years of "recovery," nobody—including the Federal Government—had anything to show for it but deficits. The emergency did not end. The Depression would not lift. . . . As the war got closer and closer, we got ready to resort to that received idea which always overrode the others. . . . We knew that in wartime you had to do whatever was necessary to win the war. We made the adjustment easily, for the idea of unbalancing the budget to kill people was more familiar to us than the idea of unbalancing it to save the lives of fellow citizens. When the war came, it was sound to do what had been unsound in the years before.[31]

Only by entering the war and remaining thereafter on a war economy, funneling vast sums into corporate hands, was the United States able to maintain a higher level of employment than in the prewar decades.

31. Hutchins, "In the Thirties, We Were Prisoners of Our Illusions," pp. 44–59, *passim*.

Politics : Who Gets What?

6

IN THE SUCCESSIVE ADMINISTRATIONS since the New Deal, be they Democratic or Republican, the government's use of public resources on behalf of private gain has never faltered. If anything, it has grown in scope. What follows is a sampling of the ways government has operated in recent years in the service of powerful interests.[1]

Welfare for the Rich

(a) In any given year the U.S. Treasury distributes about $10 billion to $13 billion in direct payments to manufacturing, shipping, aviation, communication, mining, timber, agriculture and other enterprises to enhance their profits and diminish their losses. Another $10 billion a year is paid out in benefit-in-kind subsidies, including subsidized commercial mail delivery, private airports, public lands, industrial machinery, etc. To offer some specifics: between $6 billion and $7 billion is allocated yearly to high-income farmers and

1. The best source on this subject is *The Economics of Federal Subsidy Programs* prepared by the Joint Economic Committee (Washington, D.C.: U.S. Government Printing Office, 1972). A compendium of information demonstrating the influence of big corporations in and out of government can be found in Morton Mintz and Jerry S. Cohen, *America, Inc.* (New York: Dial Press, 1971). For an excellent analysis of how government serves large producer interests see Grant McConnell, *Private Power and American Democracy* (New York: Knopf, 1966) and the numerous studies cited therein. A recent more popular treatment is Jack Newfield and Jeff Greenfield, *A Populist Manifesto, The Making of a New Majority* (New York: Praeger, 1972).

large farm corporations to limit acreage production and buy up crop surpluses, keeping profits high and, in effect, subsidizing an expansion of corporation farm ownership at the expense of millions of farm workers and small-farm families. Among those of property who receive big farm subsidies, according to Representative Silvio Conte (R.-Mass.), are numerous oil companies, some state universities, a bowling alley in Dallas, a municipal airport in Nebraska, a radio station in Ohio, a mental hospital in Alabama and even the Queen of England (the royal family owns property in the States).[2]

The federal government gives about $1 billion a year to the shipping industry and some $200 million a year to private aviation facilities used mostly by a few thousand executives and well-to-do flying enthusiasts. In order to "promote the development of air transportation" the government reimburses private air carriers for any losses they may incur: in 1971 the sum was $57.2 million. Another $83.6 million in direct gifts goes to the sugar industry to produce sugar beets and sugar cane. These kinds of government handouts are defended as necessary "to insure the health of industry" or "to provide essential services."

(b) The federal government maintains prices at noncompetitive high levels in "regulated" areas of the economy at a multibillion-dollar cost to consumers and to the lasting advantage of established producers. For many years the oil import quota system limited the supply of fuel to the consumer market and raised its price by over 50 percent, resulting in an estimated $5-billion annual transfer of income from consumers to petroleum companies. The regulation of trucking and railroad rates by the ICC "to prevent destructive competition" and to exclude new competitors results in costs of many hundreds of millions in excess of what competitive prices would allow; and the fixed prices and restrictions imposed on new airline competitors by the Civil Aeronautics Board allows for an estimated $2 billion to $4 billion in excess airline revenues.[3]

The federal government engages in preferential enforcement—or nonenforcement—of regulatory standards, as when

2. *New York Times*, July 11, 1973; see also Senator John Williams' comments as reported in the *Philadelphia Inquirer*, July 11, 1967; also Edward Higbee, *Farms and Farmers in an Urban Age* (New York: Twentieth Century Fund, 1963), pp. 139 ff.; John A. Schnittker, "The Farmer in the Till," *Atlantic*, October 1969, pp. 43–45; William Robbins, "Farm Policy Helps Make the Rural Rich Richer," *New York Times*, April 5, 1970.

3. See Peter Passell and Leonard Ross, "Mr. Nixon's Economic Melodrama," *New York Review of Books*, September 23, 1971, p. 8.

the FCC sets an "allowed rate of return" for the telephone company and then ignores it, enabling American Telephone and Telegraph to earn a $169-million yearly excess over already generous rates.[4] Private electric utilities offer another illustration of the advantages of government "regulation." Utilities are nonrisk enterprises whose expenses are virtually guaranteed by the government. They never go bankrupt; they pay high dividends to their shareholders and give their managers handsome salaries and stock options. Their rates—largely unsupervised by state regulatory commissions—are set so as to allow them a net income as high as 15 to 25 percent, which explains why private utility rates are sometimes more than twice those of municipal-owned utilities.

Municipal-owned companies not only produce lower-cost electricity but also raise revenue for a city's budget. Thus, in Boston, 500 kilowatt hours purchased from the private utility (Boston Edison) cost $13.41; in Seattle the same amount bought from the municipal-owned company costs $5. In Boston, property taxes on a home assessed at $10,000 come to $1,050 a year; in Seattle, to only $513, because Seattle's city-owned electric plant, despite lower rates, pumps millions of dollars into the city treasury.[5] While the cost of producing electricity has been steadily *decreasing*, the consumer's electric bill has been *increasing*. After a thorough investigation, Senator Lee Metcalf (D.–Mont.) concluded that consumers should be paying $1 billion *less* each year due to declining production costs.

(c) The federal government gives private corporations the use, profit and sometimes ownership of new technologies developed at public expense. Nuclear energy, electronics, aeronautics, outer-space communication, mineral exploration, computer systems—much of the basic research and developmental work in these and other fields are done for the benefit of private firms at a cost of more than $15 billion a year to the taxpayer. The Atomic Energy Commission, for example, in conjunction with such manufacturers as Westinghouse and General Electric, presides over a multibillion-dollar energy combine which is dependent upon vast federal subsidies in the form of research, uranium price supports, special exemptions from liability for accidents at atomic power plants, disposal sites for nuclear waste and a vigorous national publicity campaign to support the construction

4. *Wall Street Journal*, August 30, 1971.
5. For a thorough and telling exposé on utilities see Lee Metcalf and Vic Reinemer, *Overcharge* (New York: McKay, 1967).

of often hazardous nuclear reactors throughout the country. In its first twenty-four years, the AEC spent $49 billion, bought more than $3 billion worth of uranium ore from domestic producers at fixed prices and played a dual role as regulator and promoter of the atomic energy industry.[6]

(d) As in olden days, government continues to give away, lease or sell at bargain rates the national forests, grasslands, wildlife preserves and other public lands containing priceless timber, minerals, oil and water and recreational resources—with little consideration for environmental values or for desires other than those of the favored corporations.[7] From 1965 to 1967, for instance, several major petroleum companies leased acreage in Alaska for oil exploration, paying a sum of $12 million for leases worth upwards of $2 *billion*—or more than 150 times as much. In a subsequent oil lease auction, the companies paid the government $900 million for lands that are expected to be worth some $50 billion within a decade.[8]

Reviewing the peculiarly private dedications of public policy Senator Russell Long (D.–La.) concluded:

The government pays out many billions of dollars in unnecessarily high interest rates; it permits private-monopoly patterns on over twelve billion dollars of government research money annually; it permits billions of dollars of government money to remain on deposit in banks without collecting interest; it permits overcharging by many concerns selling services to government; it tolerates all sorts of tax favoritism; it fails to move to protect public health from a number of obvious hazards; it permits monopolies to victimize the public in a number of inexcusable ways. . . .[9]

Government performs other services designed to maximize private gain at public cost: it awards highly favorable contracts and

6. Roger Rapoport, "The Story of Nuclear Power Plants," *Ramparts*, March 1972, p. 49; also Jack Shepart, "The Nuclear Threat *Inside* America," *Look*, December 15, 1970, pp. 21–27.

7. See James Ridgeway, *The Politics of Ecology* (New York: E. P. Dutton, 1970); also The Ralph Nader Study Group Report, *The Water Lords* (New York: Grossman, 1971), James M. Fallows, project director; The Ralph Nader Study Group Report, *The Vanishing Air* (New York: Grossman, 1970), John C. Esposito and Larry J. Silverman, project directors.

8. Barry Weisberg, "Ecology of Oil: Raping Alaska," in Editors of *Ramparts* (eds.), *Eco-Catastrophe* (San Francisco: Canfield Press, 1970), p. 107 and p. 109.

9. Quoted in Richard Harris, "Annals of Politics, A Fundamental Hoax," *New Yorker*, August 7, 1971, p. 53. Senator Long should know about such matters, being himself a beneficiary of the oil depletion allowance, a holder of oil interests in at least four states, and a vigorous spokesman for the industry. See "Oil Tax Write-Off Aids Senator Long," *New York Times*, October 5, 1969.

provides emergency funding to insure the survival and continued profits of particular armaments companies; it furnishes big business with risk-free capital, long-term credits and tariff protections and provides lowered tax assessments and cost write-offs amounting to many billions of dollars yearly; it makes available to defense industries some $13.3 billion worth of government-owned land, buildings, machinery and materials, thereby in part "saving them the job of financing their own investments"[10]; and it applies the antitrust laws in a manner so lenient and lackadaisical as to make the effect of such statutes inconsequential.

THE DEFICIT SPENDER

Deficit spending is one of the ways government keeps business profits high: the process entails spending heavily on behalf of business while cutting business taxes. In 1962 liberalized depreciation write-offs for business were "equivalent . . . to a reduction in the corporate profits tax from 52 percent to 40 percent," according to then Secretary of the Treasury Douglas Dillon. These cuts, he noted, were intended "to improve the climate for business investment."[11] Two years later a new tax law distributed some $11.5 billion, mostly to the rich but with minor cuts to the wage earner to make the measure somewhat more politically palatable.[12] These cuts were accompanied by *increases* in federal expenditures and in the public debt, but as the public debt grew, so did business gains. After-tax profits for corporations increased from $22 billion in 1960 to $32 billion in 1964 to $52.9 billion in 1968. Profits increased as much as 42 percent for iron and steel and 120 percent for the automotive industry during 1960–1964. During the Kennedy-Johnson era, corporate profits grew at a rate twice as great as the economic growth rate and *by almost four times as much as a worker's weekly wages.* During this same period there was no sizeable decline in unemployment. Under the Nixon administration, real wages declined for most wage earners, but profits continued to grow.

10. Sidney Lens, *The Military-Industrial Complex* (Philadelphia: United Church Press, 1970), p. 8.
11. Quoted in Leo Huberman and Paul Sweezy, "The Kennedy-Johnson Boom," *Monthly Review*, February 1965, reprinted in Marvin Gettleman and David Mermelstein (eds.), *The Great Society Reader* (New York: Random House, 1967), p. 103.
12. *Ibid.*

In the first quarter of 1971, business had made $81.3 billion in profits. By the first quarter of 1972, profits had risen to 88.2 billion, an almost $7-billion increase. By the first quarter of 1973 total corporate profits had moved to $114.3 billion, a growth of $26.1 billion. Not only were profits growing but the *rate* of growth was increasing—without noticeable benefit to the scores of millions on the lower and lower-middle income rungs, whose food bills and taxes continued to rise. While Wall Street hailed the first half of 1973 as a boom period, it did not feel much like a boom to most Americans. Helping to feed this business prosperity was Mr. Nixon's deficit spending: in its first four years the Nixon administration added $73.8 billion to what was a national debt of over $450 billion by 1973. As economists Huberman and Sweezy had remarked some years earlier: "It is hardly surprising that businessmen are so enthusiastic about *this* kind of deficit spending. Boiled down to essentials it amounts simply to using the borrowing power of the federal government to subsidize corporate profits."[13]

As government spends more than it collects, it must borrow money from those who have it by floating risk-free, high-interest bonds. Some nonwealthy citizens buy non-marketable government bonds of modest denomination through various payroll savings plans, but the bulk of federal bonds, a high percentage of the total sum, is held by banks and very rich individuals. Most federal bond issues come in nothing smaller than $5,000 denominations. As the government continues to borrow money, the national debt increases. As the national debt increases, so does the interest on it that has to be paid to the very rich. This interest payment represents another huge subsidy to the wealthy and is one of the largest single items in the federal budget each year; in 1972 it was $22 billion, *a sum more than three times the federal money spent on all welfare payments to the poor.* The bulk of this interest is drawn from the salaried and wage-earning public; it constitutes a reverse redistribution of income, a manifestation of what one writer called the "trickle up theory" of income.[14]

THE ECONOMIC STABILIZER

In 1971 the government initiated a "wage-price freeze" which

13. *Ibid.* p. 103.
14. Robert Fitch, "Selling the Debt," *Ramparts*, April 1972, p. 20.

held down wages fairly successfully but not prices.[15] During such freezes, firms market old commodities with new packaging and higher prices; they maintain prices but cut weight and reduce quality. Products are too numerous and varied for their prices to be effectively supervised; and when government does manage to oversee prices, it does so with much compassion, as when Nixon's Price Board allowed General Motors, Ford, U.S. Steel and other giant corporations to raise prices because of something called "permissible profit margins"—at a time when profit rates already were increasing by about 15 percent each year. The *decline* in real wages coupled with the continued rise in profits would seem to indicate that it is not the worker's wage demands that determine the upward direction of prices. *The "wage-price spiral" is really a profit-price spiral, and the worker is more the victim than the cause of inflation.*[16]

In 1973 the federal government attempted to curb inflation by cutting back public assistance programs such as the school milk fund and the rural environmental program, economy measures that won the approval of the business community. The overall effect of Nixon's fiscal policies was to diminish the buying power of the wage earner, a buying power that was considered one of the causes of inflation, without stopping the inflation itself or the growing unemployment. However, the government's intent was not to achieve full employment but to insure business profits. It was presumed that high profits would eventually bring high employment, a presumption held more firmly by those who make the profits than by those looking for jobs.

In any case, from business' standpoint an occasional recession is not without its compensations, since it acts as a check on wages, though not on prices, and guarantees a pool of unemployed, cheap labor. Recessions allow the well-protected, well-subsidized, price-fixing giant corporations to tighten their hold on the market by taking over weakened smaller firms, thereby emerging all the stronger for the next boom.[17] Such phrases as "cooling off the economy" and "weeding out the

15. See "The Fantastic Rise in Corporate Profits," *Economic Trends and Outlooks* (monograph published by AFL-CIO).

16. As early as 1965, the first year of the Vietnam escalation, real wages were declining. See James Ridgeway, "Nixon's Other War," *Hard Times*, July 28–August 4, 1969; also Peter Kihss, "Factory Workers in Suburbs Are Reported on 'Treadmill,' " *New York Times*, July 29, 1969.

17. R. D. Corwin and Lois Gray, "Of Republicans and Recessions," *Social Policy*, 2, November–December 1971, p. 43.

overgrowth" are metaphors used effortlessly by those who do not suffer the chilling effects of the cooling or who in fact do the weeding. When it is said that the goal of government and business is a sound stable economy, it must be asked, "Sound and stable by whose definition? And at whose expense?"

The Pentagon: Billions for Big Brother

As measured by the federal budget, the greatest single devotion of the federal government is to an ever growing military establishment. The Department of Defense (commonly known as the Pentagon) commands more personnel and money than almost all the other departments, agencies, bureaus and commissions of government combined. Its budget, an estimated $80 billion in 1973, continues to increase steadily no matter if there is war or peace. From 1946 to 1972 the military consumed more than *one thousand billion* of the taxpayers' dollars. There has grown in our midst, President Eisenhower warned in his farewell address, a vast "military-industrial complex" whose influence "is felt in every city, every state house, every office of the Federal Government."

The leading beneficiaries of armaments contracts, the large corporations, help propagate the military's cause with skillful lobbying and mass advertising that stresses the importance of keeping America strong and the dangers of falling prey to one foe or another. In 1956 military leaders, corporation lobbyists, publicists and their congressional allies alerted the American public to a dangerous "bomber gap." Only after massive allocations were awarded to the Air Force was it acknowledged that no such gap existed and that the Soviets had no more than 150 to 200 long-range bombers as against our force of 680 B-52s and B-58s (not including the NATO air forces). In 1960 the "missile gap" scare followed the same disreputable course, with military spokesmen, political and corporate leaders and their news editors predicting that the United States would soon be reduced to a second-rate power open to attack. Only after the military budget was swollen to an all-time high was it revealed that the Pentagon had exaggerated the Russian missile threat by thirty times.[18] Rather than the four-to-one lead predicted for 1962, the Soviet Union had built only about fifty intercontinental missiles,

18. Bert Cochran, *The War System* (New York: Macmillan, 1965), pp. 86–87.

less than the number we had already possessed before our massive build-up.

In 1967 the Pentagon and corporate lobbyists and the same congressional and journalistic mouthpieces who had invented the "bomber gap" and the "missile gap" warned of a newly developing "antiballistic missile gap." The evidence in support of this latest manufactured crisis was as thin and conjectural as on the previous occasions; nevertheless, the Nixon administration spawned a $5.6-billion "safeguard" ABM system as the first step toward a more elaborate antimissile program. By 1973 "Safeguard" was heading for about a 250 percent cost overrun.[19]

As private industry became the supporter of defense preparedness, military men spoke more openly about the blessings of free enterprise and the "American Way of Life." With 90 percent of the contracts awarded with no competitive bidding on the open market, relations between corporate and military personnel became an all-important determinant of who gets what. Military officers increasingly looked forward to early retirement and to the financial and social rewards that came with entrance into high-paying corporate jobs—usually as recompense for services rendered while in the Pentagon. One congressional committee discovered that in 1960 more than 1,400 retired officers, from the rank of major upward, were employed by the top hundred weapon concerns.[20]

As a result of this military-industrial partnership, enormous portions of American purchasing power have been siphoned off by the government through taxation and channeled into the major corporations, with the ten largest companies receiving almost two fifths of the total contracts for weapons production, thereby further centralizing corporate wealth in America. Bert Cochran observes: "An immense industrial empire has developed whose sole customer is the government, and whose operations are risk-free."[21] The taxpayers' money underwrites all the risks of weapons development and war technology. What we have is "Socialism for the rich, at the poor man's expense: it is the American version of Marx."[22]

19. *New York Times*, July 23, 1973, also September 15 and 17, 1967; and Jerome Wiesner, "The Case Against an Antiballistic Missile System," *Look*, November 1967, pp. 25–27.
20. Samuel P. Huntington, *The Soldier and the State* (New York: Vintage Books, 1964), p. 361.
21. Cochran, *The War System*.
22. Edward Greer, "The Public Interest University," *Viet Report*, January 1968, p. 5.

Not only is the defense market risk-free; it provides even higher profits than those available on the private market, along with "cost overruns" many times greater than the original bids. Many firms do not explain their cost overruns, even when requested by government to do so. And the magnitude of these overruns is seldom appreciated: for instance, the C5A transport plane eventually cost $2 *billion* more than originally contracted. A study by the Brookings Institution concluded that "during the 1950's virtually all large military contracts . . . ultimately involved costs in excess of original contractual estimates of from 300 to 700 percent."[23] A report on thirteen major aircraft and missile programs since 1955 shows that while the total cost of the programs was $40 billion, less than 40 percent of them offered "acceptable electronic performance." During these years at least sixty-eight weapons systems were abandoned as unworkable. But the rewards for inefficiency have been high: the aerospace industry earned "a 12% greater return on equity than the average of all U.S. industrial firms," despite the fact that many of its programs either failed to measure up to expectations or broke down completely.[24]

The $80-billion Defense Department budget does not encompass all military-related spending. The government distributed more than $10 billion in veterans benefits and services in 1972 (and an estimated $10.7 billion in 1973). The greater portion of the national debt and the $22-billion interest (estimated $25 billion by 1974) paid every year is for deficits incurred because of the huge wartime and peacetime military budgets. In addition, $3.4 billion for space satellites and moon landings of widely proclaimed but unspecified scientific benefit, and expensive underground atomic tests allegedly essential to our defense but "harmless" to our environment, also must be considered in any calculation of what military spending costs the American people.

The influence of our military state is nowhere more heavily felt than in the academic community. Many institutions of higher education donate space, building funds and maintenance service to programs financed by the Pentagon and its various counterinsurgency agencies and draw anywhere from 10 to 80 percent of their budgets from government sources. "These schools must maintain their governmental research projects or face bank-

23. Cited in Lens, *The Military-Industrial Complex*, Chapter One.
24. See Bernard Nossiter's report in the *Washington Post*, January 26, 1969; also Lens, *The Military-Industrial Complex*.

ruptcy," Edward Greer concludes.[25] By 1971, at least ninety universities and colleges were researching such problems as counterinsurgency weaponry, combat communications, command-control systems, defoliation techniques, topographical and climatic factors pertinent to counterinsurgency, internal security and anti-riot strategies, population control and relocation methods and seismic and magnetic detection systems. At least fifty-six universities and colleges have been engaged in research on chemical and biological warfare.[26] "Academic scientists," observes Cathy McAffee, "are finding it increasingly difficult to pursue their careers without contributing to [defense] work. Not only do they depend on government contracts for support, but often they must become involved in defense projects merely to gain access to the information and equipment they need for research."[27] Representing the military's idea of a good academician is Dr. A. J. Hill, a weapons research man at MIT, who in no uncertain terms noted: "Our job is not to advance knowledge but to advance the military."[28]

Many social scientists have joined programs financed by the military apparatus, including psychological, sociological, economic and political studies devoted to counterrevolutionary techniques and the manipulation of opinion at home and abroad. In hundreds of conferences and in thousands of brochures, articles and books written by members of the intellectual community who are in the pay of the government, military and counterinsurgency propaganda is lent an aura of academic objectivity, complete with statistical and sociological embellishments. Casting a shadow on their own integrity as scholars and teachers, such intellectuals transmit to an unsuspecting public the military view of reality and the Pentagon's sense of its own indispensability.

The proliferation of Pentagon-financed "independent" corporations such as RAND and the Hudson Institute—the "think-tanks" that solve technical military problems for a fee—testifies to the growing role played by the nonmilitary man. The armed services, progressively less able to provide the brainpower for all their needs, simply buy up such human resources from the

25. Greer, "The Public Interest University"; also Clark Kerr, *The Uses of the University* (New York: Harper and Row, 1966), p. 55.
26. See the wealth of data—most of it from published government and university sources—gathered by Greer, C. Brightman, C. McAffee, M. Klare, D. Ransom, B. Leman, R. Rapoport, and M. Locker in *Viet Report*, January 1968.
27. *Ibid.*, p. 9.
28. Quoted in Cochran, *The War System*, p. 307.

universities, corporations and planning institutions. "What this means," Jules Henry points out, "is not so much that the military are being pushed out of the war, but that the civilians are being sucked into it. . . ."[29] The staggering fact is that over two thirds of all the technical research in America is being consumed by the military.

Millions of other Americans who make their living either directly or indirectly from the Pentagon's billions have committed themselves to the armaments race. Defense spending has been twice as important as private investment in expanding the American economy since 1948.[30] Taking into account the multiplier effect of a dollar spent, and the network of subsidiary services that feed on the defense dollar, possibly a fifth of all economic activity in America has been dependent on military expenditures.[31] As early as 1960 the Pentagon owned more than 32 million acres of land in the United States and 2.6 million acres in foreign countries—more than the combined areas of Delaware, Connecticut, Rhode Island, New Jersey, Massachusetts, Maryland, Vermont and New Hampshire.

If we define "military state" as any polity that devotes the major portion of its public resources to purposes of war, then America is a military state, the strongest military power in the history of mankind. Our leaders proudly proclaim that fact. Contrary to the conventional view, a civilian constitutional government is as capable of becoming a militaristic power as is a dictatorship. The political system of a nation is of less importance in determining its capacity for violence than is the level of its industry and wealth, the intensity of its anxiety about domestic and foreign enemies and the scope of its overseas investments and ambitions.

The Sword and the Dollar: Travels Abroad

The large profits from defense expenditures help feed overseas investments, and as these investments grow, so does the need for military intervention and big military budgets. Let us explore this point in some detail. The postwar growth of American corporations has been nothing less than stupendous, but prob-

29. Jules Henry, *Culture Against Man* (New York: Vintage Books, 1963), p. 106.
30. Cochran, *The War System*; also Tristram Coffin, *The Armed Society: Militarism in Modern America* (Baltimore: Penguin Books, 1964).
31. Cochran, *The War System*, pp. 142–144.

lems come with such success; enormous surplus profits remain after operational expenses are paid and even after the more than $25 billion in yearly dividends are distributed—chiefly to the wealthiest 1 or 2 percent of America's families. The remaining undistributed profits must be invested somewhere. Overseas investments— especially in underdeveloped countries—become increasingly attractive because of the cheap native labor, the absence of corporate taxes, the marketing of products at monopoly prices and the opportunity to invest a surplus capital that would only depress the profit rate at home or bring a low return in other industrialized nations.[32]

A central function of capitalist governments is, as Adam Smith said, to facilitate commerce "carried on with barbarous and uncivilized nations"[33] and to protect the overseas holdings of its private citizens. In pursuit of these goals, the government charters corporations to finance exports, subsidizes these exports with grants-in-aid, funds overseas business loans and investments, uses the International Monetary Fund and the World Bank to foster the right kind of international business climate, subsidizes the merchant marine and assures U.S. investors protection against losses due to war, revolution, insurrection, confiscation or expropriation by a foreign government.[34]

Through various foreign aid programs the government further subsidizes private business with sums amounting to several billion dollars each year. Ostensibly designed to help poorer nations help themselves, foreign aid is actually a means "by which the United States maintains a position of influence and control around the world," as President John Kennedy once proudly noted.[35] Aid from the United States must be carried in United States ships and is not available to countries which nationalize U.S.-owned assets without compensation.[36] Monies are allocated to Third World countries usually on the condition

32. See Joseph Schumpeter, "The Sociology of Imperialism," in *Two Essays by Joseph Schumpeter* (New York: Meridian Books, 1955), p. 51; also Harry Magdoff, *The Age of Imperialism* (New York: Monthly Review Press, 1969).
33. Adam Smith, *An Inquiry into the Nature and Cause of the Wealth of Nations* (Chicago: Encyclopaedia Britannica, Inc., 1952), p. 309.
34. The AID Specific Risk Investment Guarantee Program of September 1966 underwrites private investment in underdeveloped areas such as Latin America; see James Petras, "U.S. Business and Foreign Policy," *New Politics*, 6, Fall 1967, reprinted in Michael Parenti (ed.), *Trends and Tragedy in American Foreign Policy* (Boston: Little, Brown, 1971), p. 100.
35. Quoted in Teresa Hayter, *Aid as Imperialism* (Baltimore: Penguin Books, 1971).
36. *Ibid.*, pp. 15–16.

that they be used to buy U.S. goods at American prices. The roads, ports, communications, dams and utilities constructed with American funds frequently are planned around the needs of American-owned mines, oil fields, refineries and plantations. Abroad, as at home, the U.S. taxpayer pays for the "social overhead capital" needed to service private business.

Much of the aid program is nothing more than a direct export subsidy. Procurements of steel mill products by the Agency for International Development account for about one third of the American steel industry's exports. Government financing of wheat, rice, tobacco and dairy exports is approximately 30 percent of corporate agriculture's overseas trade. The government spent more than $61 million in 1960–1969 to subsidize the overseas sale of American tobacco, while another $69 million worth of tobacco was sold in foreign countries for local currencies which usually cannot be converted into dollars. "Such sales represent a nearly total loss to the U.S. taxpayer," Senator John J. Williams (R.–Del.) charged.[37] In Latin America, Alliance for Progress funds were given to native governments for the purpose of having them expropriate *unprofitable* U.S. firms at *above market prices*. "In turn," James Petras notes, "U.S. corporations used the funds procured to invest in more profitable activities, receiving special dispensation on the amount of profit which was remitted."[38]

The poor are almost always left out of such arrangements. Of the 25,000 tons of meat shipped to Brazil under the Alliance for Progress, for instance, 85 percent ended up in the hands of wealthy ranch owners. In countries such as Laos, on those rare occasions when the land of small farmers was irrigated and transformed into profitable holdings by U.S. aid, these were immediately taken over by the larger landholders.

Aid also retards the development of native-owned industry and helps U.S. capital exploit the recipient country's labor, monopolize its resources and influence its investments, tastes, markets and technical needs so that dependency on American products continues well after the aid program has ceased.[39] The military sales assistance program has a similar purpose. The

37. See Joseph Cassidy, "U.S. Subsidizes Tobacco Industry," *National Enquirer*, May 11, 1969.
38. Petras, "U.S. Business and Foreign Policy" in Parenti, *Trends and Tragedies in American Foreign Policy*, p. 98.
39. Harry Magdoff, *The Age of Imperialism* (New York: Monthly Review Press, 1969), pp. 129 ff.

multimillion-dollar overseas sale of every variety of weapon by U.S. corporations is vigorously promoted and subsidized by the Department of Defense in the hope that recipient nations will be tied more closely to American weapons systems.[40]

The net effect of overseas aid and capital investments is to retard rather than advance the economic development of Third World countries. Many liberals have wondered why the gap between rich and poor nations grows wider despite the increase in Third World investments. The answer is that the gap widens *because* of such investments. Unless we assume that corporations are in the business of social philanthropy, it is clear that investments have the ultimate purpose of *extracting* wealth from poorer nations rather than donating wealth. The intent is to control and exploit the labor, natural resources, finances, production and, if need be, the politics of the weaker nation for the purpose of gaining the greatest profits possible. Such growth brings very little development and prosperity for the poorer nation; it is not designed for that purpose. The effect of foreign investment is usually to dislocate the economy of the poorer country, retarding its productive capacity by limiting it to a few specialized extractive industries like oil, timber, tin, copper and rubber or cash crops like sugar, coffee, cocoa, cotton or tobacco. Major resources of the land are mobilized to suit the needs of the foreign corporations rather than the needs of the populace. The result is underemployment for the populace, low wages, high illiteracy and chronic poverty. Thus in a country like Guatemala, while the United Fruit Company owns three fourths of the arable land and extracts enormous profits, the rural population has a smaller per capita food supply today than during the Maya civilization. Every year fifty thousand Guatemalan children die of hunger before the age of five.[41]

The growth of American capitalism from a weak domestic position to a dominant international one has been accompanied by a similar growth in American military interventionism. Sometimes the sword has rushed in to protect the dollar, and sometimes the dollar has rushed in to enjoy the advantages won by the sword. The result is a military empire of a magnitude never

40. See Senator Eugene McCarthy, "Arms and the World," *ADA World*, September 1966, p. 4.

41. For a closer look at the effects and purposes of overseas corporate investments and government aid, see Felix Greene, *The Enemy: What Every American Should Know About Imperialism* (New York: Vintage, 1970); Paul Baran and Paul Sweezy, *Monopoly Capital* (New York: Monthly Review Press, 1968), pp. 186–207; Petras, "U.S. Business and Foreign Policy."

before equaled in the history of man. As of 1971 more than 1,517,000 American fighting men were stationed in 119 countries; the U.S. maintained 429 major military bases and 2,972 lesser bases in thirty countries, covering some 4,000 square miles and costing almost $5 billion a year. Two million native troops and large contingents of native police, under the command of various military juntas, have been trained, equipped and financed by the United States and assisted by U.S. counterinsurgency forces, their purpose being not to defend these countries from outside invasion but to protect capital investments and the ruling oligarchs from the dangers of domestic insurgency. Since World War II more than $50 billion in military aid has been given away by the U.S. to some eighty nations. No one knows precisely how much is being spent on military aid; '

estimates range from $4.8 billion to $7 billion a year. Congress exercises no effective oversight on military aid, and details of the program are withheld from the public and from Congress in "the interests of national security."[42]

This American global expansionism demands government expenditures that are greatly in excess of the business profits gleaned from overseas investments. But such considerations scarcely enter since, as Veblen pointed out in 1904, "the costs are not paid out of business gains, but out of the industry of the rest of the people."[43] The *profits* of empire flow into private hands,

42. See "Curbing Arms Aid," *Progressive*, April 1971, p. 7.
43. Thorstein Veblen, *Theory of Business Enterprise* (New York: New American Library Edition, n.d.), p. 217.

while the growing military and overhead *costs* are socialized and carried by the taxpayer.

This is not to say that U.S. expansionism has been impelled by purely material motives but that various other considerations, such as national security and patriotism, lead to policies that are closely identified with, and serve the material interests of, a particular class. Indeed, much of what passes for "the national interest" in capitalist America, not surprisingly, has been defined from the perspective of a capitalist social order. "A serious and explicit purpose of our foreign policy," President Eisenhower observed in 1953, "[is] the encouragement of a hospitable climate for investment in foreign nations."[44] Since American "security" is supposedly dependent on American power, and such power depends in part on American wealth (i.e., a "sound economy," "secure markets," "essential raw materials," etc.), then policies which are fashioned to expand U.S. corporate wealth abroad are presumed to be in the national interest. Thus we avoid any question as to whose interests are benefited by military-industrial global expansionism, at whose cost, and in pursuance of whose particular definition of "security."[45]

Taxes: The Unequal Burden

For many years liberals held two mistaken notions about the distribution of income: they believed that incomes were becoming gradually more equal and that government spending and taxing programs were accelerating that trend. But recent studies find that the gap between the very rich and very poor has increased over the last twenty-five years. The difference in the mean annual income of the richest 5 percent of U.S. families and that of the poorest 5 percent was $17,057 in 1947 but had grown to $27,605 by 1969 (weighting for inflation by using 1969 dollar value). Between 1947 and 1960 the percentage of families earning *less* than one half the median income *increased* from 18.9 percent to 20.3 percent. The poorest 20 percent received 5.1

44. *New York Times*, February 3, 1953, quoted in Magdoff, *The Age of Imperialism*, p. 126.

45. For further discussion of this and related points see Michael Parenti, "The Basis of American Interventionism," in Parenti, *Trends and Tragedies in American Foreign Policy*, pp. 215–228; David Horowitz (ed.), *Corporations and the Cold War* (New York: Monthly Review Press, 1969); Magdoff, *The Age of Imperialism;* Greene, *The Enemy*.

percent of the national income in 1947; by 1960 their share had dropped to 4.9 percent.[46] Between 1949 and 1969 the income gap—or the dollar distance—between those who have the most and those who have the least had *doubled.*

Contrary to the notion that taxes burden the rich more heavily than the poor and therefore lessen class inequalities, the tax structure never has been a means of significant redistribution of wealth.[47] The impact of state and local taxes is strikingly regressive, with those in the lower brackets paying proportionately more in sales and excise taxes than those in the upper brackets. One study estimates that persons in the $2000–4000 wage bracket pay 11.6 percent of their income in state and local taxes; those earning $6000–8000 pay 9.3 percent; those making $15,000 and above pay 5.9 percent.[48] Even taking account of federal and state income taxes, we find that individuals earning less than $2000 yearly pay a higher percent of their income in taxes than those who make over $10,000.[49] In 1968 the middle-income Americans in the $7000 to $20,000 range paid a higher percentage of their income for taxes than the richest 1 percent of Americans.

Kolko has shown that families earning less than $4,000 together contribute substantially more in federal taxes than the government spends "on what by the most generous definition may be called 'welfare.' "[50] Nor does recent tax legislation change this general pattern. According to Lekachman:

The Tax Reform Act of 1969 either retains or accentuates the elements of the federal tax structure which have the effect of sheltering income from property and capital gains, encouraging speculation, enlarging the personal fortunes of reactionary oil men, permitting a favored minority

46. See the findings reported by MIT economist Lester Thurow in *Time*, May 8, 1972, p. 9; also S. M. Miller and Pamela Roby, *The Future of Inequality* (New York: Basic Books, 1970), p. 38, and Leonard Ross, "The Myth that Things Are Getting Better," *New York Review of Books*, August 12, 1971, pp. 7–9.

47. The documentation in support of this point is quite ample; see Joseph Pechman, *Federal Tax Policy* (Washington, D.C.: Brookings Institution, 1966); Ferdinand Lundberg, *The Rich and the Super Rich* (Garden City, N.Y.: Doubleday, 1968); Philip M. Stern, *The Great Treasury Raid* (New York: Random House, 1964); Herman P. Miller, *Rich Man, Poor Man* (New York: Crowell, 1971).

48. John Mendeloff, "Taxes: Squeezing People to Support Corporations," *The American Independent Movement Newsletter*, April 1, 1969, p. 8 (published in New Haven, Conn.).

49. Leon Keyserling, "Taxes From Whom, For What?" *New Republic*, April 23, 1966, p. 18.

50. Gabriel Kolko, *Wealth and Power in America* (New York: Praeger, 1962), p. 39.

to supplement its income with huge tax-free expense-account allowances, and stimulating the accumulation of vast individual estates. . . . It amounts from its title onward to a major deception of the public.[51]

In capital gains write-offs, an estimated $5.5 billion to $8.5 billion each year goes to the very affluent. In addition there is another $1.43 billion yearly in oil and mineral depletion allowances, along with an almost $5-billion-a-year write-off for property tax allowances and home-owner mortgage interests—of benefit mostly to better-income groups. It is estimated that in the area of property and mortgage deductions, the federal government "pays 70 percent of local taxes and interest payments for the rich, 20 percent for the average man, and nothing for the poor."[52] Economist Leon Keyserling noted that tax cuts resulting from the Kennedy-Johnson "reforms" mostly benefited the upper 2 percent of the population.[53]

The steeply progressive federal tax rates on income give the misleading appearance that the rich are taxed more heavily than the poor. In reality, the wealthier the person, the greater are his opportunities to enjoy nontaxable income from capital gains, expense accounts, tax-free municipal and state bonds, stock options and various other kinds of business and professional deductions. Philip Stern calculated that families with yearly incomes of $100,000 and above—about .3 percent of the population—receive tax preferences of more than $11 billion annually.[54] In 1964 thirty-five persons making over $1 million paid no income taxes at all. In 1970 112 millionaires paid not a penny to the federal treasury.

The income of right-wing Texas oil billionaire H. L. Hunt was estimated back in 1957 to be $1 million each *week,* and oilman J. Paul Getty's income is estimated at $300,000 each *day.*

51. Robert Lekachman, "Taxes: A Gift for the Man Who Has Everything," *Dissent,* March–April 1970, p. 106.
52. Taylor Branch, "The Screwing of the Average Man: Government Subsidies: Who Gets the $63 Billion?" *Washington Monthly,* March 1972, p. 13; also Stanley Surrey, "Federal Income Tax Reform," *Harvard Law Review,* 84, 1970, p. 352. For data on other tax inequities see the works by Pechman, Lundberg, Stern and Miller cited in footnote 49 *supra;* also Joseph A. Ruskay, "The Missing Taxpayers," *New Republic,* April 29, 1967, pp. 11–14, on the difficulties of getting meaningful tax reforms.
53. Cited in Jack Newfield and Jeff Greenfield, "Them That Has, Keep: Taxes," *Ramparts,* April 1972, p. 62.
54. Stern's estimates are cited in Erwin Knoll, "It's Only Money," *Progressive,* March 1972, p. 25.

(The average worker must labor for most of his life to earn what Getty gets in twenty-four hours.) Yet both Hunt and Getty pay only a few thousand dollars a year in taxes. Many hundreds of other persons who earn over $200,000 pay little or nothing. In contrast, the low-wage earner has few opportunities for deductions and pays close to the full amount demanded by law. Estate and gift taxes provide a mere 1.7 percent (1969) of federal revenue. Loopholes to avoid inheritance taxes allow families at the top to hold onto and increase their wealth from generation to generation.[55]

Lenient taxes for the rich is a rule that extends to the corporations. Business continues to win enormously generous concessions in the form of tax relief, depreciation allowances, investment credits and other write-offs. In 1970, while 14 percent of the earnings of the lowest paid Americans went for federal taxes, more than a third of the big corporations, including companies like U.S. Steel, paid no taxes at all. The tax rates for the five largest oil companies averaged about 5 percent.[56] The Revenue Act of 1971, written and sponsored by the Nixon administration, cut income taxes by $9 billion annually, with over $7.5 billion going to large corporations. Tax sanctuaries, write-offs and abatements for the large corporations and the very rich shift the tax burden onto everyone else.

To summarize the major points in this chapter: The out-puts of the political system, as manifested by the services, subsidies, protections, taxes, leases, credits and market quotas established by public authority, affect the various areas of business enterprise and socioeconomic life mostly to benefit those who own the wealth of the nation. In almost every area of enterprise, government has provided business with unsurpassed opportunities for non-risk investments, gainful inefficiency, monopolistic pricing, lucrative contracts and huge profits. Government feeds capital surplus through a process of deficit spending, offers an endless market in the defense, space and nuclear industries, and provides for the financial aid, expansion and military protection of modern multinational corporations. From ranchers to resort owners, from doctors to bankers, from auto makers to missile

55. From a study done by the Cambridge Institute, cited in *Society*, 9, September–October 1972, p. 16.
56. In 1967 Standard Oil of New Jersey, with a *net* income of $2 billion, paid 7.9 percent in taxes; Texaco paid 1.9 percent; Mobil paid 4.5 percent; and Atlantic-Richfield with a net income of $145.2 million paid no taxes.

makers, there prevails a welfarism for the rich of such stupendous magnitude as to make us marvel at the big businessman's audacity in preaching the virtues of self-reliance and private initiative whenever lesser forms of public assistance threaten to reach hands other than his own.

Health, Education and Welfare: The Leaky Pump

7

GOVERNMENT EFFORTS ON BEHALF of health, education and welfare make up a relatively small portion of the federal budget and an increasingly smaller percentage of the Gross National Product. In the early 1970s such expenditures were cut substantially, while appropriations for the military continued to increase and allocations for "advancement of business" rose by *20 percent*.[1] In 1971 not more than 5 percent of the federal budget went to welfare, yet even these relatively modest sums seldom reached those most in need.

The Poor Get Less

The much publicized "war on poverty" of the 1960s brought no noticeable betterment to the estimated 40 million Americans living in poverty, nor to the 40 million others just above the poverty level, who suffer a precarious existence burdened by heavy debts, low wages, high taxes, inflation and lack of job security.[2]

After studying antipoverty programs in a dozen cities in 1969, the social psychologist Kenneth B. Clark concluded: "The poor serve as pawns in a struggle in which their interests are not the primary concern. The leaders talk

1. See Saul Friedman's comments in the *Progressive*, March 1972, p. 9.
2. See Richard Parker, *Myth of the Middle Class: Notes on Affluence and Equality* (New York: Liveright, 1972).

91

in the name of the poor and extensive funds are appropriated and spent in their name without direct concern for, or serious attempts at, involvement of the poor."[3] What is true of urban America seems equally true of rural America. During the 1960s, $7 billion was invested by federal, state and local governments in the Appalachia region yet, according to a *New York Times* report, the bulk of the poor "remain largely untouched" by the expenditures.[4] Some OEO officials complained that the poverty program was "chiefly a boon for the rich and for the entrenched political interests," specifically Appalachia's suburban and town "Main Streeters"—merchants, bankers, coal industry leaders, civic boosters and road contractors.[5] By concentrating funds in "small town growth areas," where businesses were located, and in a two-thousand-mile network of highways, many of which—as in urban ghettos—took advantage of a "right-of-way" displacement of poor homes, the Appalachian Regional Commission reportedly had hoped to achieve a "trickle-down economics" that eventually was to have benefited the poor with more jobs. After ten years and $7 billion the trickle had yet to begin.[6]

Low-income families are shortchanged by government programs supposedly designed to serve them. Thus one study shows that federal transfer payments, such as social security, railroad retirement, workman's compensation, unemployment benefits and veteran's disability compensation, distribute $7 billion more to people earning above $10,000 than to those below, with a person under the $5,000 income level receiving only a third the share available to someone in the $25–50,000 bracket.[7]

While conservatives often complain about "welfare chiselers" and stories are told about individuals who arrive in Cadillacs to pick up their welfare checks, the truth is that 50 percent of those on welfare are children, 13 percent are mothers, 37 percent are aged, disabled or blind, less than 1 percent are able-bodied men and about 55 percent are white. Large numbers of welfare recipients suffer from poor diet, insufficient clothing, over-

3. Quoted in the *New York Times*, November 9, 1969.
4. *New York Times*, November 29, 1970.
5. *Ibid*.
6. *Ibid*.
7. Taylor Branch, "The Screwing of the Average Man. Government Subsidies: Who Gets the $63 Billion?" *Washington Monthly*, March 1972, p. 22. Branch was referring to a study done by Joseph Pechman and Benjamin Okner for the Brookings Institution.

WARREN LINN

crowded housing, chronic illnesses and inadequate or nonexistent medical care. Approximately one fourth of all welfare children, ages five to fourteen, have never seen a dentist; at least half suffer from malnutrition.[8] An estimated 112,000 to 225,000 children of poverty, living in dilapidated housing, fall victim every year to lead poisoning; the toddlers eat chips of peeled paint containing lead, which, when ingested in sufficient amounts, causes brain damage and other serious disabilities.[9] Almost nothing has been done about this situation by federal or local authorities.

The welfare program in the United States does little to advance the life chances of persons in dire need; its funding is grossly inadequate and its administration is usually punitive in spirit and abusive of the rights of recipients.[10] One welfare expert estimates that, under the present program, for every two people receiving support, there are between two and three entitled to assistance who do not get it, not including those who receive payments smaller than they legally deserve.[11] In states like New York, Illinois, Alabama and California, the number of welfare recipients has been reduced by administrative fiat in recent years even as the need for benefits has increased.[12]

Other federal assistance programs show a similar pattern of favoritism toward the haves at the expense of the have-nots. The following are only a few of the many instances that might be cited:

(1) The Citizens' Board of Inquiry into Hunger and Malnu-

8. See data published by Children's March for Survival in the *New York Times*, March 19, 1972.

9. *New York Times*, March 26, 1969.

10. For detailed accounts of the inhumane effects of welfare programs, see Paul Jacobs, *Prelude to Riot* (New York: Random House, 1966); James J. Graham, *The Enemies of the Poor* (New York: Random House, 1970) Chapters 1–4; Gilbert Y. Steiner, *Social Insecurity* (Chicago: Rand McNally, 1966); Dorothy James, *Poverty, Politics and Change* (Englewood Cliffs, N.J.: Prentice-Hall, 1972); and the various other citations in this chapter.

11. David Steinberg, "Life Under the Plague," *Activist*, 7, Fall 1966, p. 20. See also Francis X. Clines, "Relief Clients Feel the Loss of Quarterly $25," *New York Times*, July 26, 1969; Homar Bigart, "Hunger in America: Stark Deprivation Haunts a Land of Plenty," *New York Times*, February 16, 1969.

12. Stephen Torgoff, "New York Clamps Down on Poor," *Guardian*, August 25, 1971. In New York, nursing care for the elderly indigent was cut to a maximum one hundred days. The measure was termed the "euthanasia section" by some critics, since old people would have to die or be put on the streets after their hundred days in a nursing home had expired. See Carl Davidson, "New York Welfare: Starving to Death," *Guardian*, April 12, 1969. See also Herbert J. Gans, "The Uses of Poverty: The Poor Pay All," *Social Policy*, July–August 1971, pp. 20–24.

trition noted that, under the federal school-lunch program, most lunches were being distributed to middle-class children rather than to the poor. Food programs reach only about 18 percent of the poor. The Board also found that the very poor were least likely to benefit from the food programs because they had insufficient funds to pay for them.[13] Furthermore, since the food programs were under the jurisdiction of a Department of Agriculture primarily dedicated to serving large agricultural producers, poor children often were fed whatever tended to accumulate in farm surplus programs, their diets being more "a result of economic policies rather than the types of food they really need," according to two nutrition experts.[14]

(2) The federal manpower programs, expending some $2.5 billion, have been described as a "windfall" and a "business bonanza" for the private firms that run the training programs at considerable profit to themselves, but few jobs have been generated for the mass of unemployed and unskilled.[15] The manpower training budget is padded with funds given to the Pentagon supposedly to train soldiers before discharge for civilian employment. There is not much evidence suggesting that enlisted men actually receive training for civilian employment while in the service.

"Community" programs like VISTA seem to have been of benefit primarily to corporations like General Electric which pick up the multimillion-dollar yearly training fees for program volunteers. VISTA, like OVP and other such programs, seems primarily intended to foster quiescence among the have-nots by performing minor services on their behalf. VISTA workers have readily complained of the uselessness of their efforts in helping the poor overcome the economic forces that perpetuate their poverty.[16]

(3) The use of funds on behalf of the privileged sometimes takes cruder forms. Thus the Farmers Home Administration, a

13. *Hunger, U.S.A.*, a report by the Citizens' Board of Inquiry into Hunger and Malnutrition in the United States (Boston: Beacon Press, 1968).
14. Dr. Michael Latham and Dr. Jean Mayer testifying before a Senate subcommittee, *New York Times*, December 18, 1968.
15. The training of people for jobs presumes the existence of the jobs. The training programs do nothing to answer the unemployed's first need, which is the creation of a faster expanding job market. On the shortcomings of one program, see Ivar Berg and Marcia Freedman, "The Job Corps: A Business Bonanza," *Christianity and Crisis*, May 31, 1965, pp. 115–119.
16. These are the conclusions of VISTA workers in Vermont interviewed by me in 1971–1972. Conversations with VISTA workers in eastern Kentucky and the Boston area brought forth similar complaints.

federal agency supposedly concerned with the problems of rural America, busied itself from 1962 to 1969 in providing multimillion-dollar no-risk loans for the construction of better than five hundred private golf courses. And in 1971 the government allocated $4 million from funds earmarked for "economically depressed areas" to construct a convention center to service businessmen in an affluent resort area in Missouri. (The resorts happened to be located in a county classified as "depressed.") Another $2.5 million of federal funds from the Economic Development Administration went to finance nearby airports for the convenience of the resorts' prosperous clientele.[17]

(4) Most of the federal funds intended for underprivileged school children—$4.3 billion by 1969—were used to replace rather than supplement state and local funds, often perpetuating racially segregated facilities in both North and South, with little of the monies going to instructional programs. One study group reported that the main beneficiaries of such aid have been the "textbook publishers and professional producers of education hardware," who lobbied hard for the federal act and who since have sold millions of dollars worth of their products to the schools under the act's program.[18] Another study revealed that millions of dollars intended for the education of impoverished Native American children were being used to buy expensive equipment for White students and to cover general operating expenses in order to reduce taxes for non-Indian property owners in some sixty school districts in eight states. Parents of Native American students were seldom informed about the money and programs available to them.[19]

(5) In 1969 the Office of Economic Opportunity let three contracts totaling about $500,000 to Pillsbury, Monsanto and Ballantine Beer, for the ostensible purpose of market-testing high protein foods in order to better distribute these among the poor. Actually the poverty funds were used to introduce new products into a luxury market in order to discover what prices middle-class consumers would pay for higher-quality flours and what their responses were to various new cola drinks.[20]

17. *National Enquirer*, February 21, 1971.
18. The report was prepared by the NAACP and the Washington Research Project; see the *Chicago Sun-Times*, November 9, 1969.
19. *Champaign-Urbana Courier*, January 12, 1971. By "Native American" I mean those indigenous peoples usually described as "Indians."
20. James Ridgeway, "Merchants of Hunger," *Hard Times*, December 15–22, 1969, pp. 1–4.

(6) Publicly funded "educational research" is frequently little more than publicly supported commercial research in disguise. Federal and state monies help finance the schools of business, law, agriculture and technology that provide expensively trained personnel, specialized consultations, research skills and various other services to the large firms in these respective fields. Academic entrepreneurs have been among those greatly advantaged by "social welfare" expenditures. Since 1950 hundreds of "task forces," "social laboratories," "research projects," "study programs" and "conferences" on race, poverty and urban affairs conducted by academic institutes and private consulting firms have been funded by the Department of Labor, HEW, HUD, OEO, the Economic Development Administration and other federal and state agencies.[21] Such studies, charged Ralph Nader, have cost billions, yet they "are worthless, expensive, used mainly to delay policy decisions and to get the agencies who commission them off the hook. Others are wholly ignored."[22]

(7) Almost without exception the beneficiaries of public aid to higher education have been in the upper-income quartile. Students in tax-supported as well as private institutions are drawn mainly from upper- and middle-income families, the better off among them attending the more heavily subsidized universities. Thus the students who attended the University of California in the mid-1960s and received an average subsidy of about $5,000 were mostly upper-middle class, while lower-middle- or working-class students were concentrated in the California junior colleges where the per capita subsidy was only about $1,000.[23] A similar situation exists in public support for elementary schools. Although state aid is supposed to counterbalance the great inequities between rich and poor school districts, in fact most states dispense money through matching funds, giving larger sums to upper-income districts and smaller sums to lower-income districts and thereby doing little to lessen inequities and much to intensify them.[24]

21. See the *New York Times*, September 11, 1968, for a report on the Urban Institute, a "government backed corporation" involved in this kind of enterprise.
22. Ralph Nader, "A Citizen's Guide to the American Economy," *New York Review of Books*, September 2, 1971, p. 16.
23. See W. Lee Hansen and Burton A. Weisbord, *Benefits, Costs and Finance of Public Education* (Chicago: Markham, 1969).
24. John E. Coons, William H. Clune and Stephen Sugarman, *Private Wealth and Public Education* (Cambridge, Mass.: Harvard University Press, 1970).

"Urban Removal" and Transportation

The many billions expended by government in urban renewal programs have usually forced low-income people to double up in the remaining low-rent areas so that their neighborhoods can be demolished and replaced by luxury apartments, office buildings, banks, department stores, shopping centers, throughways and parking lots, as has happened in just about every city with a housing program. Urban renewal projects might best be characterized as "land grabs." By the power of eminent domain, the municipal or state government is able to do for realty investors and corporations what they could not do for themselves —namely, forcibly buy large tracts of residential areas from reluctant small owners and small businessmen, or from "farsighted" speculators who, armed with inside information, buy up land in the "condemned" area for quick resale to the city at substantial profit. Then the city sells this land, often at less than the market value, to big developers, underwriting all investment risks on their behalf. The losses suffered by the municipality in such transactions are usually made up by federal funds and constitute another public subsidy to private capital.[25] Furthermore, the federal government directly underwrites private housing programs, dispensing multimillion-dollar "research and development" contracts through its Department of Housing and Urban Development to big developers like Levitt and Sons, a subsidiary of ITT.

In the 1970–1972 period a failing economy caused many developers to default under the Housing and Urban Development program—with the government taking the loss.[26] Defaults on FHA and HUD mortgages "created blocks and blocks of abandoned housing in American cities." One major newspaper described Secretary George Romney, in charge of HUD, as having "witnessed his own transformation from crusader for decent shelter to leading slumlord in America."[27] The chairman of the House Appropriations Subcommittee on Housing, Edward Boland, complained of the widespread "abuse, corruption and inefficiency" of the housing program. "In fact, the subsidized

25. See Paul Baran and Paul Sweezy, *Monopoly Capital* (New York: Monthly Review Press, 1968), pp. 289–300; also Edward C. Higbee, *The Squeeze: Cities Without Space* (New York: Morrow, 1960).

26. *New York Times*, July 17, 1968.

27. Appropriations to assist HUD housing payments were to reach $1.8 billion in 1972; this was apart from the $1 billion yearly urban renewal program.

housing programs have turned out to be a bonanza in too many instances for just about everyone except [the poor]."[28]

In the postwar era, the *New York Times* reports, federal housing insurance has made possible the construction of more than 10 million units for well-to-do families and only 800,000 units for the poor and the lower-middle class.[29] The chairman of the President's National Commission on Urban Problems, former Senator Paul Douglas, concluded that "Government action through urban renewal, highway programs, demolition on public housing sites, code enforcement and other programs has destroyed more housing for the poor than government at all levels has built for them."[30] Blacks, Chicanos, Native Americans, Chinese and other racial minorities occupy a disproportionate share of the nation's bad housing. According to a 1971 report by the McGovern Senate Committee on Nutrition and Human Needs, "from 1960 to 1968, the percentage of non-whites occupying substandard housing actually increased from 22 to 33 percent."[31]

The transportation system in America is a prime example of how the well-to-do get the most and the needy the least. Twenty percent of all federal transportation outlays goes to the airlines. Another 63 percent is spent on highways—of little use to the millions of very poor, elderly and others who cannot afford automobiles. Only 2.8 percent is given to mass transit systems.[32] Thus the relatively high-income air traveler is sumptuously subsidized while the urban low-income subway or bus rider is expected to pay nearly the full cost of his transportation. The urban areas "where the greatest number of persons suffer from the most severe problems deriving from transportation," including "pollution and congestion," receive the least support.[33] Even the crumbs allocated to public transportation sometimes do not reach their destination. Thus in fiscal 1971–1972, while the highway lobby was feasting on some $5.7 billion, only $750 million was budgeted for mass transportation, and only two thirds of this sum was actually spent; the remaining funds were impounded by the Nixon administration.

28. *New York Times*, October 5, 1972.
29. *New York Times*, July 17, 1968.
30. Quoted in Michael Harrington, "The Betrayal of the Poor," *Atlantic*, January 1970, p. 72.
31. Quoted in "Rural Housing Famine," *Progressive*, April 1971, p. 8.
32. Robert S. Benson and Harold Wolman (eds.), *Counterbudget, A Blueprint for Changing National Priorities 1971–1976* (New York: Praeger, 1971), p. 157.
33. *Ibid*.

As public transportation declines because of the austerity imposed on it by federal and state budgets, a growing reliance is placed on the automobile—leading to a further decline in public transportation. The social costs of the automobile are staggering. At least 55,000 people are killed on the highways each year and hundreds of thousands more are injured and maimed. More than 60 percent of the land of most U.S. cities is taken up by the movement, storage and servicing of automobiles.[34] Homes, schools, churches, recreational areas and whole neighborhoods, particularly in working-class communities, have been razed to make way for highways. The single greatest cause of air pollution in urban areas is the automobile: its carbon monoxide exhaust now claims about a thousand lives a year, and deaths from emphysema, a related lung disease, have been increasing by about 12 percent each year for the past twenty years.[35] As the number of cars grows (from 31 million in 1945 to 114 million in 1972), so do the revenues from the gasoline tax that are put into the Highway Trust Fund. As more superhighways are built with these accumulated billions, the carnage, environmental devastation and—just as significantly—the profits of the oil, auto, trucking, tire, cement, construction, motel and other businesses increase. At the same time the mass transit systems—the most efficient and safest form of transporting large numbers of people—fall into further decay. Most of the municipal transit systems are funded by deficit spending, with bond issues that are sold to wealthy individuals, banks and business firms. In any one year these transit systems pay out millions of dollars for the enrichment of privileged bondholders, while themselves coming close to bankruptcy and being forced to cut services for the ordinary citizens who pay the bill. In 1973, for example, the Chicago Transit Authority proposed an additional fare rise and threatened to cut services and lay off workers because it was $42 million in debt. Yet CTA bondholders, led by First National Bank of Chicago and Continental Illinois, collected some $7 million in interest on their holdings that same year. Much of what is called "public ownership" in transportation, roads, airports, bridges and other facilities and services is really privately bonded, with tax-free, risk-free dividends going to the rich and the costs being paid by consumers, users and taxpayers. The

34. According to the Highway Action Coalition, a public interest group in Washington, D.C., as reported in Renee Blakkan, "Profits Clog the Highways," *Guardian*, November 29, 1972.
    35. *Ibid*.

juxtaposition of private wealth and public poverty so frequently found in the United States is no mere curiosity. The two go together.

Health and Safety for Nobody

Consumer protection is another area in which government efforts seem designed to advance the interests of private producers at the expense of the public. Adulterated products, contaminated meats and fish, unsafe additives and preservatives, deceptive labeling, false advertising, overpricing, planned obsolescence, shoddy and dangerous commodities—such evils of the consumer market not only go uncorrected but are sometimes even encouraged by public authorities.[36] Consider the Food and Drug Administration. FDA does little policing of the drugs and foods that are marketed; it samples but 1 percent of the millions of yearly shipments of produce, yet issues reassuring pronouncements on the safety of numerous drugs, additives and preservatives whose long-range, or even immediate, effects are suspect. FDA's claim that it has not enough men to police the food, drug and cosmetics industries has not prevented its agents from spending much time in what Omar Garrison describes as "a host of questionable, ignoble and often illegal activities," investigating and prosecuting those health lecturers and health food innovators whose ideas about nutrition and medicine are critical of established drug and food enterprises. FDA has also found time to stigmatize as "faddists" and "crackpots" the growing number of Americans who are concerned about the safety of their food and medications.[37] Not surprisingly, many top decision-makers within FDA maintain intimate ties with drug manufacturers, food processors and AMA officials, frequently ending up as high-paid managers and consultants in firms they previously "regulated."

36. An excellent collection of articles documenting the ways consumers are cheated and endangered by business, often with the complicity of government, is David Sanford (ed.), *Hot War on the Consumer* (New York: Putnam, 1969). See also David Caplovitz, *The Poor Pay More* (New York: Free Press, 1967).

37. See Omar V. Garrison, *The Dictocrats' Attack on Health Foods and Vitamins* (New York: Arco Publishing, 1971); also Alek A. Rozental, "The Strange Ethics of the Ethical Drug Industry," *Harper's*, May 1960, pp. 73–84; Estes Kefauver, *In a Few Hands* (New York: Pantheon Books, 1965); and Richard Harris, *The Real Voice* (New York: Macmillan, 1964). One spokesman for FDA, Dr. Ogden Johnson, revealed his real concern by noting: "We have been quite frankly appalled at the degree to which the consumer does not trust the manufacturer," quoted in the *Militant*, December 24, 1971, p. 7.

CARL A. RUDISILL LIBRARY
LENOIR RHYNE COLLEGE

A pattern of collusion between business and government can be found in the area of worker safety. Lax enforcement of safety codes by the Bureau of the Mines sustains working conditions regarded as among the worst in the world and helps make it possible for mining companies to operate at 15 percent profit. A study by J. David McAteer reports that in 1948 a miner's chances of getting killed were one in 454, while in 1968 his chances were one in 273. In any given year the probabilities are *one in six* that a miner will be seriously injured. Because of intensified drilling, instances of "black lung" disability have increased greatly. Health officials in Kentucky report miners breathe 67 times the maximum amount of coal dust declared to be safe by federal law. McAteer also reports that coal mine owners routinely ignore safety regulations. Even when federal inspectors write up safety violations, there are no penalties; and state inspectors often have difficulty gaining access to mines because of lack of cooperation from mine operators, who seem to hold them in contempt.[38] At the same time, the mining communities continue to suffer from inadequate schools, roads, housing and hospitals. One expert on the subject, Harry Caudill, notes:

It is still astonishingly laissez-faire, a land where absentee owners of immense mineral deposits, and the mining companies to which they lease, rule states and counties through puppet officials, commit with impunity every conceivable assault against the physical environment, and evade their tax liabilities so thoroughly that long tiers of pauper counties huddle broke and impotent atop vast mineral reserves and amid endless industrial activity. The corporations treat mining men with the same contempt a farmer might reserve for his mules and shirk virtually all responsibility ... for the communities they so ruthlessly dominate.[39]

As in mining, so in almost every area of production, the laborer is treated as an expendable component of the production process, forced to work under unsafe conditions that remain unrectified by public agencies. Thus in one Georgetown steel factory, reports Rita Millins, *one third* the labor force suffered

38. J. David McAteer, *Coal Mining Health and Safety in West Virginia* (Morgantown, W. Va.: West Virginia University Press, 1970); also Brit Hume, *Death and the Mines* (New York: Grossman, 1971); Ben A. Franklin, "The Scandal of Death and Injury in the Mines," *New York Times Magazine*, March 30, 1969, pp. 25–27, 122–128.
39. Harry M. Caudill, "Betrayal in the Mines," *New York Review of Books*, December 2, 1971, p. 11.

injuries within a year.[40] And many thousands of asbestos workers are doomed to early deaths from cancer because government regulations fail to offer adequate protection. One cancer specialist, noting that federal standards permit workers to inhale 20 to 30 million asbestos fibers in a single working day, charged that "we face an unparalleled disaster to working people in this country."[41] In an average year more than fourteen thousand Americans lose their lives in job accidents and 2.5 million are disabled by job-related diseases and accidents. Of 1,339 companies doing business with the government, 95 percent violated minimum safety and health standards. "Corporations," Sylvia Porter noted, ". . . are doing typically little to protect employees."[42]

Workers in the low-wage brackets have the highest rate of injury. According to a study done by one labor economist, a major determinant of how much money industry expends on safety measures is the potential savings to a firm when it reduces injury. Low-wage workers are less expensive to "damage"—that is, the amount of production lost is less than when a highly skilled, better paid worker is disabled. Industries with low wages tend to have higher injury rates because it is less expensive to replace the injured worker than make safety changes.[43]

Like the corporations, government is doing almost nothing to protect the lives of workers. Enforcement of the Occupational Safety and Health Act of 1970, the first piece of federal legislation to establish a comprehensive structure for defining standards for safe working conditions, has been inadequate both because of lack of staff (often factories go for years without an inspection) and because of light penalties: one factory that

40. Rita Millins, "Georgetown Steel Company Strike," *Workers' World*, December 25, 1970. See also Jeanne M. Stellman and Susan M. Daum, *Work Is Dangerous to Your Health* (New York: Pantheon, 1973).

41. Dr. Irving Selikoff of Mount Sinai Hospital in New York, in a report quoted in the *Guardian*, June 28, 1972.

42. Sylvia Porter, "Accident Toll of Workers," *San Francisco Chronicle*, July 30, 1968, cited in G. William Domhoff, *The Higher Circles* (New York: Vintage, 1971), p. 201. See also Morton Mintz, "Danger and Death in the Trucker's Cargo," *New York Post*, September 3, 1969; Millins, "Georgetown Steel Company Strike." For a report on the plight of farm workers see Fay Bennett, "The Condition of Farm Workers and Small Farmers in 1969," *Report to the Board of Directors of National Sharecroppers Fund* (New York: 1969); Tom Foltz, "Florida Farmworkers Face Disaster," *Guardian*, April 3, 1971, p. 4; Rod Such, "New Growth in Use of Child Labor," *Guardian*, June 2, 1971, p. 5; and the *New York Times* report on migrant workers, September 16, 1971.

43. The study is by the economist Robert S. Smith, reported in the *New Haven Register*, December 22, 1972.

manufactured a highly toxic chemical was fined *six dollars* for each of its several pollution violations.[44]

When Americans fall victim to illness or injury they also are prey to a rapacious and unreliable medical profession. The quality of medical care in America has shown little improvement in recent years despite huge public expenditures. In 1966 physicians' fees jumped 11 percent, most of it charged to the Medicare program. In the New York area, doctors increased their fees for elderly patients by as much as 300 percent. Throughout the country, hospital bills have been rising five times faster than the overall cost of living.[45] High premiums and padded administrative costs have enriched private health-insurance companies, further inflating costs beyond anyone's expectations. The second largest item in the Medicare administration budget has been for data processing services, a task contracted at nearly *40 percent profit* to a private electronic data company owned by H. Ross Perot, a businessman who became a multimillionaire by servicing various state and federal welfare and medical programs.[46]

Some $9 billion spent by the federal government in 1970 on medical programs extended some assistance to the elderly and the indigent. But the major beneficiaries were the doctors who continued to charge exorbitant rates without providing any commensurate increase in the overall quality of medical care. More than anyone else, it has been the medical men who "are doing well under 'socialism.' "[47] "I am horrified," writes Senator Edward Kennedy, "that we in America have created a health care system that can be so callous to human suffering, so intent on high salaries and profits, and so unconcerned for the needs of our people."[48] The conditions Senator Kennedy found in his Senate investigation were the same throughout the nation: people denied emergency treatment because they could not show proof

44. Bob Kuttner, "When the Job Disables the Worker," *Village Voice*, May 18, 1972. See also Joseph A. Page and Mary-Win O'Brien, *Occupational Epidemic* (The Ralph Nader Task Force Report on Job Health and Safety, unpublished preliminary draft), Chapter 9, pp. 2–3.

45. "T.R.B. from Washington," *New Republic*, January 13, 1968, p. 3. The profit-seeking organization of the medical profession and its deleterious effects on lower- and middle-class people is discussed with telling effect in Barbara and John Ehrenreich, *The American Health Empire: Power, Profits and Politics* (New York: Vintage, 1970).

46. See Robert Fitch, "H. Ross Perot: America's First Welfare Billionaire," *Ramparts*, November 1971, pp. 43–51.

47. "T.R.B. from Washington," *New Republic*, January 13, 1968, p. 3.

48. Edward Kennedy, *In Critical Condition: The Crisis in America's Health Care* (New York: Simon and Schuster, 1972).

of ability to pay, others ejected from hospitals in the midst of an illness because they were out of funds, still others who were bankrupted by medical bills despite supposedly "comprehensive" insurance coverage, many who were victims of unnecessary surgery done for the sole purpose of bringing profit to the physician: in sum, a medical profession composed of doctors who are rich or nearly rich and who are busily victimizing the public in the most callous ways.

Public health programs, like poverty programs, are sometimes never implemented even after having been voted into law. In 1967 Congress enacted a law requiring the Department of Health, Education and Welfare to set up by July of 1969 a comprehensive program of early and periodic screening, diagnosis and treatment (EPSDT) for all children under the age of twenty-one. It was to provide extensive preventative dental and medical examinations—including testing for such things as lead poisoning, anemia and hearing and sight problems, as well as remedial treatment and regular follow-ups. Four years later no such program existed and in fact state officials in many places were unaware there was such a law. It is only through the efforts of a few active poor people's organizations that the issue remained alive at all.[49]

On Behalf of Pollution

The federal government's widely publicized "war on pollution" of the early 1970s, like its "war on poverty" of the decade before, has brought few results. The disastrous effects of strip mining, off-shore drilling and other such exploits have been frequently publicized but seldom prevented. The Nixon administration, for example, has permitted the petroleum companies to embark upon a five-year program of accelerated off-shore drilling, despite the continued oil spillage disasters of recent years.[50] One writer observed that the destruction of shore lines by oil seepage is actually quite functional to the oil companies, since by destroying off-shore areas for recreation, it opens them for

49. "Child Health Care: A Worsening Scandal," *Guardian*, December 20, 1972; the article is primarily the text of a National Welfare Rights Organization statement to the Congressional Black Caucus hearing on government lawlessness.

50. For an account of the Santa Barbara oil leakage, see Ross Macdonald, "Life with the Blob," in Walt Anderson (ed.), *Politics and Environment* (Pacific Palisades, Calif.: Goodyear, 1970), pp. 123–132.

drilling.[51] Enforcement of pollution laws is so rare as to be newsworthy, and the penalties invoked so minor as to be farcical: after the first oil spillage at Santa Barbara, the petroleum companies were charged with 343 violations of the Fish and Game code; upon conviction, each company was fined the grand sum of $500. The multibillion-dollar U.S. Steel Corporation was indicted on five counts of dumping poisonous industrial wastes into Lake Michigan—if convicted it could receive a maximum fine of $2,500 on each count.[52]

The Pesticide Control Act passed in 1972 made pollution a money-making venture for some industries. A little publicized provision of the law allowed the government to compensate—at retail prices—the producers of pesticides for financial losses suffered if their products were ordered off the market as unsafe. One Congressman observed: "This measure may set a precedent for the Government to pay compensation to private enterprise every time a legitimate Government action taken in the public interest results in a loss of profit for the business community."[53]

Efforts at the state level show no better record of enforcement. In Maine, one of the states in which environmental issues have received much attention, the record as of November 1970, according to the *Maine Times,* was as follows:

Water classification laws, enacted a decade ago, have yet to take effect, or to work any significant cures on the pollution wounds inflicted by industry and the public on Maine's major rivers.

A state pesticides control board, created more than four years ago, has thus far proven incapable of bringing any major pesticide reforms to Maine.

A wetlands preservation measure, voted by a legislature that is now history, has been hamstrung and declared ineffective by a state court.

No single Maine air polluter has yet been prosecuted under any existing local, state or national statute. . . .

The protection of tidal estuaries, research which could double the lobster crop, studies of practical aquacultural techniques for the cultivation of mussels, oysters and clams . . . each of these is termed a visionary idea by the state's leadership establishment, including Senator Muskie and Governor Curtis.

The prime areas of Maine's most pristine environment, the unorganized townships of the timber wildlands, are totally without protec-

51. See James Ridgeway, *The Politics of Ecology* (New York: E. P. Dutton, 1970).
52. See the *Daily Illini*, March 19, 1970.
53. Richards D. Lyons, "Pesticide Compensation Bill Seen Costing Billions," *New York Times*, October 15, 1972.

tion from developers, even though the most rudimentary protective laws have been sought in the last two legislative sessions. . . .

When you look at this record of the state you realize that no environmental law enacted by any legislature has had any significant effect on saving the environment; and that few local laws have been enacted which can protect Maine communites against the destruction wrought by greedy developers.

Examined in the harsh light of reality, the environmental crusade in Maine becomes a bleak illusion.[54]

The approach taken by state, local and federal government in regard to pollution, like the approach taken in most other problem areas, hews closely to three principles: (1) the forms of public control must never compete or interfere with the basic profit interests of private investment—that is to say, the solutions to pollution must be accommodated to the private-profit capitalist production system; (2) in keeping with the above requirement, the costs of pollution control are to be borne by the public rather than by the producers; and (3) the companies that pollute the most will get the most. Thus the larger the company's profits, the greater is its pollution subsidy under the 1969 Tax Reform Act. This measure is in pursuance of a certain perverse logic: big profits are made by big producers, and big production generally means big pollution, which, in turn, demands big clean-up subsidies and big tax credits. In sum, the polluter is rewarded rather than punished.[55]

The Nixon Approach

As of 1973 the outlook was not promising for the poor and the needy. Even the paltry sums that had been reaching them were endangered for fiscal 1973–1974; President Nixon increased the military budget by some $5 billion (despite the Vietnam "peace") and cut almost $4 billion from the "human services" budget. Among the programs to be slashed or abolished were aid to the elderly and crippled, pensions for disabled Vietnam veterans, the school milk fund, school lunches, food stamps, day

54. Editorial in the *Maine Times*, November 15, 1970.
55. See Branch, "The Screwing of the Average Man: Government Subsidies . . . ," p. 15; also "Eco-profits," *Hard Times*, May 11–18, 1970, p. 1; and Martin Gellen, "The Making of a Pollution-Industrial Complex," *Ramparts*, May 1970, pp. 22–27. For an excellent analysis of the effects of capitalism on the natural environment, see Barry Weisberg, *Beyond Repair—the Ecology of Capitalism* (Boston: Beacon Press, 1972).

care, community action, drug and addiction treatment, aid to dependent children, aid to public libraries, public transportation, pollution control, biomedical research training, dentistry training, public health services, mental health services and flood control. Besides this, Nixon vetoed bills for vocational rehabilitation of the disabled, child-care centers, hospital construction, drug rehabilitation and environmental protection and refused to spend monies that were allocated by Congress for low-income housing, food stamps, mass transportation and water pollution control.

The *methods* of funding initiated by the Nixon administration also had regressive effects. Thus in 1972 the President signed the revenue-sharing bill into law. The law rechannels 1.3 percent of federally taxed income back to the states ($5.3 billion in 1972–1973). States like Alaska, Wyoming and New Mexico, with high revenues from oil and mineral leases, get more money than industrial states with their financially impoverished cities. Many states paying the most federal taxes benefit least from revenue sharing, yet it is these states that are most in need. Thus New York's share of federal money for human services was to drop from $800 million to $223 million under revenue sharing. In addition, the funds would no longer go directly to the needy urban areas but would be funneled through state governments often dominated by conservative rural and business interests unsympathetic to the problems of the urban working class and racial minorities.[56] The revenue-sharing plan was hailed by Nixon as a way of "giving government back to the people." In giving it that description he avoided several questions: When we give money back to the communities, are we enhancing equality or increasing inequality? To whom are the funds going? For what purposes and to serve what interests? The Nixon approach to revenue sharing seems to be a way of achieving more decentralization of funding with less democratization.

56. See Renee Blakkan, "New Bill Puts Rich on the Dole," *Guardian*, November 1, 1972, p. 6.

Whose Law? Whose Order?

8　SINCE WE ARE TAUGHT TO THINK OF the law as an institution that serves the entire community and to view its representatives —from the traffic cop to the Supreme Court Justice—as guardians of our rights, it is always discomforting to discover that the law is often conceived and enforced in unjust ways and that its agents can be motivated by the most tawdry racist, class and sexist biases.

The Protection of Property

Far from being a neutral instrument, the law belongs to those who have the power to define and use it—primarily those who control the resources of society. Thus it is no accident that in most conflicts between the propertied and the propertyless, the law intervenes on the side of the former. The protection of property is deemed tantamount to the protection of society itself and of benefit to all citizens, presumably even the propertyless. Those who equate the interests of property with the "common interest" seldom distinguish between (a) large corporate property used for the production of profit and (b) consumer-use possessions like television sets, homes and personal articles. Most political conflicts are concerned with the distribution and use of (a), not (b); yet segments of the public, believing that their modest and highly mortgaged personal-use possessions (b) are being threatened in controversies arising over (a), will give sympathetic support to the corporate property system.

The law's intimate relationship to property can be seen in the curriculum of the average law school: one learns corporate law, tax law, insurance law, torts and damages and realty law chiefly from the perspective of those who own the property. Owners, trustees and landlords have "rights," but workers, students and tenants have "demands," and troublesome ones at that. Under the property law, management may call in the police or, if need be, the National Guard to lock out discontented workers, but workers cannot call in the police to drive out management. University trustees may bring in the police to control the behavior of striking students, but students cannot call on the police to control the behavior of trustees. Landlords can have the police evict rent-striking tenants, but tenants cannot demand that police evict rent-gouging landlords. In most legal contests between landlord and tenant, the landlord's rights are usually automatically upheld by the courts, the burden being on the tenant to prove violations. Low-income residents soon learn that housing laws dealing with the collection of rents, eviction of tenants and protection of property are swiftly enforceable, while those dealing with flagrant violations of building and safety codes, rent overcharging and the protection of people seem impossible to enforce.

The biases written into the law, which reflect the one-sided and often unjust property relations of the society, are compounded by the way the law is enforced. The corporate rich have the advantage both in the way the law is written and the way it is applied. For the same reasons, low-income people are gravely disadvantaged. Even when the letter of the law is on their side, the poor usually have little else working for them. Although they are in greatest need of legal protection, they are the least likely to seek redress of grievances through the courts, having neither the time nor the money to do so. And when they find themselves embroiled in court cases, it is almost always at the initiative of the bill collector, the merchant, the landlord or some such party who regularly uses the courts as a means of asserting his property interests.

Business crime is socially more damaging than most working-class crime, since it may involve the health, safety and earnings of millions of workers and consumers. Ralph Nader once estimated that each year orange-juice companies steal more money from the American public by watering down their product than bank robbers steal from banks. A Nader task force estimated that monopolies are costing American consumers $48 to $60 billion a year because of fixed prices, lost production and lack of innovation.[1] The President's Commission on Law Enforcement reported in 1967 that the property losses from crimes like robbery, burglary, auto theft and larceny accounted for only 15 percent of the money costs against property, while business crimes like embezzlement, fraud, forgery and commercial theft accounted for 78 percent.[2]

Lawlessness is endemic to the business community. A routine inspection of lumber establishments resulted in the find that approximately three fourths of them were violating major provisions of the Fair Labor Standards Act.[3] And three fourths of all banks were violating the banking laws. Long after Congress prohibited employers from interfering with the efforts of employees to organize for collective bargaining, owners continue to use spies, scabs, goons and labor racketeers to terrorize union organizers and troublesome workers—frequently with the complicity and active cooperation of local police and with the knowledge of Labor Department officials.[4] The criminality of corporations, Sutherland concludes, is persistent, "like that of professional thieves."[5] Looking at seventy of the largest corporations in the United States, he found that in several decades they had been convicted of an average of ten criminal violations each (a figure that greatly underestimates the actual amount of crime, since most violations go unchallenged or never reach court). Any ordinary citizen with such a conviction record would be judged an "habitual offender" deserving of heavy punishment. Yet the guilty companies were provided with special stipulations, desist orders, injunctions and negotiated settlements or were let off with light fines. Often they were not even required to appear in court. "The criminality of their behavior was not made obvious by the conventional procedures of the criminal law but was blurred and concealed by special procedures."[6]

1. "Nader Report: Consumers Lose Billions to Invisible Bilk," *Crime and the Law* (Washington, D.C.: Congressional Quarterly, 1971), p. 21.

2. President's Commission on Law Enforcement and Administration of Justice, 1967, reported in *Crime and the Law*, p. 20.

3. Edwin Sutherland, *White Collar Crime* (New York: Holt, Rinehart and Winston, 1949), p. 150.

4. *Ibid.*, pp. 137–144. Note the difficulties of the United Farm Workers in trying to organize the grape and lettuce pickers in California and Arizona.

5. *Ibid.*, pp. 210–222.

6. *Ibid.*, p. 42.

Nonenforcement of the law is common in such areas as price fixing, restraint of trade, tax evasion, environmental and consumer protection, child labor and minimum wages. The antitrust laws, supposedly intended to restrict the unfair practices of large firms and protect the consumer and smaller producers, have snared almost no businessmen in the eighty years of their existence: from 1890 to 1946 only seven were sentenced to prison, and all seven had their sentences suspended. In the early 1960s, thirty-two General Electric executives were found guilty of conspiracies to fix prices in contracts valued at over $27 million. Thirty were given jail sentences; twenty-three of these were suspended and the other seven served thirty days.

The business community enjoys a double standard under the law. In New York a judge imposed a small fine on a stockbroker who had made $20 million through illegal stock manipulations and, on the same day, sentenced an unemployed Black man to one year in jail for stealing a $100 television set from a truck shipment. "Contained in that small example is much of the story of American legal justice," Edward Greenberg suggests.[7] An extensive investigation of the New York State court system found that persons who committed crimes like burglary, theft and small-time drug selling received harsher sentences than persons convicted of securities fraud, kickbacks, bribery and embezzlement.[8]

The class homogeneity of lawmakers and lawbreakers is indeed a crucial factor. Persons in public office usually are drawn from the same social strata as businessmen, and many return to business when they leave office. "Almost every important person in government has many close personal friends in business, and almost every important person in business has many close personal friends in government."[9] As Sutherland writes: "Legislators admire and respect businessmen and cannot conceive of them as criminals. . . . The legislators are confident that these respectable gentlemen will conform to the law as the result of very mild pressure."[10]

7. Edward S. Greenberg, *Public Policy in the United States* (forthcoming). The incident described is taken by Greenberg from Leonard Downie, Jr., *Justice Denied* (New York: Praeger, 1971), p. 46.

8. *Guardian*, October 18, 1972.

9. Sutherland, *White Collar Crime*, p. 248.

10. *Ibid.*, p. 47.

Criminal Enforcement:
Unequal Before the Law

Looking at the criminal law enforcement process, we find that various racial, sexual, political and class factors—external to any actual criminal behavior—bear a clear relationship to the treatment accorded an individual from the time of arrest to the time of sentencing.

ARREST

An arrest is not only the first step in the enforcement process; it is often a form of punishment in itself, leading to temporary incarceration, legal expenses, psychological intimidation and possible loss of job. Of the 7.5 million people arrested in 1969 for all crimes, excluding traffic offenses, more than 1.3 million were never prosecuted or charged, and 2.2 million were acquitted or had the charges against them dismissed, according to the FBI Uniform Crime Report. The large number of arrests without charges or conviction, especially of ghetto residents and antiwar demonstrators, suggests that frequently the purpose of arrest is not to convict but to harass, intimidate and immobilize. In some cities, as many as 90 percent of arrests are made without warrants. Police have the power to jail anyone for up to two or sometimes three days without pressing charges and, once charged, a suspect can have a "hold" placed on him by the District Attorney or some law enforcement official and be kept in prison until trial time.

In many situations the prejudices of the police officer are a crucial determinant of who gets arrested. When members of the leftist DuBois Club in Brooklyn were attacked by neighborhood hoodlums in 1966, the police arrived on the scene, arrested the victims and allowed their assailants to walk off untouched. Acts of vandalism during ghetto disturbances led to mass arrests, and Chicago police were instructed to shoot looters; but when a middle-class White mob wrecked a newly constructed house in Queens—in response to rumors that it was to be occupied by non-Whites—they were merely shooed away by the police, who witnessed most of the vandalism but made no arrests.[11] Studies show that Blacks, Chicanos, Puerto Ricans and indigent Whites

11. *Guardian*, January 10, 1973.

have many more personal experiences with police brutality than middle-class White "respectables."[12]

CHARGES

The kind of charges brought against an arrested person may depend on the kind of person he is. Members of rich and influential families and persons who occupy high public positions are often able to hush up an embarrassing arrest and not be charged with anything.[13] Every arrest situation has enough ambiguity to allow authorities some discretion in determining charges. Whether a situation is treated as "disorderly conduct" or "mob action," whether it is to be "aggravated battery" or "attempted murder," depends somewhat on the judgment of the law enforcers, both police and prosecutors, and their feelings about the suspect.

A factor sometimes determining the seriousness of the charges is the degree of injury *sustained,* not inflicted, by the individual during the course of his arrest. Police are inclined to bring heavier charges against someone whom they have badly beaten—if only to justify the beating and further punish the "offender." The beating itself is likely to be taken as evidence of guilt. "I cannot believe a state trooper would hit anyone for no reason," announced one judge in a trial involving a college professor who had been repeatedly clubbed by state troopers while participating in an antiwar demonstration.[14] "In the eyes of the police," Paul Chevigny argues, "arrest is practically tantamount to guilt, and the police will supply the allegations necessary for conviction; the courts are treated as a mere adjunct to their purpose."[15]

BAIL AND LEGAL DEFENSE

After being charged and booked, the suspect is held in jail to

12. See David H. Bayley and Harold Mendelsohn, *Minorities and the Police* (New York: Free Press, 1971), p. 122.

13. The former lobbyist Robert Winter-Berger gives an interesting account of his successful efforts to cover up the arrest of a U.S. Senator in a gay bar in New York; see his *The Washington Pay-Off* (New York: Dell, 1972), pp. 82–84.

14. Michael Parenti, "Repression in Academia: A Report from the Field," *Politics and Society*, 1, August 1971, pp. 527–537.

15. Paul Chevigny, *Police Power* (New York: Pantheon, 1969), pp. 276–277.

await arraignment.[16] At arraignment the judge has the option of doing anything from releasing the defendant on his own recognizance to imposing a bail high enough to keep him in jail until his trial date—which might come a couple of years later—as was the fate of numerous Black Panthers arrested in police raids in New York, New Haven and other cities and held on bonds set as high as $100,000 and $200,000. Even if eventually found innocent, as was the case of the New York and New Haven Panthers, the defendant will have suffered the immense costs and anxieties of a trial and an extended imprisonment. This "preventive detention," commonly employed against large numbers of persons rounded up during urban disturbances, allows the state to incarcerate and punish people without having to convict anyone of any crime.[17]

"Recognizance" would be most helpful to those unable to afford bail but it is usually granted to "respectable" middle-class persons and seldom to indigents. Stuart Nagel shows that in state cases 73 percent of all indigents were denied pre-trial release as opposed to 21 percent of nonindigents.[18] The 1970 census discovered that more than half the people held in all county and municipal jails had been convicted of no crime but were awaiting either a trial or a hearing.[19] Pre-trial detention makes it almost impossible for the poor to assist their attorney in the preparation of an adequate defense. Brought into court directly from jail, a defendant is statistically more likely to be convicted and likely to be sentenced to a longer term than someone accused of the same crime who has been free on bail and whose lawyer can point to his "rehabilitation" and law-abiding life since the original arrest.[20] Poor people also are more likely to be persuaded to plead guilty to reduced charges ("plea bargaining"). Ninety

16. Procedures vary somewhat from state to state and according to the nature of the crime. For a standard textbook account of law enforcement procedures, see Delmar Karlen, *The Citizen in Court* (New York: Holt, Rinehart and Winston, 1964).

17. See Jerome Skolnik, "Judicial Response in Crisis," an excerpt from Skolnik's book, *The Politics of Protest* (New York: Simon and Schuster, 1969), reprinted in Theodore Becker and Vernon Murray (eds.), *Government Lawlessness in America*, (New York: Oxford University Press, 1971), p. 162, especially the comments by Judge Crockett of Detroit.

18. Stuart Nagel, "Disparities in Criminal Procedure," *UCLA Law Review*, 14, August 1967, pp. 1272–1305.

19. 1970 National Census, statistics reproduced in *Crime and the Law*, p. 12.

20. Ralph Blumenfeld, "The Courts: Endless Crisis," *New York Post*, May 15, 1973. See also Stuart Nagel, "The Tipped Scales of American Justice," *Transaction*, 3, May–June 1966, pp. 3–9; and Nagel's "Disparities in Criminal Procedure."

percent of all defendants plead guilty without a trial; of the other 10 percent, more than half are convicted of something. This statistic hardly fits with the image of "coddled" criminals and "soft-hearted" courts propagated by the get-tough advocates.

LAWYERS, JURIES AND JUDGES

Like medical service, legal service in our society is commercial; it best serves those who can pay for it. The man who has the $100,000 for top legal assistance experiences a different treatment from the law than the poor person with a court-appointed lawyer. Public Defender or Legal Aid lawyers are overloaded with cases and have little time for the defendant, sometimes seeing him for the first time on the day of his trial. Being mostly of White middle-class background, they often share the same prejudices about their non-White, poor clients as do police, prosecutors, judges, juries and probation officers, a factor that can further influence their efforts.

The selection of juries is weighted in favor of the more conservative elements of society. In most states prospective jurors are chosen from voter registration rolls that underrepresent racial minorities, the young, the longhairs, the working class, the poor, the transient and mobile and the politically alienated who feel voting is a waste of time. The few cultural or political "deviants" who might get called for jury duty are usually weeded out at selection time by the peremptory challenges of the prosecutor. Juries in most areas of the country will contain a disproportionately high percentage of White, middle-aged or elderly middle-class Americans of conventional and often conservative stripe. The same is true of grand juries, which commonly function as extensions of the prosecution rather than as impartial citizens' panels. The grand jury bringing indictments against prisoners who allegedly had taken part in the 1971 Attica uprising contained twelve persons who stated in open court that they had friends or relatives working as guards in Attica prison. Five jurors had friends who were hostages in the yard. The judge did not believe these connections were evidence of bias or prejudice.[21]

As portrayed in the popular media, the judges who preside over our municipal, state and federal courts are distinguished

21. See Nick Coles, "Massive Crackdown Hits Attica," *Guardian*, January 3, 1973.

looking men, possessed of a wise and commanding air, making fair-minded decisions, calming courtroom passions with measured admonitions, showing fear and favor toward none yet capable of a certain compassion for the accused. Turning from Hollywood to reality, we discover that judges are often arrogant, self-inflated persons who are not above indulging their worst prejudices by meting out harsh decisions against defendants who incur their disapproval.

As an illustration of the arbitrary, biased judgments made by men on the bench, consider the decision handed down by the Iowa Supreme Court against Harold Painter. In 1966 Mr. Painter, a widower who had remarried, was denied custody of his eight-year-old son by the nine-man Iowa court because the justices felt that his household in a San Francisco suburb was "unconventional, arty, Bohemian and probably intellectually stimulating"—hence not a desirable place to raise the boy. While Painter himself made a fairly good salary, his house was old and had weeds in the yard and needed painting, the judges noted; and, worse still, Mr. Painter "has read a lot of Zen Buddhism" and was known to have attended his wife's funeral (at a time when Painter contends he was still in shock over her sudden death in an auto accident) in improper attire, i.e., an open-necked sport shirt without a tie. Confronted with such degeneracies, the court ruled that the boy should stay with his maternal grandparents, who would provide a "stable, dependable, conventional, middle-class Middle West background."[22]

A study of state courts found that judges were considerably more inclined to send poorly educated persons to prison and less likely to give them suspended sentences or probation than better educated and better-income persons convicted of the same crimes.[23] A study of courts in Seattle, Washington, found that persons who convey the appearance of a middle-class status are treated as more worthy of leniency by judges than those who by dress or attitude do not seem to value "the same things which the court values."[24] One federal judge observes that his colleagues

---

22. *New York Times*, April 3, 1966. Painter finally got his boy back when the grandparents voluntarily gave up custody two years or so later. He wrote a book about the whole episode: *Mark, I Love You* (New York: Simon and Schuster, 1968).

23. Nagel, "Disparities in Criminal Procedure."

24. For a report on the study see Ray Bloomberg, "Court Justice Tied to Middle-Class Values," *Quaker Service Bulletin*, 54, Spring 1973, p. 8. This study found poverty to be a bigger factor in court bias than race. Nagel finds the same, although he allows that there is much overlap.

are "likely to read thick briefs, hear oral arguments, and then take days or weeks to decide who breached a contract for the delivery of onions"—such are the efforts devoted to business cases—but when dealing with criminal charges against a common defendant, "the same judge will read a pre-sentence report, perhaps talk to a probation officer, hear a few minutes of pleas for mercy—invest, in sum, less than an hour in all—before imposing a sentence of 10 years in prison."[25]

Like police, many judges are inclined to see any defendant who enters their court as guilty of something. One observer of New York City Courts concluded:

Favoritism to the prosecution is the rule among most judges here, products of a middle-class Jewish, or Italian, or Irish background that makes it impossible for them to identify with most Black and Puerto Rican suspects. Racism is the most common form of corruption. But beyond that, judges are psychologically allied with the police and prosecutors in most courtrooms.[26]

Judges not only identify with the prosecutor, they frequently *are* former prosecutors, having made their way to the bench via the office of district attorney or state attorney or the Justice Department. Thus a Justice Department lawyer, Myles Lane, one of the prosecutors in the Rosenberg "atom spies" trial, became, twenty years later, the judge who sentenced the Black revolutionary H. Rap Brown to five to fifteen years for armed robbery.

Echoing a favorite conservative theme, President Nixon complained of "softheaded judges" who showed more concern for "the rights of convicted criminals" than for innocent victims. To Mr. Nixon's charges, U.S. District Judge Marvin Frankel responded:

On the contrary, I would have to confess that we run more to the toughness and arrogance that go with a pervasive sense of righteousness and respectability. . . . Does [the judge] identify more with the criminal than with the victim? Anyone who would answer "yes" has not spent much time in criminal courtrooms. Judges actually prefer law and order

25. Marvin E. Frankel, *Criminal Sentences: Law without Order* ((New York: Hill and Wang, 1973).
26. Ralph Blumenfeld, "The Courts: Endless Crisis," *New York Post*, May 15, 1973. The description offered by Blumenfeld should not be confined to New York Jews, Italians or Irish; it fits White, middle-class judges of every national background throughout the land.

to lawlessness and disorder. Our judges give out long, hard, stern sentences in quantity. . . .[27]

An American Bar Association study found that, far from coddling criminals, American jurists imposed much severer sentences than their opposite numbers in Western European countries. Sentences of over five years for felony convictions are rare in Europe but common in the United States,[28] where jail terms sometimes have an eighteenth-century quality about them. In Norfolk, Virginia, a man received ten years for stealing eighty-seven cents; in Detroit, a Black youth was found guilty of stealing seven dollars and given three to ten years; in Urbana, Illinois, an unemployed Black caught stealing a loaf of bread from a supermarket was sentenced to half a year in prison; in Georgia, a White youth and a Black youth were sentenced to thirty years each for possession of marijuana; in Los Angeles a twenty-year-old Mexican-American drug addict was sentenced to life in prison for selling some narcotics to a police informer; a young night-club dancer was sentenced to fifteen years for possession of marijuana in Texas; a sick, twenty-three-year-old street addict received thirty years in New York City for selling one seventy-third of an ounce of heroin; a youth in Louisiana got fifty years for selling a few ounces of marijuana.

Drug laws have served handily to entrap political activists. John Sinclair, a radical in Wisconsin, was sentenced to nine years for accepting a marijuana cigarette from a friend who turned out to be a police informer. Lee Otis Johnson, a SNCC leader in Texas, did the same and was sentenced to thirty years. The hippie guru, Timothy Leary, received ten years for possession of marijuana. The Black socialist Martin Sostre, long an opponent of heroin and drug traffic in the ghetto, was convicted of dealing in heroin—on the sole testimony of a convict who was released from prison after appearing against Sostre and who subsequently admitted in a sworn statement that his testimony had been fabricated. Sostre was sentenced to forty-one years and has been in prison since 1968, mostly in solitary confinement.

In contrast, Robert F. Kennedy, Jr., received a suspended

27. Marvin E. Frankel, "An Opinion by One of Those Softheaded Judges," *New York Times Magazine*, May 13, 1973, p. 41. In his book *Criminal Sentences*, Judge Frankel describes judges as "arbitrary, cruel and lawless" in the ways they determine sentences.
28. Frankel, "An Opinion by One of Those Softheaded Judges."

sentence for possession of marijuana. The son of a well-established New York politician, arrested for possession of heroin, was paroled and placed in a narcotics treatment program. A major heroin dealer, with twelve previous arrests and important mob connections, was released on his own recognizance. Another influential heroin dealer, with two previous arrests for selling, was given a conditional discharge. A big-time racketeer had felony charges against him dismissed by a compassionate judge known for his stern rulings against longhairs and Blacks. A detective with gangland connections, caught dealing in heroin, was convicted of a misdemeanor and given a suspended sentence. "What criminal cases reveal," Mitgang writes, ". . . is that there is one law for the poor, another for the organized criminal with the expensive name lawyers."[29]

JUSTICE DENIED

The image we have in our heads of an orderly, even-handed, dignified system of justice does not coincide with the picture drawn by one reporter who spent a month observing a municipal courtroom:

Routinely, lives are ruined and families broken by 30-second decisions. Some judges quit work at 2:00 P.M. to play golf, while some 8,000 men and women presumed innocent under the Constitution wait months for trials in the city's overcrowded detention jails. Other judges have tantrums on the bench and call defendants "animals" and "scum." Cops pay court attendants ("bridgemen") $5 to call their cases first. Legal Aid lawyers defend 50 poor clients a day with not a second for preparation. The bail system lets bondsmen buy freedom for the rich and well-connected. Clerks sell advance word on court assignments and decisions. Civil cases almost always get decided in favor of the landlord or businessman, or city agency.[30]

Generally speaking, poor and working-class defendants, the uneducated and the racial minorities are less likely to be released on bail, more likely to be induced to plead guilty, more likely to go without a pre-trial hearing even though entitled to one, less likely to have a jury trial if tried, more likely to be

29. Herbert Mitgang, "The Storefront Lawyer Helps the Poor," *New York Times Magazine*, November 10, 1968.
30. Jack Newfield, "New York's Ten Worst Judges," *New York*, October 1972, p. 32.

convicted and receive a harsh sentence and less likely to receive probation or a suspended sentence than mobsters or business- men and other upper- and middle-class Whites. What breeds disrespect for the law on the part of many poor people is that it is so unevenly applied: if one is wealthy enough and well- connected enough, one can escape its impositions and exploit its resources. Many poor understand that the man who steals five dollars is called a thief while the man who steals five million is called a financier. And they see that the law rather consistently works against people like themselves who, in a private economy, are most in need of public protection and assistance.

Women of upper-class social background are more likely to receive favored treatment at the hands of the law than low- income or impoverished people of either sex, and in most kinds of cases White women receive better consideration than Black men. But race and class aside, women suffer certain legal injustices of their own. Most laws against prostitution, for exam- ple, are either written or enforced so as to place all the guilt on the prostitute and none on her male clients. In some states, wives still have not achieved equality with their husbands in regard to consent in contracts and handling of property. In most states a woman under eighteen still does not have the right to consent to sexual love without running the risk of having the act declared unlawful and her lover prosecuted for "statutory rape." But men under eighteen are under no similar consent restriction with women of "legal age." As victims of rape, women often receive little justice in the courts, it frequently being assumed by police, attorneys, judges and jurors that the rape victim "was asking for it" (an assumption that is far less likely to be made if the alleged rapist is Black).

As with Blacks, the poor and women, so with homosexuals: the oppression practiced in the wider society is reflected and reenforced in the law and the courts. Thus when gay people go to court to contest the discrimination they suffer in housing and employment, they are most likely to find that the rights of property take precedence over the rights of people, and the doctrine of equal protection under the law does not apply to them. In most states gay love is still punished under the "sodomy" or "unnatural acts" laws, and two people who love each other but are of the same sex find themselves treated as criminals or "perverts" to be hustled off to jail or a mental institution for "treatment" and "cure." Gays are barred from certain government jobs on the highly dubious assumption that their homosexuality is indicative of personal instability and leaves them open to corruption or blackmail, making them poor security risks. Gay bars are frequently raided by police or closed down by municipal authorities and gay individuals often are "cruised" by undercover police, posing as fellow gays, whose intent is to entice and entrap them, an undertaking that some law officers perform with an enthusiasm that seems to involve something more than the call of duty.

The Repression of Dissenters

Among those whom the law treats harshly are persons who oppose capitalism and advocate alternative social orders. Since capitalism is treated as an essential component of Americanism and democracy, those who are anticapitalist are portrayed as being antidemocratic, un-American, subversive and a threat to the "national security"—thus fair game for repression.

In response to this "Red Menace," at least twenty well-financed federal agencies (of which the FBI is only the best publicized) and hundreds of state and local police units actively engage in the surveillance, infiltration, entrapment and suppression of dissenting groups.[31] In addition, the Army employs an estimated 1,200 agents for *domestic* spying. Counterinsurgency methods developed by the government for use in other lands are applied at home to combat civil disturbances caused by racial minorities, student radicals and striking workers. The Army has developed contingency plans enabling it "to strike concurrently at rioters in as many as 25 major cities."[32] The Justice Department's Law Enforcement Assistance Administration provides electronic sensors, wall-penetration surveillance radar, voice-print equipment, night-vision devices, command and control systems, mobile digital teleprinters, television street surveillance systems and other electronic materials, at an estimated yearly cost of more than $400 million, to police departments throughout the nation.

31. For a lucid analysis of political repression in the United States, see Alan Wolfe, *The Seamy Side of Democracy* (New York: David McKay, 1972). A good collection of studies of government repression is Becker and Murray (eds.), *Government Lawlessness in America*. For further comments of mine on the repressive qualities of the U.S. political order see my "Creeping Fascism," *Society*, 9, June 1972, pp. 4–8. See also Murray Levin, *Political Hysteria in America* (New York: Basic Books, 1971) for a fine study of red-baiting and political repression during this century.
32. *New York Times*, March 5, 1972.

The unrestricted adoption of surveillance technology by police moved one Rand Corporation engineer, Paul Baran, to speculate that "we could easily end up with the most effective, oppressive police state ever created." He observed that "there is an unmistaken amorality which infects some of my engineering colleagues. That is, whatever we are paid to work on we automatically rationalize to be a blessing to mankind. . . . Too many of my brethren think that merely because something can be built and sold, it should be."[33]

By 1970 one of the fastest growing commodity markets involved the sale of counterinsurgency equipment to U.S. police and the fastest growing public occupation was police work. The budgets of some cities began to resemble the federal budget in their lopsided dedication to "defense spending." For example, the largest single item in the 1971 municipal appropriations of Philadelphia was the $92 million given to the police. Yet the growth in their budget did not mean the police were coming any closer to winning "the war against crime."[34] In cities like Philadelphia and Chicago and even in smaller urban areas where organized crime and corruption were rife, the new police units were devoting more time to radicals, hippies and politically conscious Blacks than to mobsters or violent criminals. The Berkeley police budget was doubled between 1967 and 1970, yet over that same period there was a 65 percent rise in major criminal offenses, including burglary, rape and murder, and a 5 percent decrease in arrests for these offenses from the previous year. The Berkeley police were simply too interested in pursuing drug users, hippies, "street people" and radicals to worry about ordinary crime. (Drug arrests of youth increased by 231 percent.)[35] In most urban areas, according to Illinois Police Superintendent James McGuire, there are more police "on political intelligence assignments than are engaged in fighting organized crime."[36] The same seems true of federal law officers, which might explain why agencies like the FBI have such lackluster records in battling the organized rackets. Files stolen

33. Quoted in Robert Barkan, "New Police Technology," *Guardian*, February 2, 1972. See also Les L. Gapay, "Pork Barrel for Police," *Progressive*, March 1972, pp. 33–36, for data on law enforcement technology.

34. Despite the huge expenditures for police, the crime rate in Philadelphia is increasing. See the *New York Times*, May 24, 1973.

35. Frank Browning, "They Shoot Hippies, Don't They?" *Ramparts*, November 1970, p. 14.

36. Quoted in Frank Donner, "The Theory and Practice of American Political Intelligence," *New York Review of Books*, April 22, 1971, p. 28 *fn.*

from a Meade, Pennsylvania, FBI office in 1971 and subsequently published in national magazines revealed that a great portion of FBI work in the mid-Atlantic region was directed against Black militants, White radicals and antiwar organizers. Large numbers of agents had infiltrated political and antiwar groups, often acting as provocateurs to criminal actions designed to entrap activists.[37] Relatively little attention had been given to organized crime.

In June 1972 a group mostly consisting of ex-CIA agents, some of whom were associated with President Nixon's campaign staff, were caught breaking into the Democratic party headquarters in the Watergate building in Washington. Subsequent investigations revealed that the burglary was only a small part of an extensive campaign involving political espionage, campaign sabotage, wire tapping, illegal entry, theft of private records, destruction of campaign finance records, illegal use of funds, perjury, conspiracy to obstruct justice and other such acts, planned and directed by White House officials and members of Nixon's campaign staff. Directly implicated were the President's former Attorney General and closest political adviser, the President's personal appointments secretary, the President's personal lawyer and political confidant, the President's White House counsel, the President's two top White House staff members, more than a dozen other members of the President's White House staff and an equal number of his campaign staff. President Nixon himself miraculously knew nothing about it, he insisted, although in subsequent statements he admitted having suppressed certain parts of the investigation, specifically an FBI probe into GOP campaign funds that had been diverted to a Mexican bank and had been linked to the Watergate conspirators—an action he said he took because "national security" might have been involved. Nixon also admitted having authorized break-ins and acts of espionage by White House

37. Various defectors from intelligence units have publicly confessed to spying on, entrapping and provoking radical activities. Undercover FBI agents arranged and committed various bombings and draft board break-ins. See, for instance, "FBI Informer Talks: We Bombed in Seattle," *University Review* no. 23 (c. 1972), pp. 3–4, 8. My own experiences might be pertinent: In 1970 a student at the University of Illinois informed me that in exchange for a suspended sentence for a marijuana arrest, he had agreed to monitor my public and campus speeches for the FBI. The following year at the University of Vermont, a member of the campus police force made a public confession that he had been working for the FBI; one of his assignments, he told me, was to keep tabs on my campus activities.

intelligence units—although he contended that Watergate occurred without his "specific" authorization or knowledge.[38] Testimony by others close to the President alleged that Nixon withheld for a month evidence of a break-in at the office of Daniel Ellsberg's psychiatrist and may have even ordered it, that he tampered with the judge presiding over the "Pentagon Papers" trial of Ellsberg and Russo by offering him the directorship of the FBI while the trial was still in progress, that he failed to respond to warnings from his acting FBI director, Patrick Gray, who informed him of cover-up efforts by high-placed members of the White House staff, and that he himself had engaged in cover-up activities.[39]

Various political leaders and editors denounced the Watergate venture as an unprecedented instance of government lawlessness. In fact, there was very little that was unprecedented about it. For more than half a century the same illegal and clandestine tactics have been employed against political heretics. What shocked the establishment politicians was that in this instance the crimes were committed against a segment of the establishment itself—specifically, the Democratic party and mass media newsmen. The White House's use of such criminal activities was consistent with Nixon's claim that he had the "inherent executive power" under the Constitution to commit even unlawful acts when impelled by considerations of national security. And "national security" seemingly embraced every conceivable area of political activity.

The intelligence business is a massive enterprise. By 1973 government agencies were expending approximately $6 to $9 billion a year on intelligence at home and abroad. This is, at best, a rough estimate, since Congress has no exact idea how much money organizations like the CIA are spending or for what purposes. Millions of dossiers are kept on individuals suspected of harboring unorthodox political views. Data on political dissenters are shared by federal, state and local intelligence units and are sometimes fed to the press and to employers, landlords and others who might have opportunity to harass the persons under surveillance. The Internal Revenue Service has a "special ser-

38. *New York Times*, May 24 and June 7, 1973.
39. At the time of this writing, August 1973, investigations of the entire affair were being conducted by several congressional committees and by a specially appointed Justice Department prosecutor. The full extent of wrongdoing was not known. Talk of impeachment was heard in the press and in Congress, along with suggestions that the President resign.

vice" unit whose function is to audit the tax statements of troublesome newsmen, congressional opponents and political groups like the Black Panthers and SDS. Various political activists, including such Black organizers as the Reverend Jesse Jackson, have complained of continual IRS harassment. In June 1973 it was made public that President Nixon had complained privately to his aides that the "Democratic bias" of IRS bureaucrats had made it difficult to extend the use of IRS audits to certain Democratic critics of his administration. In response, the IRS Commissioner announced his continued determination to apply the law in an even-handed, nonpolitical way (at least in regard to Democrats and Republicans). Meanwhile the political use of tax audits against radicals by the IRS continued.

In supposedly defending the Constitution against subversives, law enforcement agencies have had repeated occasion to violate it. Within recent years, the Justice Department has (a) engaged in illegal mass arrests, as during the May 1971 antiwar demonstration in Washington, D.C., (b) advocated and used illegal wiretapping and bugging devices against political dissenters, (c) applied conspiracy laws unjustifiably against antiwar organizers, (d) failed to seek prosecution against those guilty of killing students at Kent State University and (e) used grand jury investigations as tools for political surveillance. "Justice," as the late FBI chief J. Edgar Hoover said in a 1970 television interview, "is merely incidental to law and order. It's a part of law and order but not the whole of it." Indeed, the whole of it, the indispensable goal of law and order, Mr. Hoover made clear on many occasions, is the preservation of the American socioeconomic status quo.

When directed toward social reform, the law usually proves too weak, and public agents too few, for effective enforcement, but when mobilized against political dissenters, the resources of law enforcers seem boundless. Few social problems are pursued with such punitive vigor and imagination. "I've had more trouble with the law," Eldridge Cleaver wrote, "since I've been relating to the movement than when I was committing robberies, rapes and other things that I didn't get caught for."[40] In cities throughout the nation, radical activist groups have had their telephones bugged, their offices raided, their records and funds stolen by police, their members shot at, threatened, beaten, intimidated, maligned, arrested on trumped-up charges, held on exorbitant

40. Quoted in the *Guardian*, November 30, 1968.

bail and subjected to costly, time-consuming trials which, whether won or lost, paralyzed their leadership, exhausted their funds and consumed their energies. In a series of litigations against antiwar activists and radical organizers in the late 1960s and early 1970s the government's message came across loud and clear: people are not as free as they think. They may organize and propagandize against government policies, but they will be placed under surveillance for it and their public statements and actions will be recorded by the FBI or the equivalent local or state police agency and be used against them when they are charged with conspiracy to obstruct draft laws, or sedition or, as in the case of the eight radical leaders who participated in the street demonstrations at the 1968 Democratic National Convention in Chicago, conspiracy to violate the anti-riot provisions of the Civil Rights Act of 1968.[41]

At numerous universities, students and faculty who espouse Marxist or other unorthodox political ideas have been hounded by campus police and university authorities. Radical faculty members often find their contracts not renewed or, in rarer instances, their tenure revoked. The number of cases handled by the American Association of University Professors has tripled in recent years. At Dartmouth College in 1969 a dozen radical faculty regularly met together for lunch, but within three years all but one had been terminated—a dramatic but not unique example of the quiet purge conducted on campuses throughout the nation.[42] Sometimes the crassest political considerations are revealed in these actions. One of the charges made by the trustees at the University of Vermont against an outspokenly radical political scientist whose contract was not renewed despite unanimous recommendations from faculty and administration was that he had been seen carrying a "Viet Cong" flag in a downtown peace demonstration, an action they cited as a violation of "professional conduct." When teaching and research cannot be faulted, this vague category of "professional conduct"

41. For an account of the conspiracy trial of the "Chicago Eight" see Jason Epstein, *The Great Conspiracy Trial* (New York: Vintage, 1971); for an account of the Spock-Coffin conspiracy trial see Jessica Mitford, *The Trial of Doctor Spock* (New York: Knopf, 1969).

42. Michael Miles, "The Triumph of Reaction," *Change, The Magazine of Higher Learning*, 4, Winter 1972–1973, p. 34. This article provides a good summary of recent repressive actions on campuses. Another analysis is J. David Colfax, "Repression and Academic Radicalism," *New Politics*, 10, Spring 1973, pp. 14–27.

is conjured up and then applied to nonprofessional areas of political activity and expression.

The repression of dissent is usually a violent affair, revealing something of the criminal nature of those who say they are dedicated to fighting crime. This account of a police attack against a peace demonstration in New York in 1969 is typical of many such incidents that occurred throughout the United States during the antiwar protests.

A number of policemen came charging into the crowd, many, but not all, with their clubs in hand raised to the levels of their heads. . . . I saw other people being beaten. Some were arrested and others were not. It appeared to me that the police were just beating people at random with no clear indication that the people they were attacking had committed an illegal act. I saw none of the people being attacked fight back or attempt to hit the police. Most attempted to protect themselves by covering their heads or tried to run.[43]

Witness this assault on an antiwar protestor in front of the Pentagon in 1967:

At least four times that soldier hit her with all his force, then as she lay covering her head with her arms, thrust his club swordlike between her hands onto her face. Two more troops came up and began dragging the girl toward the Pentagon. . . . She twisted her body so we could see her face. But there was no face there: all we saw were some raw skin and blood. We couldn't even see if she was crying—her eyes had filled with the blood pouring down her head. She vomited, and that too was blood. Then they rushed her away.[44]

Police brutality can occur with impunity within the very halls of justice. In the trial of the surviving Soledad Brothers, Clutchette and Drumgo (the third defendant, George Jackson, had been murdered by prison guards), the two prisoners entered the court one day reporting that they had been beaten and burned with cigarettes by guards. When defense attorneys tried to draw the attention of the presiding judge to the marks and bruises that were visible to court spectators, he denied being

43. Quoted in Peggy Kerry, "The Scene in the Streets," in Becker and Murray (eds.), *Government Lawlessness in America*, p. 61.
44. Eyewitness testimony by Harvey Mayes, *New York Times*, December 3, 1967. Descriptions of brutality at the Pentagon were not carried in the *Times* or other newspapers. Mayes' account along with numerous others appeared in a full-page paid advertisement.

able to see anything of the kind and refused to step forward at the attorneys' request to get a closer look. At this point Drumgo's mother fled the courtroom crying and Clutchette's mother began to sob uncontrollably, cursing the judge. One news report reconstructs what happened next:

Suddenly, the San Francisco Tactical Squad, standing with clubs ready in the back of the sealed-spectator section of the courtroom, waded in with clubs flailing. . . . It was two Black men whom the Tac Squad chose to attack. They began one of the longest, most bloody beatings ever witnessed in a demonstration or riot—not to mention inside a courtroom. For long moments, the Tac Squad beat Phil Price, a cousin of Fleeta Drumgo, as he lay on the ground, bending his leg over a chair and slamming a club on the leg repeatedly, trying to break it. Then the sheriff's deputies moved in. Lifting Price to his feet, slamming his already profusely bleeding head repeatedly, then forcing him against the wall where they continued to beat him. Marty Price, Phil's older brother was being shoved around the neck with a Tac Squad club but he wasn't beaten. Instead, both were dragged inside to a prison holding cell where the guards forced Marty to watch as his younger brother was clubbed and beaten some more. When they finished, an officer said, "We need some injured men," and several officers wiped their hands in Phil's blood, rubbed it on their own faces and went off to have their pictures taken. The brothers were charged with assaulting an officer.[45]

The brutality is often fatal. In recent years there have been literally hundreds of killings of members of low-income groups and non-Whites by police in situations which have every appearance of murder: a Black man is forced to lie face down in a Detroit motel and a policeman cold-bloodedly pumps a bullet into his head. A Black man, father of five children, is killed by an angry off-duty San Francisco policeman whose car has been accidentally scraped by someone else. In Newark a grinning state trooper, holding a Black youth captive in an alley, repeatedly shoots him in the head and body, pausing only to place a knife in the victim's hand. A White working-class youth is beaten to death by police in a paddy wagon in Cambridge, Mass. A patrolman in Eureka, Calif., accosts a thirty-eight-year-old Native American father of five and shoots him through the forehead for no reason. A twelve-year-old Chicano boy, arrested in Dallas as a "burglary suspect," is shot through the head and killed while sitting handcuffed in a patrol car. A Black man,

45. *Guardian*, September 8, 1971. For a somewhat similar incident see the *New York Times*, April 28, 1970.

father of three, driving without a license, becomes frightened when finding himself followed by police and flees from his car in Urbana, Ill., only to be shot dead by a policeman who utters no warning. A White hippie, finding his house surrounded by armed, unidentified men in Humboldt County, Calif. (they turn out to be county police and narcotics agents raiding the wrong place), flees in terror out the back door and is shot dead. A Puerto Rican teenager is killed by a patrolman while climbing a park fence one night in New York. A ten-year-old Black boy walking with his foster father in Queens, New York, is killed by a plainclothes policeman who leaps from his unmarked car without identifying himself, shouts "Hey, niggers!" and opens fire.[46]

Few of the law officers involved in these cases and others like them have ever been indicted for murder. Most have been exonerated by review boards despite the highly incriminating testimony of eyewitnesses. A few have been suspended from the force, and a few have been tried for "justifiable homicide" or "manslaughter" and acquitted.[47]

The police have killed unarmed people participating in collective protest actions. Of the one hundred or so murders of persons associated with the civil rights movement during the 1960s, almost all were committed by police and White vigilantes. Few of the murderers were caught; none was convicted of murder. From 1968 to 1971 local police stormed into and wrecked Black Panther headquarters in more than ten cities, stealing thousands of dollars in funds and arresting, beating and shooting the occupants in what were well-planned, unprovoked attacks. More than forty Panthers were killed by police in that period, including Chicago leader Fred Hampton, who was shot

46. For accounts of these and similar incidents the reader is referred to Tom Hayden, *Rebellion in Newark* (New York: Vintage Books, 1967); John Hersey, *The Algiers Motel Incident* (New York: Knopf, 1968); Art Goldberg and Gene Marine, "Officer O'Brien: 'I Want to Kill a Nigger So Goddamned Bad I Can Taste It!' He Killed George Baskett," *Ramparts*, July 1969, pp. 9–16; Murray Kempton, "The Harlem Policeman," in Becker and Murray (eds.), *Government Lawlessness in America*, pp. 47–49; Joe Eszterhas, "Death in the Wilderness: The Justice Department's Killer Nark Strike Force," *Rolling Stone*, May 24, 1973, pp. 28–34, 44–54. See also various back issues of the *Guardian*, the *Militant* and the *Daily World* for accounts of criminal and murderous actions against radicals and racial minorities. *Akwesasne Notes*, official publication of the Mohawk nation, has carried numerous accounts of atrocities committed against Native Americans in recent years by law officers and other Whites. The *Black Panther Intercommunal News Service* has carried similar accounts involving Black victims.
47. See Sara Blackburn (ed.), *White Justice: Black Experience Today in America's Courtrooms* (New York: Harper, 1972).

to death in his bed. More than 300 were arrested and many of these were imprisoned for over two years without bail. In Orangeburg, S.C., Black students were killed by state and local police who fired into a demonstration; no guns were seen, heard or ever found among the students, and some of the victims had been shot in the back while fleeing.

In the demonstrations of 1970, unarmed Black students at Jackson State were murdered by police, and at Kent State, White students were murdered by National Guardsmen. In both instances, the evidence gathered by the FBI and other government agencies clearly indicated that the lives of the law enforcement officers and Guardsmen were never in danger and that the men who did the shooting got together after the event and agreed to tell investigators the false story that their lives had been in danger. In both cases, state grand juries refused to indict the murderers but did indict demonstrators, including several who had been wounded.[48] While the President's Commission on Campus Disorder found the Kent State shootings "unnecessary, unwarranted, and inexcusable," the Ohio grand jury ruled that the Guardsmen were justified in firing their weapons because they held the "honest and sincere belief . . . that they would suffer serious bodily injury had they not done so." Attorney-General John Mitchell refused to move on the case because he claimed to know, without benefit of investigation, that there would not be sufficient evidence to indict the Guardsmen.

During the prison rebellion at Attica State Penitentiary in New York, Governor Nelson Rockefeller, asserting that the uprising was the work of "revolutionaries," ordered an armed assault by troopers. Blasting their way into the prison yard, they killed thirty inmates and ten prison guards who had been held as hostages and wounded more than a hundred other prisoners. Not a single gun was found among the prisoners. Some months later, during a nonviolent demonstration at Louisiana State College, two unarmed Black students were killed by police.

The list of killings could go on and on, but the pattern remains the same: law enforcement agents have used lethal weapons against antiwar activists, ghetto protestors, rebellious prisoners and political radicals, none of whom were armed, a few of whom were reported to be hurling rocks or making "obscene

48. I. F. Stone, "Fabricated Evidence in the Kent State Killings," *New York Review of Books*, December 3, 1970, p. 28. The Kent State case was reopened by the Justice Department in early August 1973, perhaps as part of the outbreak of government lawfulness that followed in the wake of the Watergate investigations.

gestures." In almost every instance, an "impartial investigation" by the very authorities responsible for the killings exonerated the uniformed murderers and their administrative chiefs. The few killers who are indicted are not usually convicted.

The law and its enforcement agents, the police, do many worthwhile things. Many laws are intended to enhance public safety and individual security. The police sometimes protect life and limb, direct traffic, administer first aid, assist in times of community emergency and perform other vital social services with commendable dedication and courage. But aside from this desirable *social service* function, the police and the law serve a *class control* function—that is, they protect those who rule from the protests and confrontations of those who are ruled. And they protect the interests of corporate and institutional property from those who would challenge the inequities of the private-property system. The profiteering corporate managers, plundering slumlords, swindling merchants, racist school boards, self-enriching doctors, special-interest legislators and others who contribute so much to the scarcity, misery and anger that lead to individual crimes or mass riots leave the dirty work of subduing these outbursts to the police. When the police charge picket lines —beating, gassing and occasionally shooting farm workers—they usually are operating with a court injunction which allows them to exert force in order to protect the interests of the corporate owners. When police harass and terrorize radicals, racial minorities and slum dwellers, they usually have the support of the White middle-class community and government officials, who want problems like protest and poverty swept under the rug—even if it takes a club or gun. Repressive acts by police are not the aberrant behavior of a few psychotics in uniform but the outgrowth of the kind of class control function law officers perform and rulers insist upon—which explains why the police are able to get away with murder.

It is very difficult to have a "nice" repression. If it is the unenviable task of police to keep a lid on the anger and frustration of the victims of economic, racial and political oppression—a task assigned to them by those in power—then criminal acts by law officers inevitably occur. If it is the job of law officers to suppress radical political ideas and organizations and keep surveillance on every imagined political "troublemaker," then it is not long before the police, the FBI, the CIA, Army Intelligence and other such units begin to see the Constitution as little more than an obstacle to be circumvented or brushed aside. Before long, the police become a law unto themselves.

By now, it should be apparent that what is called "law and order" is a system of authority and interest that does not and usually *cannot* operate with equitable class effect and neutral political effect. The laws are themselves *political* rulings and judgments, the outcome of a legislative process that is most responsive to the pressures of the politically stronger, as we shall see. Rather than being neutral judgments, laws are the embodiment of past political victories and therefore favor the interests of the victors. The law is inevitably an outgrowth of the established order which produced it, and by its nature it serves the established interests far better than the unestablished ones. When discussing law and order, then, it is imperative to ask *whose* law and *whose* order we are talking about. While the courts, the police and the lawmakers claim to be protecting order as such, they really are protecting a particular kind of order, one that sustains the self-appointed, self-perpetuating oligarchs who rule most of our economic, technological, educational, communicational, medical and social institutions.

Psycho-controls for Law and Order

In their never-ending campaign to control behavior that is unacceptable to the existing order, authorities have moved beyond the clubs, bullets and eavesdropping devices of the police and are resorting to such things as electroshock, electrode implantations, mind-destroying drugs and psychosurgery. Since the established powers presume that the present social system is a benign and virtuous one, it follows that those who are prone to violent or disruptive behavior, or who show themselves to be manifestly disturbed about the conditions under which they live, must be suffering from *inner* malfunctionings which can best be treated by various psycho-controls. Not only are political and social deviants defined as insane, but sanity itself has a political definition. The sane and normal person is the obedient one who lives in peace and goes to war on cue from his leaders, is not too much troubled by the inhumanities committed against people, is capable of fitting himself into one of the mindless job slots in a profit-oriented hierarchical organization and does not challenge the established mores and conventional wisdom. If it happens that he actually has been victimized by class conditions—if, for instance, he has been raised in poverty, has received no education, has been repeatedly discriminated against because of his race, cannot find decent housing or even a dull and meaningless job and sees his children go hungry and his family and his life falling apart—then he must be able to handle these distresses without resorting to aggressive and troublesome behavior or other "abnormalities." What are called sanity and insanity, normal and abnormal, in many cases are political judgments made by privileged professionals who are imbued with, and committed to enforcing, establishment rules that protect the status quo—even as they insist they are making only "scientific" and "medical" diagnoses.

In almost all the instances in which individuals have been treated by psycho-control methods, the victims are selected because of their socially deviant and "disturbed" (i.e., disturbing) attitudes and behavior. Seldom do the scientists engaged in this kind of work manifest any awareness of the class, racial and political biases influencing their selection of subjects. Their eagerness to work with law enforcement authorities reflects the ideological presumption under which they operate. Since they accept the present politico-economic system as a good one, then anything that increases its ability to control dissident and unhappy persons—whose rebellion is rarely thought of as a justifiable response to an unjust social system—is also seen as good. A scientist working at Yale and financed by Washington, José Delgado, has proposed a billion-dollar government project to control minds through the use of electrode implants. Delgado already has experimented on human beings in mental institutions and has demonstrated his ability to produce placid, euphoric persons through electrical brain controls. His vision is of a "psycho-civilized society" in which unsavory, destructive, and disruptive emotions are done away with by electric controls.[49]

Among the psycho-control methods employed, probably the most inhumane is psychosurgery, a treatment that modifies behavior by destroying certain brain cells. About six hundred psychosurgical operations are performed each year, and the number is rising. In most cases, drastic personality changes result: individuals become placid and compliant; their emotions are greatly dulled; they become less able to cope with new

49. José M. Delgado, *Physical Control of the Mind: Toward a Psychocivilized Society* (New York: Harper and Row, 1969).

situations, have disoriented reactions to things around them and suffer a marked deterioration in intelligence.[50] After the Detroit ghetto rebellions in 1967, three doctors of the Harvard Medical School, leading proponents of psychosurgery, wrote in the AMA journal:

It is important to realize that only a small number of the millions of slum dwellers have taken part in the riots. . . . Is there something peculiar about the violent slum dweller that differentiates him from his peaceful neighbors? . . . We need intensive research and clinical studies of the individuals committing the violence. The goal of such studies would be to pinpoint, diagnose and treat those people with low violence thresholds.[51]

These same doctors now run the Neuro-Research Foundation in Boston, funded in part by a $100,000 grant from the Justice Department's Law Enforcement Assistance Administration. The foundation's function is to diagnose and treat persons who are "potentially violent offenders," both those with "brain diseases" and the "nondiseased."[52]

Prison inmates who are proponents of revolutionary or Black nationalist ideas or who have engaged in organizing protests among fellow inmates or who are generally unsubmissive have been singled out for "Behavior Modification" programs in various penal institutions. These programs use several approaches. One technique is to put the prisoner in solitary confinement under excruciating conditions of filth, cold, insufficient food and sensory deprivation, and make piecemeal improvements in each of these conditions as a reward if he develops the kind of attitude and behavior patterns desired by the authorities. Another method is "aversion therapy." By the use of electric shock a prisoner is made to associate pain with whatever the authorities consider bad. In Vacaville, California, for instance, inmates

50. See "Violence Upon the Brain, Information on the New Lobotomists," unpublished monograph prepared by the Greater Boston Medical Committee for Human Rights, c. 1972. Although hailed as a "new" method for treating mental illness, psychosurgery today is nothing more than the lobotomies of the 1930s and 1940s with some minor technical improvements and a new name.

51. Correspondence to the *Journal of the American Medical Association*, 201, September 1967, p. 217. Two of the authors of the letter wrote a book advocating psychosurgery for "violent, irrational behavior"; see Vernon Mark and Frank Ervin, *Violence and the Brain* (New York: Harper and Row, 1970). For critiques of the repressive and morally criminal uses of mental hospitals and treatment like psychosurgery, see the literature issued by the Medical Committee for Human Rights, Cambridge, Mass.

52. Dr. Sweet, quoted in "Violence Upon the Brain."

accused of homosexuality are shown erotic gay films and shocked whenever a polygraph indicates the prisoner is sexually excited. Sometimes Anectine is used, a drug which induces a death panic by paralyzing one's breathing for a couple of minutes.[53] A letter from a group of prisoners at Dannemora provides some personal testimony of how old and new techniques are blended:

Anyone who has spent any amount of time in [Dannemora State Hospital] must know at least one person who was sent for punishment, and returned with the mind of a vegetable or moron if he returned at all. . . . The box [solitary] is jam-packed since February, on the pretext of phony "conspiracies."

Many of us have been notified of our "selection" to the Rx Program, and the goons have been kidnapping us two or three a day. In fact, one of our brothers . . . made a valiant but futile stand by refusing to leave his cell and accompany the beasts.

The goons used this as a pretext to gas the brother into submission and gas the entire box, which they did with unconcealed pleasure and jest. When the brother had been rendered helpless the beasts then took him away [for treatment in the medical program].[54]

"Hyperkinetic" children, guilty of "rebellious" behavior in schools, orphanages or reformatories, have been the victims of psychosurgery. More commonly, hyperactive children—many of whom come to school hungry, physically ill, and under emotional stress from growing up in impoverished, unhappy slum conditions—are treated with amphetamines and with drugs like Ritalin and Enterovioform, "whose safety has never been documented and whose efficacy has never been proved."[55] Upwards of 300,000 school children are being treated, at a yearly profit of some $13 million to the drug industry and with side effects to themselves like weight loss, growth retardation and acute psychosis.

Other kinds of medical aggressions are perpetrated against poor people, especially Blacks and other racial minorities. Some doctors perform involuntary sterilizations on low-income White and Black women, without the knowledge or consent of the women. In Alabama in 1973 two Black girls, aged twelve and

53. Joel Meyers, "Electrode Torture and Starvation Legal 'Therapy' in U.S. Prisons," *Workers' World*, May 25, 1973, p. 6.

54. Letter by Dannemora inmates Chester Gibson, Isaac Richards, Felix Huerta, Che Avada, Juke Elmore, Makau-Chuh Champelle in *ibid.*, p. 15.

55. "Minimal Brain Dysfunction (MBD): Social Strategy or Disease?" unpublished report by the Medical Committee for Human Rights, New York.

fourteen, from a family on welfare were sterilized. Their illiterate mother put her "X" on a document she could not read, under the impression she was signing a permission slip for vaccinations. The clinic performing the operation said the operations had been ordered because "boys were hanging around the girls" and it believed sterilization was "the most convenient method to prevent pregnancy."[56]

People confined involuntarily in mental institutions number three times more than inmates of all state and federal prisons. Like prisoners, they compose a population "notably devoid of white middle-class Americans."[57] Legal protections for mental patients are even less sound than those afforded ordinary criminals. In many instances commitment comes without the benefit of investigation, trial or other procedural safeguards, and is based on considerations and "scientific" criteria that betray a marked class and racial bias. A worker in a New York State mental hospital offers this testimony:

One Black woman was admitted . . . because she began screaming at the landlord who had come to evict her and her several children. . . . The Bureau of Child Welfare took her children. This upset her even more. She came to the Admissions Committee, crying, hysterical and angry. Obviously a "paranoid schizophrenic," as the racist officials would label her. The comfortable middle-class psychiatrist said so, and after all he knows. . . .

Patients [upon release] are often secured jobs working for companies which pay them considerably less than other workers. Social workers advise the patient not to join unions and "make trouble" or they will be returned to the hospital.[58]

When prisoners are transferred to mental hospitals from regular correctional institutions because of their rebellious ways, they often end up staying many years after their prison terms expire. Others are brought into mental institutions for having committed sexually deviant or other taboo acts, including using drugs like marijuana. Many are incarcerated on the testimony of hostile relatives, social workers or police. In places like the

56. *New York Times*, June 28, 1973, and August 1, 1973.
57. For a good study of the class, racial and legal injustices of mental hospitals, see Bruce J. Ennis, "Mental Commitment," *Civil Liberties* (publication of the American Civil Liberties Union), October 1969, p. 3; also Thomas Szasz, *Law, Liberty and Psychiatry* (New York: Macmillan, 1965).
58. "Mental Hospitals and the Poor," *Workers' World*, December 25, 1970, p. 7. The author is identified only as a "woman worker" within the hospital.

Correctional Institution at Bridgewater, Mass., one of the worst of its kind, inmates are forced to live naked in barren cells without bed or toilet.[59] Many are subjected to the sadistic sport of the guards. Some who are quite rational when they first arrive eventually begin to deteriorate. Presumed insane (guilty) by virtue of their presence in the institution, they find it impossible to prove their sanity (innocence). The protests they make against their cruel treatment are interpreted as symptoms of "hostility" and "paranoia"; their cries of anguish and hurt are taken as manifestations of "hysteria"; and their bitter withdrawal in the face of such inhumanity is diagnosed as "schizophrenic," or whatever. One reporter records these impressions of his visit to Bridgewater:

One could see a man walking in a small circle, round and round [in his cell]. "He doesn't talk to anyone any more," my guide said. "He just walks in circles now."

"And before?"

"I don't know just what he's supposed to have done. He used to be all right though. I remember when he came in, he was rational, could carry on a conversation, all that stuff. Then the doctor started telling him he'd be out of here soon. Every month or so they'd say he'd get out that month. Went on like that for two years. Then one day he stopped talking. No contact with anyone after that. He's been like that for years now."

We walked on down the hall. The guide told me about one 60-year-old inmate who had been in since the age of 7. His offense: running away from home.

A thin man, old and dry, stopped the guide and said, "When the hell you gonna get me a suit and let me outa here? How about it?. . ." The guide said something indefinite and the man walked away, nodding. This was the section for killers, I had been told, so I asked what the thin man had done.

"He painted a horse."

"He what?"

"He painted a horse."

"What's wrong with that?"

"It was in a field. A live horse. He was drunk and somebody bet him he couldn't make a horse look like a zebra, I think, so he painted it and they put him here. For being drunk probably."

"How long has he been in?"

"Thirty-seven years. By the time they got around to letting him out

59. Frederic Wiseman did a documentary film of Bridgewater entitled "Titicut Follies"; it is so devastating that institutional authorities succeeded in having it banned in the state of Massachusetts.

he really was crazy. . . . For his own good we just can't let him go out of here."[60]

Police, judges, surveillance technicians, psycho-surgeons, drug-pushing school authorities, prison guards and the attendants in mental institutions all have one thing in common: they work to make the world safe for those on top by exercising arbitrary power over those below—all in the name of peace and security, normality and well being, law and order.

60. Bruce Jackson, "Our Prisons Are Criminal," *New York Times Magazine*, September 22, 1973, pp. 54, 57.

The Sound
and the Fury:
Elections and Parties

AS NOTED EARLIER, MOST INSTITU-
tions in America are ruled by self-appointed,
self-perpetuating business elites that are answerable to no one. But presumably the same
cannot be said of government, for a necessary
condition of our political system is the provision for free and regular elections of those who
govern, the function being to hold officeholders accountable to the people who elect them.
Whether or not the electoral process keeps
government responsive to public needs is a
question to be treated in the pages to follow.

The Harvesting of Votes

The harvesting of votes is the specialized task
of the political parties. The job has gone to
men who have enjoyed a class and ethnic
familiarity with the common voters and who
have been sufficiently occupied by the pursuit
of office and patronage to remain untroubled
by questions of social justice. Alan Altshuler
provides an apt description of the machine
politicians:

Though they distributed favors widely, they concentrated power tightly. Though their little favors
went to little men, the big favors went to land
speculators, public utility franchise holders, government contractors, illicit businessmen, and of
course the leading members of the machines
themselves. . . .

The bosses were entrepreneurs, not revolutionaries. They provided specific opportunities for individual representatives of deprived groups, but they never questioned the basic distribution of resources in society. Their methods of raising revenue tended toward regressivity. On the whole, the lower classes paid for their own favors. What they got was a *style* of government with which they could feel at home. What the more affluent classes got, though relatively few of them appreciated it, was a form of government which kept the newly enfranchised masses content without threatening the socio-economic status quo.[1]

Today, the party politician still performs little favors for little men but seldom addresses himself to the larger problems facing ordinary citizens. He might investigate a complaint by a mother that her welfare checks are not arriving, but he would not challenge the more demeaning features of the welfare system nor the conditions that fostered it. He might find a municipal job for a faithful precinct worker, but he will not advance proposals for an attack on unemployment. He might procure an apartment for a family, but he will not ask the landlord, who himself is sometimes a party contributor, to make housing improvements, nor would he think of challenging his right to charge exorbitant rents. The party regular will "look into" everything except certain of the more harrowing realities of lower-class life and the wider social forces that help create those realities.[2] Party regulars take "the existing socio-economic structure . . . as given," Dahl notes. They assume "that the physical and economic features of the city are determined by forces beyond their control."[3]

These same politicians, however, are quite ready to serve those "forces beyond their control." "When Mayor Daley took office," reports Banfield in his study of Chicago, "he immediately wrote to three or four of the city's most prominent businessmen asking them to list the things they thought most needed doing. . . . He may be impressed by the intrinsic merit of a proposal . . . but he will be even more impressed at the prospect of being well-regarded by the highly respectable people whose proposal it is."[4] The machine depends on the sufferance and direct aid of urban capitalist interests. In most cities

1. Alan A. Altshuler, *Community Control: The Black Demand for Participation in Large American Cities* (New York: Pegasus, 1970), pp. 74–75.
2. See Michael Parenti, "Power and Pluralism: A View from the Bottom," *Journal of Politics*, 32, August 1970, p. 514.
3. Robert Dahl, *Who Governs?* (New Haven: Yale University Press, 1961), p. 94.
4. Edward Banfield, *Political Influence* (New York: Free Press, 1961), p. 251.

this alliance is one of the important assets of the political organization.[5] Since their primary concern is to maintain their own positions of influence within society's established order, machine politicians, like most churchmen, union leaders and college administrators, generally take a conservative approach, showing little sympathy for new and potentially disruptive ideas and demands and little taste for the kind of dialogue and confrontation that one associates with the democratic process. "The man who raises new issues," observed Walter Lippmann more than a half century ago, "has always been distasteful to politicians."[6]

Democrats and Republicans: Fraternal Twins

"The rigidity of the two-party system is, I believe, disastrous," added Lippmann. "It ignores issues without settling them, dulls and wastes the energies of active groups, and chokes off the protests which should find a civilized expression in public life."[7] That scathing judgment has stood the test of time. Today the two parties are still more ready to blur than clarify political issues, adopting stances that seldom move beyond conventional formulas. Electoral contests, supposedly providing democratic heterodoxy, have generated a competition for orthodoxy. In politics, as in economics, competition is rarely a safeguard against monopoly and seldom a guarantee that the competitors will offer the consumer a substantive choice.

This is not to say there are no differences between (and within) the major parties or that one party is not preferred by some people over the other. Generally the racial minorities, union workers, lower-income urban groups and more liberally oriented professionals support the Democratic party, while the White Protestant, rural, upper-income groups, big and small businessmen and the more conservative elements of the electorate make their home in the Republican party. These differences are sometimes reflected in the voting records of Democratic and Republican legislators, albeit in a most imperfect way and within a narrow range of policy alternatives.

5. Gerald Pomper, "The First, New-Time Boss," *Transaction*, January 1972, p. 56.
6. Walter Lippmann, *A Preface to Politics* (Ann Arbor: University of Michigan Press, 1962), p. 195. Originally published in 1914.
7. *Ibid.*, p. 197.

When magnified by partisan rhetoric, the differences between the parties appear worrisome enough to induce many citizens to vote—if not *for* then *against* someone. While there is no great hope that the party of their choice will do much for them, there persists the fear that the other party, if allowed to take office, or remain in office, will make things even worse. This lesser-of-two-evils approach is perhaps the most important inducement to voter participation.[8] It is not quite accurate to characterize the Republicans and Democrats as Tweedledee and

8. See Murray Levin, *The Alienated Voter* (New York: Holt, Rinehart and Winston, 1960), pp. 37–39; a similar sentiment was expressed by many lower-income voters in Newark and New Haven when explaining their somewhat reluctant preference for the Democratic party. See my "Power and Pluralism."

Tweedledum. Were they exactly alike in all manner of image and posture, they would have even more difficulty than they do in maintaining the appearances of choice. Therefore, it is preferable that the parties be fraternal rather than identical twins.

From the perspective of those who advocate "a fundamental change in our national priorities," the question is not, "Are there differences between the parties?" but "Do the differences make a difference?" For the similarities between the parties in organization, funding, electoral methods, ideological commitment, priorities and policy output loom so large as frequently to obscure the differences. The Democratic and Republican parties are both committed to the preservation of the private corporate economy; the use of subsidies, deficit spending and tax allowances for the bolstering of business profits; the funneling of public resources through private conduits, including whole new industries developed at public expense; the concoction of domestic programs which are supposedly to assist the less fortunate segments of the population but which provide little assistance to anyone but private contractors; the use of repression against opponents of the existing class structure; the defense of the multinational corporate empire and forceful intervention against social revolutionary elements abroad. In short, Republicans and Democrats are dedicated to strikingly similar definitions of the public interest, at great cost to the life chances of underprivileged people at home and abroad. Disagreements between the two parties focus principally on which of them is better qualified to achieve commonly shared goals within a fairly narrow range of means.

The similarities between the parties do not prevent them from competing vigorously and even vehemently for the prizes of office, expending countless hours and huge sums in the doing. The very absence of significant disagreement on fundamentals makes it all the more necessary to stress the peripheral, personalized and stylistic features that advantageously differentiate oneself from one's opponent. As with industrial producers, the merchants of the political system have preferred to limit their competition chiefly to techniques of packaging and brand image. With campaign buttons and posters, leaflets and bumper stickers, television commercials and radio spots, sound trucks and billboards, with every gimmick and ballyhoo devoid of meaningful political content, the candidate sells his image as he would a soap product to a public conditioned to such bombardments.[9] His family and his looks; his experience in office and devotion to public service; his sincerity, sagacity and fighting spirit; his military record, patriotism and ethnic background; his determination to limit taxes, stop inflation, improve wages and create new jobs by attracting industry into the area; his desire to help the workingman, the farmer, and the businessman, the young and the old, the rich and the poor and especially those in between; his eagerness to fight poverty but curb welfare spending, while ending government waste and corruption and making

9. On the methods of selling a candidate as one might sell a commodity, see Joe McGinnis, *The Selling of the President 1968* (New York: Simon and Schuster, 1970). For an earlier collection of case studies of mass media merchandising of political issues and candidates, see Stanley Kelley, Jr., *Professional Public Relations and Political Power* (Baltimore: Johns Hopkins Press, 1956).

the streets and the world itself safe by strengthening our laws, our courts and our defenses abroad, bringing us lasting peace and prosperity with honor and freedom and so forth—such are the inevitable appeals which like so many autumn leaves, or barn droppings, cover the land, only to be collected in piles and carted away each November.

The Two-Party Monopoly

The two major parties have long cooperated in various stratagems to maintain their monopoly over electoral politics and discourage the growth of radically oriented third parties. "Each views with suspicion the third party movements in America," writes one Washington observer. "Each in effect is committed to the preservation of the other as its chief competitor."[10] For all their election-time rancor, Republicans and Democrats understand something about each other: they know that neither will go "too far"; neither will move beyond a narrow range of goals and means; neither has much appetite for the risks of social change; each helps to make the world safe for the other.[11]

All fifty states have laws, written and enforced by Republican and Democratic officials, regulating party representation on the ballot. Frequently the provisions are exacting enough to keep smaller parties from participating. In order to win a place on the ballot, minor parties are required to gather a large number of signatures on nominating petitions, an expensive, time-consuming task. In some states they must pay exorbitant filing fees ($5,000 in Louisiana for an independent candidate) and observe exacting deadlines when collecting and filing nominating petitions. In Pennsylvania, in 1972, third-party candidates for statewide office had to obtain the signatures of 36,000 registered voters within a three-week period. Sometimes a 5-percent requirement for signatures of registered voters has been interpreted to mean 5 percent of voters from every district within the state—an impossible task for a third party whose base might be confined to a few urban areas. Persons who sign nominating petitions for unpopular third parties sometimes find their names

10. Douglass Cater, *Power in Washington* (New York: Random House, 1964), p. 180.
11. At least this was true until the Nixon administration began its campaign of political espionage and sabotage against the Democrats—some of which was exposed in the Watergate hearings.

publicized by town clerks in an effort to embarrass them into withdrawing their names, as happened in Vermont in regard to Communist party petitions in 1972. In some states voters who are registered with the major parties are not allowed to sign or circulate minor-party nominating petitions. Petitions are often thrown out on technicalities arising from ambiguities in election laws, compelling the minor party to pursue costly court battles which, whether won or lost, usually are decided *after* the election.

The system of representation itself limits the opportunities of third parties. The single-member district elections used throughout most of the United States tend to magnify the strength of the major parties and the weakness of the smaller ones, since the party that polls a plurality of the vote, be it 40, 50 or 60 percent, wins 100 percent of a district's representation with the election of its candidate, while smaller parties, regardless of their vote, receive zero representation. This is in contrast to a system of proportional representation that provides a party with legislative seats roughly in accordance with the percentage of votes it wins, assuring minor parties of some parliamentary presence. Duverger notes that under the winner-take-all system "the party placed third or fourth is under-represented compared with the others: its percentage of seats is lower than its percentage of votes, and the disparity remains constantly greater than for its rivals. By its very definition proportional representation eliminates this disparity for all parties: the party that was at the greatest disadvantage before is the one to benefit most from the reform."[12]

The winner-take-all, single-member-district system not only deprives the minority parties of representation but eventually of voters too, since not many citizens wish to "waste" their ballots on a party that seems incapable of achieving legislative representation. Some political scientists argue that proportional representation is undesirable because it encourages the proliferation of "splinter parties" and leads to legislative stalemate and instabil-

12. Maurice Duverger, *Political Parties* (New York: Wiley and Sons, 1955), p. 248 and the discussion on pp. 245–255; also E. E. Schattschneider, *Party Government* (New York; Holt, Rinehart and Winston, 1960), pp. 74–84. Not long after World War II, Benjamin Davis, a Communist elected to the city council in New York, lost his seat when the city shifted from PR to single-member districts. The change was explicitly intended to get rid of Davis and limit the growth of other dissident parties. Proposals were introduced to abolish PR in local elections in Cambridge, Mass., in 1972 after victories by a few radically oriented candidates.

ity. In contrast, the present two-party system muffles rather than sharpens ideological differences and allows for the development of a consensus politics devoid of fragmentation and polarization. But one might question why the present forms of "stability" and "consensus" are to be treated as innate social virtues. Whose stability and whose consensus are we talking about? And one might wonder whether stalemate and fragmentation—with their consequent ill effects on the public interest—do not characterize the *present* political system in many important policy areas.

If, despite rigged rules and official harassments, radical groups continue to prove viable, then authorities are likely to resort to more violently coercive measures. Almost every radical group that has ever managed to gain some grass-roots organizational strength, from the Populist movement in the last century to the Black Panther party of today, has become the object of official violence. The case of the American Socialist party is instructive. In 1919, after having increased its vote dramatically in various locales and having won control of some thirty-two municipal governments, the Socialists suffered the combined attacks of state, local and federal authorities. Their headquarters in numerous cities were sacked by police, their funds confiscated, their leaders jailed, their immigrant members deported, their newspapers denied mailing privileges and their elected candidates denied their seats in various state legislatures and in Congress. Within a few years, the party was finished as a viable political force. While confining themselves to legal and peaceful forms of political competition, the Socialists discovered that their opponents were burdened by no similar compunctions. The guiding principle of the establishment was (and still is): *when change threatens to rule, then the rules are changed.*

The weeding out of political deviants is carried on *within* as well as outside the major parties. It begins long before the election campaign and involves social forces that extend beyond the party system. First, the acceptable candidate must be born or educated into the middle or upper class, displaying the linguistic skills and social styles of a bourgeois personage. This requirement effectively limits the selection to business and professional people. Then he must express opinions of a kind that win the support of essentially conservative community leaders, party bosses and other established interests. Finally the aspiring candidate must have large sums of money of his own or access to those who do. As one Senator remarked: "The fundamental problem is that the ability to raise money starts the screening-out process. If you can't get the money, you don't get the nomination."[13] On election day, John Coleman reminds us, "the voters will have their choice between *two* such carefully chosen candidates. But the real election in which the candidates compete for the backing of business and of its representatives in the parties and the press, has already occurred."[14]

Money is not just one of many campaign resources; it is the life blood of electoral politics, helping to determine the availability of manpower, organization, tactical mobility and media visibility. Without money, the politician's days are numbered. Commenting on the plight of reformers in Congress, Representative Charles Vanik observed: "As things are now, the public-interest members here have no reward except personal satisfaction. In the long run most of them face defeat by the big-money people. Many of the best men who come here lose after one or two terms."[15]

The abortive attempt by Senator Fred Harris of Oklahoma to win the Democratic presidential nomination is instructive. Harris had been considered one of the more promising men in his party until, in the early stages of the 1972 primary campaign, he announced his intention to build a new coalition of working-class and underprivileged groups to wage a war against monopoly corporations. Within a short time Harris' campaign was without funds, and he withdrew from the race, being unable to pay his telephone bills and travel expenses. He noted that principal backers had become alienated by his anti-business stand. (One erstwhile donor had urged him to confine his attentions to such "safe" subjects as drug addiction and the Vietnam war.) The Senator concluded that this kind of financial control "explains why our Government is approaching such paralysis. For now it is very difficult to get American politicians, including many who are quite liberal, to advocate more than just *tinkering* with fundamental wrongs or simply adding a little more to existing New Deal-type programs."[16]

The man who became the Democratic presidential candidate in 1972, Senator George McGovern, found himself abandoned in the early stages of his campaign by wealthy liberal

13. Senator Mathias quoted in Richard Harris, "Annals of Politics: A Fundamental Hoax," *New Yorker*, August 7, 1971, p. 54.

14. John Coleman, "Elections Under Capitalism, Part 2," *Workers' Power*, September 1–14, 1972, p. 11.

15. Quoted in Harris, "Annals of Politics," p. 59.

16. Quoted in Erwin Knoll, "It's Only Money," *Progressive*, March 1972, pp. 25–26 (italics in the original).

financiers who opposed his proposals for tax reform and income redistribution.[17] McGovern quickly retreated from these positions, placing an advertisement in the *Wall Street Journal* to assure its readers of his faith in the private-enterprise system. In subsequent speeches he informed businessmen that if he were elected, profits would "be bigger than they are now under the Nixon Administration." McGovern eventually did receive support from some wealthy donors, although hardly as much as Nixon.

The radical candidate faces far greater difficulties than do candidates like McGovern. Besides severe money problems, he or she must try to develop some kind of plausible image among a citizenry that has been conditioned for more than a century to hate and fear "anarchists," "socialists," "communists," "leftists," etc. He finds himself dependent for exposure on mass media that are owned by the conservative interests he is attacking. He sees that, along with the misrepresentations disseminated by a hostile press, the sheer paucity of information and haphazard reportage can make any meaningful campaign dialogue nearly impossible. The dissenter competes not only against well-financed opponents but against the media's many frivolous and stupifying distractions. Hoping to "educate the public to the issues," he discovers that the media allow little opportunity for the expositions needed to make his position comprehensible to those voters who might be willing to listen.

Dissenters who, in the face of all obstacles, decide to make the long march through the electoral process soon discover that it absorbs all their time, money and energy while leaving them no closer to the forces that make the important decisions of this society. Those few reformers who do win elections may subsequently find themselves redistricted out of existence, as happened during the 1970–1972 period in New York City to three of the more outspokenly liberal Democratic Congressmen and five of the more liberal Democratic state legislators. Once in office dissenters are often relegated to obscure legislative tasks and receive little cooperation from legislative leaders or bureaucratic agencies.

To achieve some effectiveness in an institution whose dominant forces easily outflank him, the newly arrived representative frequently decides that "for now" he must make his peace with the powers that be, holding his fire until some future day

17. "McGovern's Views Alarm Big Donors on Wall Street," *New York Times*, July 3, 1972.

when he can attack from higher ground. To get along he decides to go along; thus begins the insidious process that lets a person believe he is still opposing the ongoing arrangements when in fact he has become a functional part of them.[18] There are less subtle instances of co-optation, as when reformers are bought off with promotions and favors by those who hold the key to their advancement. Once having won election, they may reverse their stands on fundamental issues and make common cause with established powers, to the dismay of their supporters.

In sum, of the various functions a political party might serve—(1) selecting candidates and waging election campaigns, (2) articulating and debating major issues, (3) formulating coherent and distinct programs, (4) implementing a national program when in office—our parties fulfill only the first with any devotion or success. The parties are loose conglomerations of local factions organized around one common purpose: to gain power. Issues come and go, but the party's *raison d'être* is the pursuit of office. For this reason, American parties have been characterized as "non-ideological." And indeed they are—in the sense that their profound ideological commitment to capitalism at home and abroad and to the ongoing class structure is seldom made an explicit issue. But even as they evade most important policy questions and refrain from commitment to distinct, coherent programs, the parties have a real conservative effect on the consciousness of the electorate and on the performance of representative government. They operate from a commonly shared ideological perspective which is best served by the avoidance of certain ideas and the suppression or co-optation of dissenters.

Democratic Competition: Does It Exist?

According to democratic theory, electoral competition keeps political leaders accountable to their constituents: politicians who wish to remain in office must respond to voter preferences in order to avoid being replaced by their rivals at the next election. This model presumes that the conditions of electoral competition actually exist. But as noted earlier, a host of political,

18. See Chapter Thirteen, "Congress: The Pocketing of Power," for a brief discussion of the conservative socializing influences within the national legislature.

legal and economic forces so limit the range of alternatives as to raise serious questions about the meaning of popular participation.

Furthermore, with so much of electoral politics reduced to an issueless publicity contest, the advantages go to the incumbent, he who has the financial support, legitimacy, exposure and other resources that come with public office, be he an ordinary Congressman or President of the United States.[19] Obviously, the man who has won office already has built some kind of winning combination of money, organization and influence. But even if appointed as a replacement, he can use the resources of office to promote his own subsequent election, catering to the needs of important financial groups and performing favors that win him backing from special interests. He gets roads, irrigation projects, airports, bridges, harbors, post offices and various other government "pork barrel" projects for his home district, carries on a correspondence with thousands of voters, uses his official staff and mailing privileges for publicity purposes and enjoys an access to the local newspapers and radio and television stations that helps establish him as a "brand name." The most important and often most difficult task facing any candidate for public office is getting his name known to the voters, and here the incumbent has a usually decisive advantage over the challenger.

The trend in Congress over the last century has been for members to serve for longer and longer periods and to suffer fewer defeats by challengers. In the 1870s about 50 percent of the Representatives in each new Congress were newcomers; in 1970 the number had dropped to 12 percent.[20] From 1924 to 1956, 90 percent of the Congressmen who stood for reelection were victorious. In 1970 94 percent of those seeking reelection to the House were returned by the voters. (Three percent were

19. If the advantages of incumbency are great for the average member of Congress, they are all the greater for the President, especially in modern times when the presidency has become the object of mass attention and the repository of much popular sentiment. The only White House incumbents in the twentieth century who failed to be reelected were William Howard Taft in 1912, because the Republican party was split in two by Teddy Roosevelt's Bull Moose party, and Herbert Hoover, who was swept away by the Great Depression. Lyndon Johnson chose not to run in 1968, but it is not certain he would have lost in a reelection bid. His poll ratings in early 1968 were not much lower than Nixon's rating in early 1972, and the latter won a smashing victory the following November.

20. Mark J. Green, James M. Fallows and David R. Zwick, *Who Runs Congress?* (New York: Bantam Books/Grossman, 1972), p. 229.

defeated in primaries, and 3 percent lost in the election.)[21]

Over the last two decades there has been a noticeable breakup of one-party regions: Republicans are now winning victories in Mississippi and Democrats get elected in Maine. Yet one-party dominance is still the rule in a good many locales throughout the rural Northeast, Midwest and South and in many cities. In 1970 one out of every ten Representatives was elected to Congress with *no opposition in either the primary or the general election.* In states like Vermont it is common for a majority of state and local officeholders to be elected to uncontested seats. One-party rule, considered the peculiar disease of "communist tyranny," is not an uncommon condition of American politics.

Death and voluntary retirement seem to be the important factors behind the turnover in representative assemblies. In this respect, legislative bodies bear a closer resemblance to the nonelective judiciary than we would imagine. One study of municipal governments found that upwards of half the city councilmen anticipated their own voluntary retirement after one term and about one fourth held nonelective appointments to fill unexpired terms. Many of the councilmen admitted that they paid little heed to constituent complaints. They entered and left office "not at the whim of the electorate, but according to self-defined schedules," a procession of like-minded men of similar social background.[22]

The prevalence of victorious incumbents is both a cause and an effect of low voter participation. As voters become increasingly discouraged about the possibility of effecting meaningful change through the ballot box, they are less likely to mobilize or respond to reformist electoral movements, thus increasing the unassailability of the incumbents. As the incumbents show themselves unbeatable, their would-be challengers become

21. See David Leuthold, *Electioneering in a Democracy* (New York: Wiley and Sons, 1968), p. 127. For the breakdown on the 1970 election I am indebted to Garrison Nelson.

22. Kenneth Prewitt, "Political Ambitions, Volunteerism, and Electoral Accountability," *American Political Science Review*, 64, March 1970, pp. 5–17; the quotation is from p. 10. Prewitt presents data on eighty-two municipal governments. The noncompetitive leadership selection he found at the local level exists to a lesser extent in the more visible and prestigious U.S. Congress, but as Prewitt points out, the more than 35,000 municipalities, towns and townships and the equal number of school boards have a cumulative impact that may be more important than the influence exercised by the Congress or any of its special committees.

fewer in number and weaker in spirit. This is not an iron law of politics and the cycle has sometimes been dramatically reversed; but the reversals are usually the notable exceptions. The predominant situation is one of officeholders who are largely unresponsive to unorganized voters and voters who are often cynical and skeptical of officeholders. In the next chapter we will explore this situation in more detail.

The Politics
of Discouragement:
Nonvoters and Voters

10   MUCH HAS BEEN WRITTEN ABOUT THE
deficiencies of ordinary voters, their prejudices, lack of information and low civic involvement. More should be said about the
deficiencies of the electoral-representative system that serves them. It has long been presumed that since the present political system
represents the best of all worlds, those who
show an unwillingness to vote must be manifesting some failing in themselves. Seldom
is nonparticipation treated as a justifiable reaction to a politics that has become somewhat meaningless in its electoral content and
disappointing in its policy results.

In the United States during the nineteenth century, the small-town democratic
system "was quite adequate, both in partisan
organization and dissemination of political
information, to the task of mobilizing voters,"
according to Walter Dean Burnham.[1] But by
the turn of the century most of the political
means for making important decisions had
been captured by powerful industrial elites.
Business interests perfected the arts of pressure politics, wielding a heavy influence over
state legislatures, party organizations, governors and Congressmen. At the same time, the
judiciary extended its property-serving controls over the national and state legislatures,
imposing limitations on taxation powers and

1. Walter Dean Burnham, "The Changing Shape of the
American Political Universe," *American Political Science
Review*, 59, March 1965, p. 22.

on regulatory efforts in the fields of commerce, industry and labor. "Confronted with a narrowed scope of effective democratic options an increasingly large proportion of the eligible adult population either left, failed to enter or—as was the case with the Southern Negro . . . was systematically excluded from the American voting universe."[2] Much of the blame for the diminishing popular participation, Burnham concludes, must rest with "the political system itself."

Nonvoting as a Rational Response

The percentage of nonvoters has climbed to impressive levels, running as high as 55 to 60 percent in congressional contests and 40 to 45 percent in recent presidential elections. In many local elections, voter participation is so low as to make it difficult to speak of "popular" representation in any real sense. Observing that in a municipality of 13,000 residents an average of 810 voters elected the city council, Prewitt comments:

Such figures sharply question the validity of thinking that "mass electorates" hold elected officials accountable. For these councilmen, even if serving in relatively sizable cities, there are no "mass electorates"; rather there are the councilman's business associates, his friends at church, his acquaintances in the Rotary Club, and so forth which provide him the electoral support he needs to gain office.[3]

The political significance of low participation becomes apparent when we consider that nonvoters are disproportionately concentrated among the rural poor, the urban slum dwellers, the welfare recipients, the underemployed, the young, the elderly, the low-income and nonunion workers and the racial minorities. The entire voting process is dominated by middle-class styles and conditions which tend to discourage lower-class participation.[4] Among the reasons poor Whites in one city gave for not voting were the humiliating treatment they had been subjected to by poll attendants in previous elections, the intimidating nature of voting machines, the belief that they were

2. *Ibid.*, p. 26.
3. Kenneth Prewitt, "Political Ambitions, Volunteerism, and Electoral Accountability," *American Political Science Review*, 64, March 1970, p. 9.
4. Penn Kimball, *The Disconnected* (New York: Columbia University Press, 1972); Giuseppe Di Palma, *Apathy and Participation: Mass Politics in Western Societies* (New York: Free Press, 1970).

WARREN
LINN

not entitled to vote because they had failed to pay their poll tax (a misapprehension encouraged by tax collectors and town clerks), the feeling that they lacked whatever measure of education, specialized information and ability gives one the right to participate in the electoral process, and the conviction that elections are a farce and all politicians are ultimately out to "line their own pockets."[5] Residency requirements and the registration of voters at obscure locations during the political off-season discriminate against the less informed and less established community elements, specifically the poor, the unemployed and transient laborers.[6]

Working long hours for low pay, deprived of the kind of services and material security that the well-to-do take for granted, made to feel personally incapable of acting effectively and living in fear of officialdom, those of lower-class background frequently are reluctant to vote or make political commitments of any kind. The entire social milieu of the poor militates against participation. As Kimball describes it:

Tenements, rooming houses, and housing projects—the dormitories of the ghetto electorate—provide . . . a shifting, changing human environment instead of the social reinforcements that encourage political involvement in more stable neighborhoods. And the immediate struggle for subsistence drains the reservoirs of emotional energy available for the distant and complex realms of politics. . . . Elections come and go, and the life of poverty goes on pretty much as before, neither dramatically better nor dramatically worse. The posturing of candidates and the promises of parties are simply irrelevant to the daily grind of marginal existence.[7]

Nor is it unreasonable that lower-strata groups are skeptical that any one candidate can change things. Their suspicions might be summarized as follows: (1) the reform-minded candidate is still a politician and therefore is as deceptive as any other; (2) even if he is sincere, the reformer is eventually "bought off" by the powers that be; (3) even if he is not bought off, the reformer can do little against those who run things. The conviction that politics cannot deliver anything significant leaves many citizens

5. Opinions reported by Democratic campaign workers in Burlington, Vt., in 1972. I am indebted to Cheryl Smalley for gathering the information.
6. See Charles E. Merriam and Harold F. Gosnell, *Non-voting, Causes and Methods of Control* (Chicago: University of Chicago Press, 1924), pp. 78 ff.; and Kimball, *The Disconnected*, p. 15.
7. Kimball, *The Disconnected*, p. 17.

unresponsive, even if not unsympathetic, toward those who promise meaningful changes through the ballot box.[8]

It has been argued that if nonvoters tend to be among the less informed, less educated and more apathetic, then it is just as well they do not exercise their franchise. Since they are not all that capable of making rational choices and are likely to be swayed by prejudice and demagogy, their activation would constitute a potential threat to our democratic system.[9] Behind this reasoning lurks the dubious presumption that the better-educated, upper-income people who vote are more rational, less compelled by narrowly defined self-interests, and less bound by racial, political and class prejudices, an impression which itself is one of those comfortable prejudices that upper- and middle-class people (including social scientists) have of themselves. As Kimball reminds us: "The level of information of the most informed voters is not very high by objective standards. The influence of ethnic background, family upbringing, and party inheritance is enormous in comparison to the flow of political debate. The choices in a given situation are rarely clearcut, and the decision to vote for particular candidates can be highly irrational, *even at the highest levels of education and experience.*" [10]

Some writers argue that the low voter turnout in the United States is symptomatic of a "politics of happiness": people do not bother to participate because they are fairly content with the way things are going.[11] But the 40 to 50 million adult Americans outside the voting universe are not among the more contented but among the less affluent and more alienated, displaying an unusual concentration of socially deprived characteristics.[12] The "politics of happiness" may be nothing more than a cover for the politics of discouragement or what Lane describes as the "alienation syndrome": "I am the object not the subject of political life.

8. Michael Parenti, "Power and Pluralism: A View from the Bottom," *Journal of Politics*, August 1970, p. 515; and Kimball, *The Disconnected*, pp. 61–62.

9. A typical example of this kind of thinking is found in Seymour M. Lipset, *Political Man* (Garden City, N.Y.: Doubleday, 1960), pp. 215–219.

10. Kimball, *The Disconnected*, p. 63. Italics added. Occasionally there is an admission by the well-to-do that voting should be limited not to protect democracy but to protect themselves. A letter to the *New York Times* (December 6, 1971) offered these revealing words: "If . . . everybody voted, I'm afraid we'd be in for a gigantic upheaval of American society—and we comfortable readers of the Times would certainly stand to lose much at the hands of the poor, faceless, previously quiet throngs. Wouldn't it be best to let sleeping dogs lie?"

11. Heinz Eulau, "The Politics of Happiness," *Antioch Review*, 16, 1956, pp. 259–264; Lipset, *Political Man*, pp. 179–219.

12. Burnham, "The Changing Shape of the American Political Universe," p. 27; and Kimball, *The Disconnected*.

... The government is not run in my interest; they do not care about me; in this sense it is not my government. ..."[13] The nonparticipation of many people often represents a feeling of powerlessness, a conviction that it is useless to vote, petition or demonstrate, useless to invest precious time, energy and hope and risk insult, eviction, arrest, loss of job and police assault, useless to do anything because nothing changes and one is left only with an aggravated sense of affliction and impotence. For many ordinary citizens, nonparticipation is not the result of brutish contentment, apathy or lack of civic virtue but an understandable negative response to the political realties they experience.[14]

With that in mind, we might question those public-opinion surveys which report that underprivileged persons are more apathetic and less informed than better-educated, upper-income citizens. If by *apathy* we mean the absence of affect and awareness, then the poor, the elderly, the young, the racial minorities and the industrial workers who have repeatedly voiced their outrage and opposition to various social conditions can hardly be described as "apathetic." Apathy should not be confused with antipathy and alienation. Nor is it clear that these dissident groups are "less informed." What impresses the investigators who actually take the trouble to talk to low-income people is the extent to which they have a rather precise notion of what afflicts them. Certainly they have a better sense of the difficulties that beset their lives than the many middle-class officials who frequently do not even recognize the reality or legitimacy of their complaints.[15]

Voting as an Irrational Response

Civic leaders, educators and opinion-makers usually characterize nonvoters as "slackers" and seldom as people who might be justifiably cynical about the electoral system. Conversely, they

13. Robert Lane, *Political Ideology* (New York: Free Press, 1962), p. 162.
14. A similar conclusion can be drawn from Studs Terkel, *Division Street: America* (New York: Pantheon, 1967); Kimball, *The Disconnected;* Levin, *The Alienated Voter;* Harold V. Savitch, "Powerlessness in an Urban Ghetto: The Case of Political Biases and Differential Access in New York City," *Polity,* 5, Fall 1972, pp. 17–56; Parenti, "Power and Pluralism"; Lewis Lipsitz, "On Political Belief: The Grievances of the Poor," in Philip Green and Sanford Levinson (eds.), *Power and Community* (New York: Pantheon, 1969), pp. 142–172.
15. See the citations in the previous footnote.

determined less by the majoritarian principle and more by the economic strength of policy advocates and the strategic positions they occupy in the wider social structure. The fact that government does little for the minority poor, and even shares in the middle-class hostility toward the poor, does not mean that government is devoted to the interests of the great bulk of belabored "middle Americans" nor that it operates according to majoritarian principles.

To summarize some of the observations offered in the last two chapters: important structural and material factors so predetermine the range of electoral issues and choices as to raise a serious question about the representative quality of the political system. Mass politics requires mass resources; being enormously expensive affairs, elections are best utilized by those interests endowed with the resources necessary to take advantage of them. Politics has always been largely "a rich man's game." Ironically enough, the one institutional arrangement that is ostensibly designed to register the will of the many serves to legitimize the rule of the privileged few. The way people respond to political reality depends on the way that reality is presented to them. If people have become apathetic and cynical, including many of those who vote, it is at least partly because the electoral system and the major party organizations tend to resist the kind of creative involvement that democracy is supposed to nurture. It is one thing to say that people tend to be uninvolved, ill-informed and given to impoverished and stereotyped notions about political life. It is quite another to maintain a system that propagates these tendencies with every known distraction and discouragement. Elections, then, might better be considered a symbol of democratic governance than a guarantee of it, and voting often seems to be less an exercise than a surrender of sovereignty.

The Mass Media: By the Few, For the Many

11

IT IS SAID THAT A FREE AND INDE-
pendent press is a necessary condition for
democracy, and it is frequently assumed that
the United States is endowed with such a
press. While the news in "totalitarian" nations
is controlled, we Americans supposedly have
access to a wide range of ideas and information
from competing sources. In reality, the controls exerted over the media in the United
States, while more subtle and less severe than
in some other countries, leave us with a press
that is far from "free" by any definition of the
word.

The news media are important to any
study of American politics. They implant the
images in our heads that help us define
socio-political reality. Almost all the political
life we experience is through newspapers,
radio and television. How we view issues
—indeed, what we even define as an "issue"
or "event"—what we see and hear and what
we do *not* see and hear are greatly determined
by those who control the media. By enlarging
our vision through technology, we have actually surrendered control over much of our own
sensory experience.[1]

It is argued that the mass media are not a
crucial factor in political life: one can point to
the many Democratic Presidents who won

1. Robert Cirino, *Don't Blame the People* (Los Angeles:
Diversity Press, 1971), pp. 30–31. Cirino's book is a
well-documented study of how the news media distort and
manipulate public opinion; recently reissued by Vintage,
it is highly recommended to the reader.

elections despite the overwhelming endorsement of their Republican opponents by the press. But despite a low rate of editorial endorsement, Democratic candidates do manage to buy political advertisements and receive coverage by the mass media during their campaigns, unlike radical candidates, who receive almost no exposure and almost no votes.[2] The argument also overlooks the subtler and more persistent influences of the media in defining the scope of respectable political discourse, channeling public attention in certain directions and determining—in ways that are essentially conservative and supportive of the existing socioeconomic structure—what is political reality.[3]

He Who Pays the Piper

The primary function of television, radio and newspapers is not to keep the public informed but to make money for their owners, a goal that frequently does not coincide with the need for a vigilant democratic press. The number of independently owned newspapers has been declining in the United States, with most of the big-circulation dailies coming under the ownership of chains like Hearst, Gannett and Copely. In the last twenty years some thirty dailies have disappeared. Today only 45 out of 1,500 American cities have competing newspapers under separate ownership. According to James Aronson, more Americans "are reading fewer papers and fewer points of view than ever before."[4] (In many cities where there is a "choice," like Chicago with its four dailies, the newspapers are all quite conservative in editorial policy.)

But if they are declining in numbers, the papers are *not* declining as business ventures. In fact, they are doing quite well. Through mergers, packaged news service and staff cutting, the larger conglomerates have paid off handsomely. In 1969 newspapers grossed $5.4 billion in advertising revenues, or 22 percent more than the total for radio and television combined. For the

2. For a discussion of this point see Chapter Nine, "The Sound and the Fury: Elections and Parties."

3. See Cirino, *Don't Blame the People*, pp. 181–182.

4. James Aronson, *Packaging the News, A Critical Survey of Press, Radio, TV* (New York: International Publishers, 1971), p. 14. Monopoly ownership extends across the various media. As of 1967 there were seventy-three communities in the United States in which one company or one rich individual owned or controlled *all* newspapers and local broadcast outlets.

businessmen who own them, "newspapers are no longer entities in themselves, with individual character, courage, and a dedication to the public service, but simply properties to be listed among holdings along with real estate, fertilizer, electronics, and aerospace rocketry."[5]

As with the newspapers, so with television: big media are big business. The three major networks, CBS, NBC and ABC, made $179 million in profits in 1968 and $226 million in 1969—an increase of 12 percent in one year. Many radio and television stations and publishing houses are owned by corporations like RCA, ITT, Westinghouse and General Electric. The networks themselves have substantial international investments, owning television stations throughout Asia, the Middle East and Latin America.[6]

The influence of big-business ownership is reflected in its political content. The media are given over to trivialized "features" and gossip items. Coverage of national, state and local affairs is usually scant, superficial and oriented toward "events" and "personalities," consisting of a few short "headline" stories and a number of mildly conservative or simply banal commentaries and editorials As one group of scholars noted after a study of the news media: "Protection against government is now not enough to guarantee that a man who has something to say shall have a chance to say it. The owners and managers of the press determine which person, which facts, which version of the facts, and which ideas shall reach the public."[7]

The business-owned media have had little to say about the relationship between the capitalist system and such things as pollution, bad housing, poverty and inflation, the relations between political and business leaders and the role of the multinational corporations in shaping American interventionist policy abroad. Almost no positive exposure is given to the socialist alternatives emerging throughout the Third World or the socialist critique of capitalism at home. Despite some recent manifestations of liberalism on such issues as Vietnam and military spending, news media content remains fundamentally conservative. There are almost no strongly liberal or radical biases expressed in the mass media. In contrast, reactionaries,

5. *Ibid.*, p. 15.
6. Herbert Schiller, *Mass Communications and American Empire* (New York: Augustus Kelly, 1969).
7. *A Free and Responsible Press* (Report by the Commission of Freedom of the Press, 1947), quoted in Cirino, *Don't Blame the People*, p. 47.

militarists and ultra-rightist elements have an estimated $14-million yearly propaganda budget donated by some 113 business firms and 25 public utilities, and each week across the country they make over ten thousand television and radio broadcasts—with much of the air time freely donated by sympathetic station owners.[8] In one three-week period the ultraconservative billionaire H. Ross Perot was able to present his viewpoints "supporting President Nixon's Vietnam policy in 300 newspapers with full-page advertisements and in a half hour television program. His qualifications? He had the $1 million it required."[9]

On the infrequent occasions when liberals muster enough money to buy broadcasting time or newspaper space, they still may be denied access to the media. Liberal commentators have been refused radio spots even when they had sponsors who would pay. A group of scientists, politicians and celebrities opposing the Pentagon's antiballistic missile program were denied a half hour on television by all three major networks despite the fact that they had the required $250,000 to buy time. All three networks refused to sell time to the Democratic National Committee to reply to Nixon's televised statements on the Vietnam war. And on various occasions the *New York Times* would not sell space to citizens' groups that wanted to run advertisements against the war tax or against the purchase of war bonds. A *Times* executive turned down the advertisement against war bonds because he judged it not to be in the "best interests of the country."[10]

Denied access to the mass media, the political left has attempted to get its message across through local newspapers and magazines of its own, but this "underground press" has suffered many financial difficulties and official harassments. In Cambridge, Mass., street vendors for the *Avatar* were arrested fifty-eight times within a short period on trumped-up charges, and newsstand owners, under threat of arrest, refused to carry the paper, thus causing a sharp decline in circulation. In Atlanta the radical newspaper *Great Speckled Bird* was subjected to repeated police harassments in 1972; its offices were then attacked by unknown persons three times in three weeks and were finally

8. Arnold Forster and Benjamin Epstein, *Danger on the Right* (New York: Vintage, 1964), p. 273.
9. Cirino, *Don't Blame the People*, p. 299.
10. *Ibid.*, p. 90 and p. 302.

destroyed by fire bombs. Police seemed unable to find a clue as to who did it.

In Montgomery County, Maryland, the editor of the *Washington Free Press* was given six months in prison for publishing an allegedly obscene cartoon of a judge. In San Diego the *Street Journal and San Diego Press* suffered bullets through its office windows, theft, destruction of equipment, fire bombings and repeated staff arrests on charges that were later thrown out of court. In Urbana, Ill., the editor of the *Walrus* was arrested in 1969 for nonpossession of his draft card and imprisoned for three years. In the same city a radical printing cooperative was burglarized and destroyed by unknown persons. And in Peoria, Ill., another printer of radical publications had his press closed by authorities under a seldom enforced zoning law.[11]

The Politics of Entertainment

While the entertainment sector of the media, as opposed to the news sector, supposedly has nothing to do with politics, entertainment programs in fact undergo a rigorous political censorship. In the late 1960s the "Smothers Brothers Comedy Hour," after being cut several times for introducing antiwar comments and other mildly political statements, was finally removed from the air. CBS censored appeals for world peace made by Carol Burnett and Elke Sommer in their respective appearances on the Merv Griffin show. Songs that contained references to drugs, prison conditions, the draft and opposition to war have been cut from entertainment shows.[12] When David Susskind submitted five thousand names of people he wished to have appear on his talk show to the advertising agency that represented his sponsor, a third of the candidates were rejected because of their political viewpoints. The censorship code used by Proctor and Gamble for shows it sponsored stated in part: "Members of the armed forces must not be cast as villains. If there is any attack on American custom, it must be rebutted completely on the same show."[13]

11. Most of these incidents are reported in Aronson, *Packaging the News*, pp. 67–69. See also the *Guardian*, May 17, 1972, and the *Militant*, January 21, 1972. The information on Illinois is from my own observations.

12. See Cirino, *Don't Blame the People*, pp. 305–306, for various examples.

13. Murray Schumack, *The Face on the Cutting Room Floor*, quoted in *ibid.*, pp. 303–304.

While critical socio-political commentaries are censored out of entertainment shows, there is plenty of politics of another sort. In soap operas and situation comedies, adventure programs and detective stories, comic strips and children's cartoon shows, conventional American values are preached and practiced. Various kinds of aggressive behavior are indulged in and even glorified, although dissident elements like student demonstrators and radicals have been portrayed unfavorably as violent and irrational characters. Foreign agents are seen as menacing our land and the military as protecting it. Establishment figures like judges, executive heads, businessmen, doctors and police are fair and competent—never on the take, never corrupt, never racist or oppressive. Or, if there *are* a few bad ones, they are soon set straight by their more principled colleagues. In the media world, adversities usually are caused by ill-willed individuals rather than by the economic system in which they live, and problems are solved by individual effort within the system rather than collective effort against it. Conflicts are resolved by generous applications of violence. Nefarious violence is met with righteous violence, although it is often hard to distinguish between the two. In many films the brutal and often criminal behavior of law officers has been portrayed sympathetically, as one of those gutsy realities of life. Violence on television and in Hollywood films is almost omnipresent, often linked to sex, money, dominance, self-aggrandizement and other attributes that represent "manliness" in the male-chauvinist, capitalist American culture.

In the media, women appear primarily in supportive roles as housewives, secretaries and girl friends. They usually are incapable of initiating actions of their own; they get into difficulties from which they must be extricated by their men. When not treated as weak and scatter-brained, women are likely to be portrayed as devious, dehumanized sex objects, the ornaments of male egoism. In media advertisements women seem exclusively concerned with getting a fluffy glow shampooed into their hair, waxing "their" floors, making yummy coffee for hubby, getting Johnny's clothes snowy white, and in other ways serving as mindless, cheery household drones.

Working-class people, as mentioned earlier, have little representation in the entertainment media except as uncouth, ignorant persons, hoodlums, servants and other such minor stock characters. The tribulations of working-class people in this society—their struggle to make ends meet, the specter of unem-

ployment, the lack of decent recreational facilities, the machinations of unscrupulous merchants and landlords, the loss of
pensions and seniority, the battles for unionization and union
reform, the dirty, noisy, mindless, dangerous, alienating quality
of industrial work, the abuses suffered at the hands of bosses, the
lives wrecked and cut short by work-connected injury and
disease—these kinds of reality almost never are thought worthy
of dramatic treatment in the plastic, make-believe world of the
mass media. The experiences of millions of working-class people
are ignored because they are not deemed suitable subjects by the
upper-middle-class professionals who create the programs and
because the whole question of class struggle and class exploitation is a forbidden subject in media owned by the corporate rich.

Repressing the Press

On those infrequent occasions when the news media do give
attention to controversial events and take a critical view of
official doings, they are likely to encounter intimidating discour-
agements from public officials. Almost without exception, government officeholders treat any kind of news that places them in
an unfavorable light as "slanted" and seek to exert pressure on
reporters in order to bring them around to the "correct" and
"objective" (i.e., uncritical and supportive) viewpoint. Few
political leaders have been more intolerant toward the press than
President Nixon, who (before Watergate, and even to a large
extent thereafter) regarded all critical reporting of his administration as biased and all opposition as bordering on disloyalty. Nixon
professed little confidence in the American people, once observing that "the average American is just like the child in the
family. . . . [If you] pamper him and cater to him too much, you
are going to make him soft, spoiled and eventually a very weak
individual." Beset by such paternalistic anxieties, the Nixon
administration did its best to control the kind of information the
childlike American was fed. Some examples:

(1) For several years Vice-President Spiro Agnew with an
occasional assist from Attorney General John Mitchell leveled a
series of attacks on the press for its supposedly "liberal" biases,
calling upon the media to be more "responsible" in its news
reports and commentaries. (This kind of attack allows the media
to appear as liberal defenders of free speech against government
censorship, instead of supporters of the established order as they

usually are.) The effect on the already timid news media of the Agnew-Mitchell assault was a palpable one. "I think the industry as a whole has been intimidated," complained CBS newscaster Walter Cronkite.[14] At the same time, the FBI approached various network executives concerning reporters who have done stories which displeased the President.[15] While covering a story, reporter Leslie Whitten was arrested by the FBI on a trumped-up charge. Whitten's real crime, some people speculated, was having vigorously pursued the story of collusion between ITT and the CIA to stage a coup in Chile, as well as the story of ITT's illegal contribution to the Nixon campaign fund and the dairy owners' successful attempts to buy favors from the Nixon administration.[16]

(2) In June 1971 the Nixon administration tried to get a court order preventing the publication of the Pentagon Papers (a collection of classified government memoranda and documents on how American policy in Vietnam was secretly shaped). It was the government's most serious attempt in American history to enforce prior censorship of the press. When the Supreme Court ruled in favor of the press, the Justice Department then charged Daniel Ellsberg and Anthony J. Russo, the two former government employees who had released the Pentagon Papers, with espionage. A political scientist, Samuel Popkin, who had seen the papers before their publication and refused to implicate other scholars who had studied them, was jailed for refusing to violate professional confidences before a grand jury.

(3) For most of our history, under the First Amendment guarantee against abridgements of free speech, reporters were not required to reveal those informants who gave them information about malfeasance in high places, political scandals or any other events about which the public had a right to know. In June 1972 the Supreme Court ruled that reporters could be required to disclose their information sources to grand jury investigators. With the Nixon appointees providing the winning balance, the Court decided in a 5–4 decision that the public interest involved in bringing a criminal to justice overrode the reporter's need to protect his news source.[17] The newsman who lost this decision, Earl Caldwell of the *New York Times*, declared that the decision

14. Quoted in Aronson, *Packaging the News*, p. 80.
15. David Wise, "The President and the Press," *Atlantic*, April 1973, pp. 55–64.
16. Stephen Torgoff, "Press Freedom in Danger," *Guardian*, February 14, 1973.
17. *United States* v. *Caldwell*, 33 L. Ed. 2d 626 (1972).

made it "really impossible to do serious reporting in the U.S. if the government doesn't want you to." Dozens of reporters have since been jailed or threatened with long prison terms on the basis of that decision.

(4) Nixon vetoed an appropriations bill for the Public Broadcasting System because he disliked several of the public affairs programs that have appeared under its auspices. Almost all the news analysis programs that the White House disapproved of were canceled. In April 1973 the chairman of the Corporation for Public Broadcasting, Thomas Curtis, a Republican and Nixon appointee, resigned in protest, warning that public broadcasting should not become "a propaganda arm for the Nixon Administration or for any succeeding administration."[18]

(5) In 1973 Nixon proposed a law giving the Federal Communications Commission the power to refuse to renew the license of any radio or television station that persisted in "bias." Nixon's spokesman, Clay Whitehead, explained that stations will be required to demonstrate "responsibility" and avoid "ideological plugola." "Station managers and network officials who fail to act to correct imbalance or consistent bias in the network, *or who acquiesce by silence*, can only be considered willing participants, to be held fully accountable . . . at license-renewal time," he concluded.[19] The government, of course, was to determine to its own satisfaction who was and was not "biased."

(6) The Nixon administration increased second-class postal rates, thereby doubling the mailing costs of publications. The increases would be a serious and perhaps fatal burden for the small, unprofitable journals that offered the kind of opposition viewpoints seldom heard in the mass media. The government defended the increase as an economy measure while at the same time continuing the heavy postal subsidy of the more than 12 billion pieces of junk mail sent out every year by business and advertising firms.

Much of the government pressure on newspapers and networks occurs outside the public view. On repeated occasions the government has subpoenaed, and received, documents, films, tapes and other materials used by news media in the reporting of events. And the government interferes in other ways: "The telephone calls from White House assistants and the visits to network executives by presidential aides are seldom

18. *New York Times*, April 24, 1973.
19. "Mr. Nixon and the Media" ("Playboy Forum" report), *Playboy*, April 1973, p. 61. (Italics added.)

publicized."[20] Such interferences impose "a chilling effect" on the news media, an inclination to think twice before reporting something, a propensity—already marked in most news reports—to slide over the more troublesome and damning aspects of a story—in all, a tendency to police and censor oneself to avoid the discomforts and risks of clashing with those in power.[21]

When not trying to control public opinion, the government is busy manufacturing it. After Nixon's speech announcing the mining of Haiphong harbor in the spring of 1972, a flood of telegrams in support of his policy came pouring in. Later on, it was revealed that the bulk of the mail had been sent by the Committee to Re-elect the President and had been fabricated to look like a spontaneous public response. There are certain hazards to this kind of manipulation: in December 1969, Spiro Agnew taped a speech that was scheduled by UPI news service to be broadcast one weekend over dozens of radio stations. Because of a mix-up, not a single station aired the speech. Just the same, the following Monday the UPI office was inundated with fourteen thousand pieces of mail praising Agnew for his latest attack on liberals.[22] (Not one of the letters was critical.)

Attempts to control or fabricate the news are not unique to the Nixon administration. Presidents like Johnson, Kennedy and Eisenhower and their various aides were repeatedly successful in killing unfavorable stories and planting favorable ones. Much of what is reported as "news" in all our newspapers, broadcasts and telecasts is nothing more than the reporting of official releases. In more instances than can be counted, the "independent press" transmits what the government wants transmitted to an unsuspecting public.

From what has been said so far it should be clear that one cannot talk about a "free press" apart from the economic and political realities that determine who owns and controls the media. Freedom of speech means not only the right to hear both

20. Wise, "The President and the Press," pp. 63–64. For a further discussion of government's use of secrecy and deception, see Chapter Fifteen, "The Politics of Bureaucracy."

21. Staggering from the blows of the Watergate exposé, the Nixon administration temporarily took a more conciliatory tack with the press in April 1973. Agnew admitted publicly that he had been too "harsh" in his choice of words. Nixon asked that the press keep giving him "hell" when he deserved it. And his press secretary, Ron Ziegler, apologized for various disparaging remarks he previously had made to reporters. Only when they no longer feel omnipotent do aggressors act civil toward others.

22. Ian Sven, Liberation News Service release, January 1970. This incident received little publicity in the establishment press.

sides of a story (Republican and Democratic) but the right to hear *all* sides. It means not only the right to *hear* but the right to *be heard,* to talk back to those in government and in the network offices and newsrooms, something few of us can do at present.

What also should be clear to anyone who understands human communication is that there is no such thing as unbiased news. All reports and analyses are selective and inferential to some inescapable degree—all the more reason to provide a wider ideological spectrum of opinions and not let one bias predominate. Some measure of ideological heterodoxy could be achieved if public law required all newspapers and broadcasting stations to allot substantial portions of space and time to a vast array of political opinion, including the most radical and revolutionary.

Ultimately the only protection against monopoly control of the media is ownership by community people themselves, with legally enforceable provisions allowing for the maximum participation of conflicting views. In Europe, some suggestive developments have taken place: the staffs of various newspapers and magazines like *Der Stern* in Germany and *Le Figaro* in France have used strikes to achieve greater editorial control of the publications they help to produce. And *Le Monde*'s management agreed to give its staff a 40 percent share in the profits and a large share in policy-making and managerial decisions, including the right to block any future sale of the paper.[23]

While interesting because they point to alternative forms of property control, these developments are themselves not likely to transform the property relations of a capitalist society and its mass media. With few exceptions, those who own the newspapers and networks, and make enormous profits on them, will not relinquish their hold over private investments and public information. Ordinary citizens will have no real access to the media until they come to exercise direct community control over the material resources that could give them such access, an achievement that would take a different kind of economic and social system than the one we have. In the meantime, Americans should have no illusions about the "freedom of speech" they are said to enjoy.

23. Aronson, *Packaging the News*, p. 99.

Who Governs?
Leaders and Lobbyists

12 IT WAS TOCQUEVILLE WHO ONCE SAID that the bourgeoisie have little interest in governing the working people, they simply want to use them.[1] Yet, in truth, members of the propertied class seldom have been slow in assuming the burdens of public office. The political party, said Secretary of State Seward in 1865, using an image that fit his class experience, is "a joint stock association, in which those who contribute most direct the action and management of the concern."[2] The same might be said of government itself. While the less glorious tasks of vote herding fell to persons of modest class and ethnic origins, the top state and federal offices, to this day, have remained largely in the hands of White, Protestant, middle-aged, upper-income males of conventional political opinion, drawn from the top ranks of corporate management, from the prominent law and banking firms of Wall Street and less frequently from the elite universities and foundations and the scientific establishment. Serving as Presidents, governors, cabinet members, administrators, high ranking advisers, Senators, Representatives, judges and ambassadors, they have carried into the public world many of the same class values, interests and presumptions that shaped their private worlds.

1. Alexis de Tocqueville, *Democracy in America*, vol. 2 (New York: Vintage, 1945), p. 171.
2. Quoted in Matthew Josephson, *The Politicos, 1865–1896* (New York: Harcourt, Brace, 1938), p. 13.

"Those Who Own the Land Shall Govern It"

From the beginning of the American Republic in 1789 to modern times, the great majority of those who have occupied the top political offices of the nation—including the presidency and vice-presidency and positions in the cabinet and the Supreme Court—have been from wealthy families (the upper 5 or 6 percent of the population) and most of the remainder have been from well-off, middle-class origins (moderately successful businessmen, farmers, professionals). Of those who went to college, more than one third attended the elite Ivy League schools.[3] Of the 125 top government appointments made by the liberal President and former small businessman Harry Truman in 1945–1947, forty-nine were bankers and industrialists, thirty-one were military men, and seventeen were lawyers, mostly with corporate connections, a situation that caused one newsman to observe: "The effective focus of government seemed to shift from Washington to some place equidistant between Wall Street and West Point."[4] Of the fifty or more top appointments in the first Eisenhower administration, three fourths were linked with industry, finance and corporate law firms, while the remainder might be classified as government administrators or professional party politicians. The men who ran the nation's defense establishment between 1940 and 1967, according to Richard Barnet, "were so like one another in occupation, religion, style and social status that, apart from a few Washington lawyers, Texans, and mavericks, it was possible to locate the offices of all of them within fifteen city blocks in New York, Boston and Detroit."[5] The policies they pursued in office frequently were directly connected to the corporate interests they represented in their private lives. Consider the White House decision-makers involved in America's armed intervention against the worker-student uprising in the Dominican Republic in 1965.

3. See the data in C. Wright Mills, *The Power Elite* (New York: Oxford University Press, 1956), pp. 400–402, fn., and *passim*; also Harold Lasswell et al., *The Comparative Study of Elites* (Stanford, Calif.: Stanford University Press, 1952), p. 30; G. William Domhoff, *Who Rules America?* (Englewood Cliffs, N.J.: Prentice-Hall, 1967), especially Chapters 3 and 4; G. William Domhoff, *The Higher Circles: The Governing Class in America* (New York: Vintage, 1970); Richard J. Barnet, *Roots of War* (New York: Atheneum, 1972); John C. Donovan, *The Cold Warriors* (Lexington, Mass.: D.C. Heath, 1973); George W. Pierson, *The Education of American Leaders* (New York: Praeger, 1972).

4. Howard K. Smith, *The State of Europe* (New York: Knopf, 1949), p. 83.

5. Barnet, *Roots of War*, pp. 48–49.

New Dealer Abe Fortas was a director of the Sucrest Corporation for 20 years, third largest East Coast cane sugar refiner; Adolf A. Berle, Jr., known Latin American expert and advisor to several presidents, was Chairman of the Board of Sucrest for 18 years and is still a director and large stockholder; Ellsworth Bunker was Chairman, President, and 38-year Director of the second largest East Coast cane sugar refiner, National Sugar Refining Corp. and one-time stockholder in a Dominican sugar mill; roving Ambassador W. Averell Harriman is a "limited partner" in the banking house of Brown Brothers, Harriman, which owns 5 percent of National Sugar's stock (his brother, E. Roland Harriman, sits on the board of National Sugar); J. M. Kaplan, molasses magnate, is a large contributor and influential advisor to many Democratic Party candidates and the ADA; Joseph S. Farland, State Department consultant and ex-U.S. Ambassador to the Dominican Republic, is a director of South Puerto Rico Sugar Company; Roswell Gilpatrick, Deputy Secretary of Defense, is the managing executive partner in the Wall Street firm of Cravath, Swaine and Moore, legal counsel to National Sugar; and Max Rabb, partner in the Wall Street firm of Strook, Strook, and Lavan, legal counsel for Sucrest, is an influential Johnson supporter. The above sugar refiners, plus the largest U.S. refiner, American Sugar, depend directly on the Dominican sugar and molasses supply for their operations. Any disruption in the supply would seriously hamper price stability. Even without these direct economic interests, it would be difficult for these gentlemen in their "neutral" decision making roles to escape the assumptions, inclinations and priorities inculcated by their economic and social milieu.[6]

Within the lower echelons of government, recruitment is less selective in regard to class background, but measures have been taken to filter out those who might entertain views that run contrary to the established political order. Ralph Miliband describes it this way:

In all capitalist countries, though with different degrees of thoroughness (the United States easily leading the field), candidates to the civil service and members of it are subjected to screening procedures and security checks which have become a familiar and permanent feature of Western administrative life. The official reason given for these procedures is that they are required to exclude "security risks" from employment by the state, particularly in important and "sensitive" posts. But the notion of what constitutes a "security risk" is an elastic one and can easily

6. Fred Goff and Michael Locker, *The Violence of Domination: U.S. Power and the Dominican Republic* (New York: North American Congress on Latin America, n.d.), cited in James Petras, "U.S. Business and Foreign Policy," *New Politics*, 6, Fall 1967, p. 76.

be stretched to encompass anyone whose opinions and ideas on important issues depart from a framework of "soundness" defined in terms of the prevailing conservative consensus.[7]

Plutocracy—rule *by* the rich *for* the rich—also prevails in Congress. In the 1970 senatorial elections, of fifteen major candidates in seven of the largest states, eleven were millionaires. Various Senators and Congressmen, like James Buckley (R.–N.Y.) and Russell Long (D.–La.), have substantial holdings in oil and gas and are staunch defenders of depletion allowances for these industries. The late Senator Robert Kerr (D.–Okla.) exercised control over legislation affecting gas, uranium, oil and other natural resources. By 1960 he owned a number of oil wells, 25 percent of America's uranium mines and 75 percent of the world's richest helium pool. Much of his wealth was accumulated after he was elected to the Senate.

Certain members of Congress who are owners of large farm holdings sit on committees that shape the farm loan and subsidy programs that directly enrich them. In 1969 ninety House members had substantial financial investments in banks, savings and loan associations or bank holding companies. Included were twelve members of the House Banking Committee and six on the Ways and Means Committee, both of which pass on legislation that serves the banking industry. In the 92nd Congress, forty out of one hundred Senators were either on the boards of national banks or among the top stockholders. Most were investors in state banks and loan associations. The 535 members of Congress in 1970 included (with some overlap) 184 from banking and business, 310 lawyers, 50 farmers (mostly large successful ones) and others from various professions such as teaching, medicine, and journalism.[8] The great bulk of the American population belongs to occupations and income levels that have no direct representation in Congress.

There are persons who entertain political views that are strikingly incongruous with their class origins, such as the very few rich individuals who espouse socialism. But usually the wealthy and the well-to-do, be they of "old families" or newly arrived, "reform-minded" or conservative, are not known to advocate the demolition of the economic system under which they prosper. Nor are they inclined to support the kind of

7. Ralph Miliband, *The State in Capitalist Society* (New York: Basic Books, 1969), p. 124.
8. *New York Times Encyclopedic Almanac*, 1970.

changes that might work against their class interests. Political leaders of relatively modest class origins, like Lyndon Johnson, Richard Nixon and Spiro Agnew, are unlikely to retain a strong identity with the low and the humble throughout their ascension. As already noted, one of the preconditions of the rise of such men is their willingness to accommodate themselves at a fairly early point in their careers to the interests of those privileged circles whose ranks they aspire to join. The frequent references they make to their humble origins are usually intended to enhance their popular appeal or to serve as proof that the system provides opportunities for individuals who have what it takes.

Campaign Contributions: What Money Can Buy

The way campaigns are funded is a reflection of the way wealth is distributed in the society. A small number of big donors pay the bulk of campaign expenses. In the 1968 campaign a mere eighty-nine persons contributed more than $6.8 million.[9] It cost an estimated $100 million to elect a President in 1968, including all expenditures from the first primary to election day; some 85 percent of this money came from businessmen and their families.[10] While politicians insist that campaign contributions do not influence them, few are inclined to go against those who support them financially. A former assistant to two prominent Democratic Senators made the following observation:

Any member of Congress who says donations don't influence him is lying. All of them are corrupt. The only question is the degree of corruption. One reason members of Congress insist that money doesn't influence them is that they . . . often become convinced of the rightness of their backers' causes without admitting it even to themselves. In time, they come to really believe that the guy who gives the big dough is the best guy and that helping him is in the public interest. But campaign money *has* to influence even the most incorruptible men here, because most people don't give away large sums of money for nothing.[11]

9. *New York Times*, November 14, 1971.
10. Herbert E. Alexander, *Financing the 1968 Election* (Lexington, Mass.: D.C. Heath, 1971); also Herbert E. Alexander, *Money in Politics* (Washington, D.C.: Public Affairs Press, 1972); G. William Domhoff, *Fat Cats and Democrats* (Englewood Cliffs, N.J.: Prentice-Hall, 1972); and Morton Mintz and Jerry S. Cohen, *America, Inc.* (New York: Dial Press, 1971).
11. Quoted in Richard Harris, "Annals of Politics: A Fundamental Hoax," *New Yorker*, August 7, 1971, p. 54.

Republicans generally receive from three to five times more from big corporate donors than do Democrats, although Democratic lawmakers of tested conservative predilections and with strategic committee positions have little difficulty in being funded. Thus the former chairman of the House Interior Committee, Wayne Aspinall (D.–Col.), received 79 percent of his reported campaign contributions from outside his district, from oil, mining and timber companies. Aspinall was "one of those men who did most to determine profit rates" in those industries.[12] In 1970 a group of bankers contributed more than $200,000 to some forty members of Congress of *both* parties who were on banking and finance committees.[13] And the gratitude of the favored interests is fitting to the services performed. Thus in 1965, after Congressman Thomas Ashley (D.–Ohio) was instrumental in passing a bill that allowed for the merger of six Ohio banks, the Ohio Banker's Association sent letters to every bank in the state urging that Áshley's re-election be supported "by any means necessary," since he had "shown an understanding of banking matters and a willingness to help develop sound laws on this subject."[14] The chairman of the House Merchant Marine committee, Edward Garmatz (D.–Md.), received $37,000 in campaign funds from the shipping industry; contributions from shipowners also went to at least sixteen other Congressmen and Senators of both parties who have been helpful to them. In 1971 some thirty House members and nine Senators, including liberal Democrats, received campaign donations totaling about $1 million from the dairy industry for their efforts on behalf of higher milk price supports. It was estimated that the dairymen would get back as much as three hundred times that amount from the supports.[15]

Small wonder that campaign gifts are seen by their contributors as *investments*—"monetary bread cast upon the water, to be returned a thousandfold," as one Senator describes it.[16] Indeed, at least one wealthy contributor was able to get a judicial ruling to that effect. Edith R. Stern spent $60,000 to back candidates for governor of Louisiana and mayor of New Orleans

12. Mark J. Green, James M. Fallows and David R. Zwick, *Who Runs Congress?* (New York: Bantam Books/Grossman, 1972), p. 26.

13. Harris, "Annals of Politics," p. 51.

14. "The Senate: Call It Millionaires' Row," *Workers' World*, December 25, 1970, p. 4.

15. Frank Wright, "The Dairy Lobby Buys the Cream of the Congress," *Washington Monthly*, May 1971, pp. 17–21.

16. Harris, "Annals of Politics," p. 53.

in the early 1960s. Usually this money would be subject to a federal gift tax which could run as high as 57 percent, a restraint on the rich requiring them to go through various circuitous routes to donate their large sums. Mrs. Stern protested the gift tax, claiming she had spent the money "to protect my property and personal interest by promoting efficiency in government." Both the district and appeals courts agreed with her; the latter concluded: "In a very real sense, then, Mrs. Stern was making an economic investment that she believed would have a direct and favorable effect upon her property holdings and business interests in New Orleans and Louisiana."[17]

The bipartisan influence of business is so pronounced as to move one Democratic Senator to remind his party colleagues that they were neglecting to keep up appearances as "the party of the people." In a speech on the Senate floor urging that the scientific patents of the $25-billion space program not be given away to private corporations but applied for public benefit, Russell Long made these candid remarks:

I submit that there is no more outrageous thing that can be done to the public interest. Many of these [corporate] people have much influence. I, like others, have importuned some of them for campaign contributions for my party and myself. Nevertheless, we owe it to the people, now and then, to save one or two votes for them. This is one such instance. If any Senator should suspect that he might lose his campaign contributors by voting with me today, I might assure him that I have been able to obtain contributions from some of those people, even though they knew I voted for the public interest as I see it on such issues as this. We Democrats can trade on the dubious assumption that we are protector of the public interest only so long if we permit things like these patent giveaways.[18]

In election financing, labor unions are seldom able to match the contributions of business. One Senator noted in 1967: "Most campaign money comes from businessmen. Labor contributions have been greatly exaggerated. It would be my guess that about 95 percent of campaign funds at the congressional level are derived from businessmen. At least 80 percent of this comes from men who could sign a net worth statement exceeding a quarter of a million dollars."[19] To juxtapose Big Labor with Big Business in

17. Reported in *Ramparts*, June 1971, p. 12.
18. *Congressional Record*, vol. 112, part 9, June 2, 1966.
19. Senator Long again, quoted in Green et al., *Who Runs Congress?*, pp. 12–13.

the manner of some American Government textbooks is to overlook the fact that the great bulk of the spending and lobbying is dominated by business groups. Frequently when labor does enter the pressure contest it is with too little, too late, or as a junior partner to a particular industry seeking a subsidy or tariff protection. This is not to discount organized labor as an interest group, but to indicate the insufficiency of its political strength, especially when measured against the needs of the working class it claims to represent.

Some unions have been instrumental in increasing minimum wage standards and improving work conditions for workers in various industries. Yet, as previously noted, fewer than one in four employees are unionized, and a great portion of the work force, including many unionized persons, suffer the hardships that come with low wages, layoffs, underemployment, "sweetheart" contracts, unhealthy and unsafe work conditions, speed-ups, inadequate transportation, substandard housing, poor medical care and other deficient or nonexistent human services. On the many issues that crucially affect the life chances of the ordinary wage earner, unions generally have shown themselves uninterested in, or incapable of, performing effectively as a public-interest lobby.

Lobbyists and Their Ways

Campaign money buys what one House aide called that "basic ingredient of all lobbying"—*accessibility* to the officeholder[20] and, with that, the opportunity to shape his judgments with data and arguments of the lobbyist's own choosing. Accessibility, however, involves not merely winning an audience with a Congressman—since even ordinary citizens sometimes can get to see their Representatives and Senators—but winning his active support. In one of his more revealing moments, Woodrow Wilson pointed out:

Suppose you go to Washington and try to get at your Government. You will always find that while you are politely listened to, the men really consulted are the men who have the big stake—the big bankers, the big manufacturers, and the big masters of commerce. . . . The masters of the

20. Quoted in Harris, "Annals of Politics," p. 55. See also Robert Winter-Berger, *The Washington Pay-Off* (New York: Dell, 1972).

Government of the United States are the combined capitalists and manufacturers of the United States.[21]

Much the same can be said of state and local governments. On economic issues of any importance, reports Martin Waldron in the *New York Times,* most state legislative bodies give first consideration to banking and business lobbyists. The idea (popular among political scientists in the 1950s) that strong party leadership would be an effective bulwark against such pressure groups appears to be without much foundation. Individual legislators vote as their party leaders want, but these leaders, in turn, are "being told what to do by lobbyists," Waldron concludes.[22] The influence exercised on state legislatures by big-money pressure groups "is so widespread in this country it appears endemic."[23]

Surveying the organized pressure groups in America, E. E. Schattschneider notes: "When lists of these organizations are examined, the fact that strikes the student most forcibly is that *the system is very small.* The range of organized, identifiable, known groups is amazingly narrow; there is nothing remotely universal about it."[24] The pressure system, he concludes, is largely dominated by business groups, the majority of citizens belonging to no organization that is effectively engaged in pressure politics. Almost all organized groups, even nonbusiness ones such as community, religious, educational and professional associations, "reflect an upper-class tendency";[25] low-income people rarely have the time, money or expectation level that would enable them to participate.

The pressure system is "small" and "narrow" only in that it represents a highly select portion of the public. In relation to government itself, the system is a vast operation. "Most of the office space in Washington that is not occupied by government workers is occupied by special-interest lobbyists, who put in millions of hours each year trying to get special legislation enacted for the benefit of their clients," writes Richard Harris. "And they succeeed on a scale that is undreamed of by most

21. Quoted in D. Gilbarg, "United States Imperialism," in Bill Slate (ed.), *Power to the People* (New York: Tower, 1970), p. 67.
22. Martin Waldron, "Shadow on the Alamo," *New York Times Book Review,* July 10, 1972, p. 2.
23. *Ibid.*
24. E. E. Schattschneider, *The Semi-Sovereign People* (New York: Holt, Rinehart and Winston, 1960), p. 31. Italics in the original.
25. *Ibid.*, pp. 33–34, and the studies cited therein.

ordinary citizens."[26] A favorable adjustment in rates for interstate carriers, a tax write-off for oilmen, a high-interest bond issue for investors, a special charter for a bank, tariff protection for auto producers, the leasing of some public lands to a lumber company, emergency funding for a faltering aeronautics plant, a lenient occupational health code for employers, a postal subsidy for advertising firms, a soil bank for agribusiness, the easing of safety standards for a food processor, the easing of pollution controls for a chemical company, an investment guarantee to a housing developer, a lease guarantee to a construction contractor—all these hundreds of bills and their thousands of special amendments and the tens of thousands of administrative rulings which mean so much to particular interests and arouse the sympathetic efforts of legislators and bureaucrats will go largely unnoticed by a public that pays the monetary and human costs, and has not the organization, information and means to make its case—or even discover that it has a case.

Pressure activities are not directed only at the legislators and administrators but encompass entire segments of the public itself. Grant McConnell offers one description of this "grass-roots lobbying":

The electric companies, organized in the National Electric Light Association, had not only directly influenced Congressmen and Senators on a large scale, but had also conducted a massive campaign to control the substance of teaching in the nation's schools. Teachers in high schools and grammar schools were inundated with materials purporting to be aids to learning on such topics as the wonders of electricity and the romance of the kilowatt. Each pamphlet included carefully planted disparagement of public ownership of utilities. The Association took very active, if inconspicuous, measures to insure that textbooks that were doctrinally impure on this issue were withdrawn from use and that more favorable substitutes were produced and used. College professors, notoriously a needy lot, were given supplemental incomes by the Association and, in return, not infrequently taught about the utility industry with greater sympathy than before. . . . Public libraries, ministers, and civic leaders of all kinds were subjected to the propagandistic efforts of the electric companies.[27]

The purpose of grass-roots lobbying is to build a climate of opinion favorable to the corporate giants rather than to push a

26. Harris, "Annals of Politics," p. 56.
27. Grant McConnell, *Private Power and American Democracy* (New York: Knopf, 1966), p. 19.

particular piece of legislation. The steel, oil and electronics companies do not advertise for public support on behalf of the latest tax depreciation bill—if anything, they would prefer that citizens not trouble themselves with thoughts on the subject —but they do "educate" the public, telling of the many jobs the companies create, the progress and services they provide, the loving care they give to the environment, etc. This kind of "institutional advertising" eschews explicit policy content; its purpose is to place the desires of the giant firms above politics and above controversy—a goal that is itself highly political.

Propaganda and public relations activities now consume the greater portion of the budgets of organizations like the National Association of Manufacturers. Douglass Cater describes how the NAM, like other business groups, has refined its techniques over the years:

The "old" NAM bribed congressmen and employed legislative spies; the "new" prefers to work in public, openly offering advice and assistance to politicians. The "old" NAM sent paid intermediaries to "influence" the drafting of the Republican Convention Platform; the "new" prepares a "Platform of American Industry" and offers to testify at both party conventions. . . . Today the NAM refers to its "bank account" theory of public relations, which "necessitates making regular and frequent deposits in the Bank of Public Good-Will so that valid checks can be drawn on this account when desirable. . . ."[28]

Like a number of other students of lobbying, Cater may be overestimating the changes that have occurred in pressure-group tactics. The development of new lobbying techniques does not necessarily mean that the older, cruder ones have been dis-carded. Along with the slick brochures, expert testimonies and technical reports, corporate lobbyists still have the slush fund, the kickback, the stock award, the high-paying job offer in private industry, the meals, transportation and housing accommodations and the many other hustling enticements of money. Many large corporations have a special division dedicated to performing personal favors for legislators. The services include furnishing everything from hotel accommodations to private jet planes for Senators and their families. An employee at ITT's congressional liaison section publicly complained about the fact that Con-gressmen continually called her office for favors "on a big scale."

28. Douglass Cater, *Power in Washington* (New York: Random House, 1964), p. 208.

This situation "shocked" her, she said, even though "very little in Washington would shock me."[29]

Corruption as an American Way of Life

When Americans refer to "corrupt regimes" they usually are thinking of "underdeveloped" countries rather than their own nation. Yet in recent years there have been reports on corruption involving federal, state and local officials in every state of the Union. In Congress, according to George Agree, director of the National Committee for an Effective Congress: "Corruption is so endemic that it's scandalous. Even the honest men are corrupted—usually by and for the major economic-interest groups and the wealthy individuals who together largely dominate campaign financing."[30] "In some states—Louisiana, for instance—scandals are so prolific that exposure of them has absolutely no impact," reports one observer.[31] A Republican member of the Illinois state legislature estimated that one third of his legislative colleagues accepted payoffs.[32] In 1970–1971, county-level officials in seven of New Jersey's eleven urban counties were indicted or convicted for graft and corruption, along with the mayors of the two largest cities, the minority leader of the state assembly, the former speaker of the state assembly, a prominent state senator, a state prosecutor, a former secretary of state, and a Port Authority commissioner.[33] At about the same time, major scandals were occurring in Texas, Illinois, West Virginia, Maryland and New York. In New York City alone half the Police Department was reported by the Knapp Commis-

29. Quoted in the *New York Times*, March 31, 1972. For evidence that corrupt practices still flourish, see Winter-Berger, *The Washington Pay-Off*; Drew Pearson and Jack Anderson, *The Case Against Congress* (New York: Simon and Schuster, 1968); and Lawrence Gilson, *Money and Secrecy: A Citizen's Guide to Reform of State and Federal Practices* (New York: Praeger, 1972). For a description of how local politicians are bought off by large corporations, see Jack Shepherd, "The Nuclear Threat Inside America," *Look*, December 15, 1970, pp. 24–25.
30. Quoted in Harris, "Annals of Politics," p. 62.
31. Waldron, "Shadow on the Alamo," p. 2. See also Peter Cowen, "Graft Held Fact of Life in Boston," *Boston Globe*, October 2, 1972.
32. Paul Simon, "The Illinois State Legislature," *Harper's*, September 1964, p. 74.
33. For recent accounts of corruption in states like West Virginia, Maryland and New Jersey, see the articles by John Rothchild, Mary Walton, Thomas B. Edsall and Michael Rappeport published together under the title "Revenue Sharing with the Rich and the Crooked," *Washington Monthly*, February 1972, pp. 8–38.

sion to be accepting payoffs, highly corrupt practices were reported in municipal tax assessments, municipal and federal narcotics agents were found "to be some of the mob's most successful pushers,"[34] and doctors were cheating the Medicaid program of many millions in kickbacks for unnecessary, expensive tests.[35] On a grander scale in Washington, the Nixon administration was being implicated in major scandals involving the sale of wheat, an out-of-court settlement with ITT, price supports for dairy producers, corruption in the Federal Housing Administration, stock market manipulations, and political espionage—the "Watergate Affair." And Vice-President Agnew was forced to resign because of his involvement in acts of bribery, extortion, graft and income-tax evasion.

Corruption in America is so widespread that, as Lincoln Steffens pointed out long ago, throwing the rascals out only means bringing more rascals in. Through all this, the public looks on with growing cynicism, uttering jokes about the habits of politicians and sometimes failing to appreciate how the corrupt officeholder is part of the same individuated acquisitive system that includes the plundering corporate manager, the lying advertiser, the rent-gouging landlord, the price-fixing merchant, the cheating lawyer, the fee-gouging doctor and, at a more modest level, the pilfering auto mechanic and television repairman.

34. Brooklyn District Attorney Eugene Gold, as quoted by Nicolas Pileggi in *The Mafia at War*, (New York: New York Magazine, Inc., 1972), p. 85. Gold testified that 70 percent of Brooklyn's detectives were taking graft.
35. *New York Times*, January 11, 1973.

Congress:
The Pocketing of Power

13　　AS WAS NOTED IN CHAPTER FOUR, OUR
Founding Fathers fashioned a Constitution
with the intent of diluting and deflecting what
they considered to be a tempestuous popular
will.[1] In order to guard against democratic
excesses and ensure the rule of the wise and
prudent elements of society—that is, themselves and other men of their class and
convictions—they separated the powers of
state into executive, legislative and judicial
branches and installed a system of checks and
balances designed to forestall action and make
fundamental class-structural change most unlikely. They understood what some theorists
today seem to have forgotten: that the
diffusion of power among the various segments of government does not necessarily
mean its *democratization* but more likely the
opposite—that is, diffusion leads to the pocketing of power by entrenched and compartmen-
talized groups which can resist and deter
popular desires. Power that is elaborately
fragmented is more accessible to specialized,
well-organized interests, less likely to be
swept along in a tide of popular opinion and
less responsive to the mass public.

　　Looking specifically at the United States
Congress, one is struck by how effectively the
diffusion of power has operated for undemo-
cratic purposes. The deficiencies of Congress have been documented by journalists,
political scientists and Congressmen them-

1. See the discussion in Chapter Four, "What the
Founding Fathers Did."

selves.[2] Without hoping to cover everything that might be said about the legislative branch, let us consider some of the more important points.

Rule by Special Interest

Power in Congress rests with the twenty or so standing committees in each house which determine the destiny of all bills —rewriting some, giving affirmative action to a few and burying most. These committees are dominated by chairmen who rise to their positions by seniority—that is, by being repeatedly elected from mostly rural or Southern districts and from states not known for two-party competition, liberal opinion or high electoral participation, often districts or states with a high percentage of nonparticipating poor Whites and Blacks. By having the good fortune of representing a constituency that never changes its mind, and by using the resources of office to ensure the retention of office, a Congressman, after many years, can accumulate the seniority that brings him to a position of influence. Explaining why he chose to retire from the House in 1964 after serving only one term, Representative Everett Burkhalter said, "I could see I wasn't going to get anywhere. Nobody listens to what you have to say until you've been here ten to twelve years. These old men have got everything tied down so you can't do anything. There are only about 40 out of the 435 members who call the shots. They're all committee chairmen and the ranking members, and they're all around 70 or 80."[3] (In the 92nd Congress, half of the thirty-eight committee chairmen were seventy or older. Most of the others were well into their sixties.)

The commitment to seniority is the most pervasive unwritten norm of Congress. Seniority "is more than a means of choosing committee chairmen; it is a means of assigning members to committees, of choosing subcommittee chairmen and conference committee members. It affects the deference shown legislators on the floor, the assignment of office space, even

2. I think the best of recent works is Mark J. Green, James M. Fallows and David R. Zwick, *Who Runs Congress?* (New York: Bantam Books/Grossman, 1972). See also Joseph S. Clark, *Congress: The Sapless Branch* (New York: Harper and Row, 1964); Joseph C. Clark and Other Senators, *The Senate Establishment* (New York: Hill and Wang, 1963); Drew Pearson and Jack Anderson, *The Case Against Congress* (New York: Simon and Schuster, 1968); and Richard Bolling, *House Out of Order* (New York: E. P. Dutton, 1965).

3. Quoted in Green et al., *Who Runs Congress?*, p. 52.

invitations to dinners. In short, 'it is a spirit pervading the total behavior of Congress.' "[4] (As testimony to the socializing powers of seniority, at the beginning of the 93rd Congress the House Democratic Caucus voted to abolish the seniority system as a method of choosing committee chairmen and then promptly re-elected by large majorities all the incumbent chairmen.) However, seniority is readily ignored by the senior members themselves when it is in their interest to do so. Former Senator Joseph Clark notes that during one session of the Senate the seniority rule was violated when filling vacancies to eight important standing committees, to the advantage of conservative Senators and the disadvantage of the already underrepresented Senate liberals.[5] Over the years, Clark himself was repeatedly denied appointment to the Foreign Relations Committee, sometimes because of lack of seniority and sometimes in violation of seniority.

The party with a majority, be it in the House or the Senate, is the one that controls the chairmanships of that house. Since World War II, except for brief interludes, control of Congress has been in the hands of the Democrats or, more specifically, of the senior members of the Democratic party—as just noted, mostly conservative Southerners. In their efforts at dominating their more liberal and more numerous Northern and Western Democratic colleagues, the Southern Democrats rely on the conservative Republican minority to vote with them, in what is known to some critics as "the Unholy Alliance." This bipartisan coalition, according to former Senator Paul Douglas of Illinois, "really carries out the Republican platform, operates against Democratic senatorial and congressional candidates from the North and the West, operates against our presidential candidate, and is indeed an albatross around the neck of the Democratic Party."[6]

Not surprisingly, the more powerful committees in both houses are those related to taxes and spending: House Ways and Means, House Appropriations, Senate Finance and Senate Appropriations. Among the most influential is the House Rules Committee. All potential legislation of Congress must pass through this committee on its way to the House floor. The function of the Rules Committee is to control the House calen-

4. George Goodwin, "The Seniority System in Congress," *American Political Science Review*, 53, June 1959, p. 412. In the last sentence of the above quotation, Goodwin is quoting Ernest Griffith.
5. Clark, *The Senate Establishment*, pp. 40 ff.
6. Douglas in *ibid.*, p. 124.

dar, deciding which bills reach the floor in what order, postponing some bills indefinitely and rewriting others. The Rules Committee can specify the conditions under which the rest of the House must consider bills; for instance, it invariably imposes a closed rule on all tax bills, preventing members from offering amendments and thereby giving the chairman of the Ways and Means Committee—for many years Wilbur Mills, a conservative Democrat elected from a rural one-party district in Arkansas —virtual one-man control of all such measures. Not surprisingly, positions on the Rules Committee are highly coveted and are filled by the most senior and usually the most conservative members of the House.

The major committees are themselves broken down into numerous subcommittees, each working with a staff of its own under the directorship of a subcommittee chairman. "More than mere specialization, the subcommittee permits development of tight little cadres of special interest legislators and gives them great leverage," reports one Washington newsman.[7] In agriculture, for instance, cotton, corn, wheat, peanut, tobacco and rice producers compete for federal support programs; each interest is represented on the various subcommittees of the Senate and House Agricultural Committees by Senators and Representatives ready to do battle on their behalf. The fragmentation of power within the subcommittees simplifies the lobbyist's task of controlling legislation. *It offers the special-interest group its own special-interest subcommittee.* To atomize power in this way is *not* to democratize it.[8] The separate structures of power tend to monopolize decisions in specific areas for the benefit of specific people. Into the interstices of these substructures fall the interests of large segments of the unorganized, unalerted public.

On those rare occasions when public opinion *is* aroused about some particular issue like auto safety, pollution, or unsafe foods, Congress might move with noticeable velocity. Yet even then the final bill usually will be sufficiently diluted to accommodate producer groups. One of Congress' more predictable ploys is to respond to an aroused public by producing legislation that gives every *appearance* of dealing with the problem but which is usually wanting in *substance:* thus we have a lobbyist registration act that does little to control lobbying practices, a

7. Douglass Cater, *Power in Washington* (New York: Random House, 1964), p. 158.
8. See Grant McConnell, *Private Power and American Democracy* (New York: Knopf, 1966), p. 193 and *passim*.

legislative reorganization act that reorganized almost nothing, a campaign financing act that is easily circumvented, a civil rights act that is seldom enforced and a tax reform act that worsens rather than lessens tax inequities.

Given the demands made on his or her time by job and family, and the superficial and often misleading coverage of events by the media, the average wage earner has little opportunity to stay informed about or give sustained attention to more than a few broad issues, if that. But throughout the legislative process the organized interests remain alert and actively engaged in shaping the substantive details of bills. Hence the people get their tax reform bill and industry gets its tax write-offs. The people get their campaign fund control bill and the politicians get their campaign funds. The people get their land conservation bill and the corporations get the land.

Sometimes, even in the face of an aroused public and sustained media exposure, Congress will make no positive response. After several years of intensive and massive public demonstrations against the Vietnam intervention and with polls indicating that a majority of the people favored withdrawal from Vietnam, Congress was still voting huge appropriations for the war by lopsided majorities, and large numbers of Senators and Representatives—a majority in the House, as Garrison Nelson revealed—still adhered to a "hawk" position.[9] In April 1973, in the face of a nationwide meat boycott, demonstrations and a deluge of letters and telephone calls protesting inflation, Congress voted down all proposals for price freezes and price rollbacks. Opposing them were "cattlemen, banking and business interests and food merchants."[10] The consumer and citizens' groups lost; the cattlemen, bankers and businessmen won.

Congress is inclined to remove itself from scrutiny whenever the public starts getting too interested in its affairs. The Senate Armed Services Committee responded to the public's growing concern about military spending by increasing its percentage of secret hearings from 56 percent in 1969 to 79 percent in 1971. The Senate Agriculture Committee held 33 percent of its meetings behind closed doors in 1971. Other secret sessions: Senate Finance Committee, 47 percent; Senate Public Works, 50 percent; House Appropriations, 92 percent; House

9. See Nelson's excellent analysis: "Nixon's Silent House of Hawks," *Progressive*, August 1970, pp. 13–20.
10. The Associated Press report carried in the *Schenectady Gazette*, April 17, 1973.

Standards of Official Conduct, 93 percent.[11] Business interests often enjoy a special access to congressional committee reports while newsmen and public-interest advocates are kept in the dark. "The thing that really makes me mad is the dual standard," complained a staff member of one key Senate committee. "It's perfectly acceptable to turn over information about what's going on in committee to the auto industry or the utilities but not to the public."[12]

Sometimes secrecy envelops the entire lawmaking process: the Nixon-sponsored bill cutting corporate taxes by $7.3 billion was (a) drawn up by the House Ways and Means Committee in three days of secret sessions, (b) passed by the House under a closed rule after only one hour of debate with (c) about thirty members of the House present for the (d) non-roll-call vote.[13] Under such conditions even the highly motivated muckraker, experienced journalist, or academic specialist has difficulty ascertaining what is going on.

As was noted in the previous chapter, Congressmen not only respond to corporate lobbyists and big campaign donors; they themselves act as lobbyists on behalf of favored business groups. Some members allow their offices to be used regularly as bases of operation for lobbying activities. According to the former lobbyist Robert Winter-Berger, one very influential Washington lobbyist, Nathan Voloshen, regularly operated out of Speaker John McCormack's office, paying McCormack a substantial "rent" along with a percentage of the take in return for use of the Speaker's name and influence on behalf of Voloshen's business clients;[14] Voloshen was later convicted of fraud. Former Republican minority leader of the House, Vice-President Gerald Ford, also had close and profitable arrangements with professional lobbyists, like most other key members of Congress. Again according to Winter-Berger:

The main part of a lobbyist's job in practice is to circumvent the legislation that already exists, to cut through red tape, to get priorities

11. See the *Washington Monthly*, September 1972, p. 17.
12. Green et al., *Who Runs Congress?*, p. 56.
13. See the observations of Thomas H. Stanton reported in the *Washington Monthly*, April 1972, p. 18.
14. Robert Winter-Berger was a lobbyist who worked closely with Voloshen and McCormack. Winter-Berger offers a good deal of astonishing eyewitness testimony in his book, *The Washington Pay-Off* (New York: Dell, 1972). At Voloshen's trial, McCormack testified that he had no idea that Voloshen was using his office for private deals.

and preferences for clients who have no legal rights to them. To achieve this, he needs the cooperation of one or more members of Congress—the more influential they are, the fewer he needs—who will write the letter or make the telephone call to the government department or agency handling the matter. He gets this cooperation by paying for it—preferably in cash. . . .

Most lobbying is underground, because more than opinions are exchanged. Money is exchanged: money for favors, money for deals, money for government contracts, money for government jobs. The members of Congress need the money primarily to pay for their campaigns, and campaigns are becoming more expensive all the time.[15]

It is "a very common occurrence" for Congressmen to telephone or write the Justice Department on behalf of business interests, according to former Attorney General Richard Kleindienst, who added, "We have a responsibility to permit that kind of thing to occur."

Frequently a Congressman acts without benefit of prodding by any pressure group, either because he is so well attuned to its interests or because he himself has lucrative holdings in the same areas that engaged the attention of his pet lobbyists. Thus Representative Clarence Brown of Ohio owns a broadcasting station—and sits on the House subcommittee that regulates broadcasting. The late Representative Robert Watkins of Pennsylvania was the chairman of a trucking firm whose profits depended on rules passed by Watkins' Commerce Committee. Senator James Eastland of Mississippi sits on the Agriculture Committee, votes for generous farm subsidies and as a result of such legislative diligence himself received $159,000 in 1971 in subsidies. Senator Russell Long of Louisiana made a great deal of money in oil wells and is chairman of the Senate Finance Committee which supports oil depletion clauses in its tax bills.[16] What is called "conflict of interest" in regard to the judiciary is defined as "expertise" in Congress. What we have are men who use their public mandate to legislate for their private fortunes. That they seldom see any incongruity or conflict in these roles itself shows how readily they define the public good in terms that are compatible with their private interests.

Congressmen pilfer from the public treasury in more modest ways. Among the bad habits they have developed, the most common are: (1) junketing—traveling for fun at government

15. *Ibid.*, p. 14 and p. 38.
16. Green et al., *Who Runs Congress?*, pp. 140–141.

expense under the guise of conducting overseas committee investigations; (2) having relatives on the payroll and pocketing their salaries; (3) taking salary kickbacks from other staff members; (4) double-billing—charging both the government and a private client for the same expense; (5) using their franking privilege for mailing campaign literature; (6) using committee staff workers for personal campaign purposes.[17] From 1968 to 1972 eight Congressmen or their aides were convicted of bribery, influence-peddling or perjury. In this century, twenty-four Senators and Representatives have been indicted for crimes; sixteen were convicted and one case is pending. And these are only the few clumsy enough to get caught.

The Legislative Labyrinth

The very constitutional structure of Congress operates with conservative effect—as the Founding Fathers intended. The staggered terms of the Senate (only one third selected every two years) makes any sweeping turnover impossible, even if there were a mass sentiment among voters for a thorough change. The division of the Congress into two separate houses makes legislative action all the more difficult. Reform legislation passed by the House, like the 1969 Patman bill to restrict the powers of bank holding companies, may not be acted upon by the Senate. And humanitarian bills passed by the Senate, like the one to allow free food stamps for families with monthly incomes of less than $60, can perish in the House.

A typical bill before Congress might go the following route: After being introduced into, say, the House, it is (1) committed to a committee where it is most likely summarily ignored, pigeonholed or gutted by the chairman (only about one out of every twenty-five bills ever finds its way out of committee), or (2) parceled out to various subcommittees for extensive hearings and then perhaps (3) greatly diluted or completely rewritten to suit influential lobbyists and their clients, some of whom, as was just noted, sit on the committees as Representatives. In the unlikely event that it is reported out of committee, the bill (4) goes to the Rules Committee where it might be buried forever, or subjected to further mutilation, or replaced entirely by a bill of the Rules Committee's own preference. Upon reaching the floor

17. *Ibid.*, pp. 131–159.

WARREN LINN

of the House (5) it might be further amended during debate or voted down or referred back to committee for further study. If passed, *it must repeat essentially the same process in the Senate,* assuming the Senate has time and interest for it.

If the bill does not make it through both houses before the next congressional election, it must be reintroduced and the entire process begins anew. Not surprisingly, the House and Senate frequently fail to pass the same version of a bill; differences then have to be ironed out in ad hoc conference committees composed of several senior members from each house. More than one conference committee has rewritten a bill to better suit special interests.

The bill that survives the legislative labyrinth and escapes an executive veto to become an *act* of Congress, and the law of the land, may be only an *authorization* act—that is, it simply brings some program into existence. Congress then must vote *appropriations* to finance the authorized policy; hence, *the entire legislative process must be repeated for the appropriations bill.* Not infrequently legislation authorizing the government to spend a certain amount for a particular program is passed, but no appropriations are subsequently voted to finance it.

The 435 members of the House and 100 members of the Senate have neither the time nor the staff to inform themselves in any depth about the many problems of the nation or the many doings of the executive. The Defense Department has more people preparing its budget than Congress has for all its functions combined (which tells us not only how understaffed is Congress but how immense is the Defense Department). Congress does not have the ability to produce a comprehensive national program. For almost all its technical information and legislative initiatives it must rely on the executive departments or on lobbyists from private industry, who often actually write the bills that friendly Congressmen later introduce as legislation.

The bulk of a Congressman's time is taken up in performing ministerial services for constituents, making calls to public agencies on behalf of businessmen and other interested parties back home, introducing private bills to permit alien relatives of constituents to enter or remain in the country and answering the huge quantity of mail that comes in. In the time he has left for legislative tasks, the Congressman devotes himself to several specialized subcommittees, trying to build up some expertise in limited areas, in effect making himself that much more of a special-interest representative who defines the legislative task in terms of distinct "problems" (e.g., trade, defense, forestry) and who focuses little attention on the interrelatedness and *systemic* nature of politico-economic problems. On matters that are outside his domain he defers to his other special-interest colleagues.

Congress is not just bicameral; with its quasi-independent committee potentates and minority pockets of power, it is almost "multicameral." These special-interest congressional factions achieve working majorities through various trade-offs and mutual accommodations, a "log-rolling" process that is not the same as compromise. Rather than checking one another as in compromise situations, and thus blunting the selfish demands of each —possibly with some benefit to the general public—interest groups end up supporting one another's claims, at the expense of those who are without power in the pressure system. Thus the oil lobby will back farm supports in exchange for farm bloc support of oil depletion allowances. In both cases the ordinary consumers and taxpayers bear the costs. *Log-rolling is the method by which the various haves reconcile their differences, usually at the expense of the have-nots.* The net effect is not a *check* on competing claims but a *compounding* of claims against the interests of the unorganized public.

Congress: A Product of Its Environment

While Congress is a body supposedly dedicated to a government of laws, not of men, its procedures "are founded all too much on unwritten, unspoken, and largely unnoticed informal agreements among men."[18] The norms and customs that are so much a part of life in the House and Senate are generally conservative in their effect—not surprisingly, since the leaders in both houses who play such a crucial role in defining and maintaining these norms are themselves usually conservative. The emphasis on elaborate forms of courtesy and on avoiding public remarks that might be construed as personally critical of colleagues discourages a good deal of discussion of things that are deserving of criticism. The tendency to minimize differences usually works to the advantage of those who prefer to keep things quiet and against the kind of confrontation needed to effect change. The unlimited debate in

18. Clark, *The Senate Establishment*, p. 15. Senator Clark was referring specifically to the Senate, but his observation applies equally to both houses.

the Senate allows a small but determined number of Senators to filibuster a bill to death or kill it by exercising the *threat* of filibuster. The quorum call stops all legislative business until enough members are rounded up and a roll call is taken. These kinds of parliamentary devices make it easier for minorities to thwart action.[19]

The freshman legislator is socialized into a world of cronyism that makes the mobilization of legislative majorities around broad issue-oriented programs difficult to achieve. He learns not to give too much attention to issue politics—since issues can be divisive—but to develop personal loyalties to senior members, defer to their judgments, avoid exacerbating debates and become a reliable member of the club. The longer he stays in Congress the more his commitment to issues seems to blur.[20] He soon realizes that opportunities for choice committee assignments and other favors are extended to him by leaders in accordance with his willingness to go along with things as they are. Most Congressmen succumb to these inducements. The few who persist in trying to change things experience an increasing sense of futility and are usually discriminated against in the distribution of benefits for home districts, in committee assignments and in getting bills seriously considered.[21]

The dilemma faced by the reformist element in Congress, as with all reformers who try to "work within the system," is that the system itself is constructed to resist change. Reform measures must pass through channels that are deliberately designed to prevent reform. Thus, in the Senate, proposals to liberalize procedures and reduce the powers of the conservative Senate elders repeatedly have been referred to, and buried forever in, the Committee on Rules and Administration—dominated by conservative Senate elders.[22]

19. In the second session of the 87th Congress, the House sat for about 657 hours, of which 163 hours or almost 25 percent were given to finding out whether a quorum was present or to voting by roll call. Swifter electronic forms of voting have been rejected by the House leadership because the delays in process that are caused by quorum calls are often just what they want. See Robert Bendiner, *Obstacle Course on Capitol Hill* (New York: McGraw-Hill, 1964), excerpt in Joseph S. Clark (ed.), *Congressional Reform* (New York: Crowell, 1965), p. 113.

20. Garrison Nelson gave me some helpful insights concerning the conservative functions and effects of personalism and leadership selection within the House. See also his *Party Control Periods in the U.S. House of Representatives and the Recruitment of its Leaders, 1789–1971*, Ph.D. dissertation (University of Iowa, Iowa City, Iowa, 1973).

21. For one Congressman's confession of frustration, see Richard Madden, "Pike Tells of Futility in House," *New York Times*, July 1, 1972.

22. Clark, *The Senate Establishment*, p. 27.

Although conservative bills sometimes get caught in the congressional log jam, generally when conservatives want action, they get it. As Senator Clark was not the first or last to complain, progressive bills are treated by congressional leaders with painfully slow deliberateness, if at all, while bills which interest them are expeditiously acted upon.[23] Without hesitation, Congress voted $6.75 million for a market news service to furnish timely reports on major agricultural commodities to enable agribusiness to better determine when to sell and how to price its products. But this same Congress debated at great length the passage of a minor pilot project supplying breakfast in school for hungry children, a program that would reach only a tiny number of the millions of malnourished American children.[24] In almost everything Congress does, the pattern remains the same. Multibillion-dollar tax depreciation bills for big business are passed in a matter of days with little debate, amendment or open hearings, while occupational safety bills are talked to death or languish in committee. Multibillion-dollar defense bills are passed in a matter of hours, while paltry and pitifully inadequate welfare measures are haggled over with that kind of ungracious stinginess and meanness which the haves so frequently display toward the have-nots.

Yet it is not quite accurate to call the legislature "unrepresentative." In a way, Congress is precisely and faithfully representative of the power distributions of the wider society. As Ralph Nader observes, "Power goes to those senior legislators who service powerful interests, while isolation goes to those who merely represent powerless people."[25] And as long as Congress reflects the distribution of economic power in the wider society, it is not likely to change much even if liberals in both houses manage to gain control of the major committees, and even if the cloture rule is changed to enable the Senate to rid itself of the filibuster, and even if the Rules Committee is deprived of its arbitrary powers, and even if seniority is done away with. For what remains is the entire system of organized corporate power with its elitist institutions, business-controlled media and mass propaganda, organized pressure groups, high-paid lobbyists and influence-peddling lawyers, campaign contributions and

23 *Ibid.*, p. 77.

24. *Hunger, U.S.A.*, a report by the Citizens' Board of Inquiry into Hunger and Malnutrition in the United States (Boston: Beacon Press, 1968), p. 80.

25. Ralph Nader, "Making Congress Work," *New Republic*, August 21 and 28, 1971, p. 19.

bribes—all of which operate with such telling effect on legislators, including most of the professedly liberal ones.

It might be noted in passing that the situation within the various state legislatures is comparable to that in the Congress except that state lawmakers seem to be even less visible, less accountable and possibly even more corrupt than their national counterparts. More secluded from public scrutiny than is Congress, the state legislatures are, in the words of one national magazine, "the willing instrumentalities of an array of private corporate entities."[26] While most of the public has no idea what their state representatives are doing, the banks, loan companies, gambling interests, big franchise holders, insurance firms, utilities, manufacturers, oil and gas companies and Farm Bureau lobbyists carry on a regular liaison with them, showering them with campaign contributions, legal retainers, liquor and entertainment, special-term "loans," business tips and opportunities to participate in growing investment areas. One former state senator described his legislature as "polluted beyond belief."[27] Corruption is so widespread in the state legislatures as to be more the norm than the exception. And subservience to business is so pervasive as to make it almost impossible to tell the lawmakers from the lobbyists. State legislators usually work only part-time at their tasks, devoting the better part of their days to their private law practices, insurance firms, realty agencies and other such enterprises, which often benefit from their legislative efforts.

To be sure, a representative system *should* be a pressure system, enabling constituents to exercise control over their lawmakers. But what is usually missing from the lawmaker's own view is any real appreciation of the one-sidedness of the pressure system. For many in the state legislatures, as in Congress, the existing pressure system *is* the representative system; that is to say, those groups having the money, organization, visibility and expertise to *take* an interest in legislative affairs are presumed to be the only ones that *have* an actual interest in legislative affairs. The muted levels of society are left pretty much out of the picture. This might partly explain the arrogance displayed by some officeholders when confronted by working-class protestors. Not only are the politicians unresponsive to the protests of lower-income groups; they often do not believe such people

26. "The Sick State of the State Legislatures," *Newsweek*, April 19, 1965, p. 31.
27. Paul Simon of Illinois, quoted in *ibid*.

have a right to make the kinds of demands they occasionally do. I can recall one "representative of the people," a Democrat from New Haven, Conn., who greeted a delegation of poor Blacks and a few sympathetic Whites who wanted to speak to him about welfare practices with the words: "Who do you people think you are, coming into my office like this?"

The Special - Interest President

14

MUCH HAS BEEN MADE OF THE "uniqueness" and "sanctity" of the presidency. More should be said about how the men who have occupied the office have operated within the same system of power and interest as other politicians. Our task here is not to join those who would mystify the presidency, thereby placing it beyond the criticisms of alert citizens, but to take a nonworshipful look at the office and at the special-interest politics commonly practiced by its occupants.

Guardian of Capitalism

While Congressmen are the captives of the "special interests," the President, occupying the highest national office and elected by the entire country, tends to be less vulnerable to the monied pressure groups and more responsive to the needs of the unorganized public —at least this is what political scientists taught after years of observing Presidents like Roosevelt, Truman and Kennedy tussling with conservatives in Congress. Actually, our various Presidents resemble the average pressure politician much more than we were taught to believe.

The presidency is often described as a composite of many roles. The President, we are told, is not only the chief executive, he is "chief legislator," commander-in-chief, head-of state, head of foreign relations, and leader of his party. Seldom mentioned is his role as guardian and spokesman of capitalism. Far from being an opponent of the special interests, the President is the embodiment of the political system that serves them and, given his uniquely strategic position in the system, he plays an active part in fortifying modern capitalism at home and abroad. Whether a Democrat or a Republican, a liberal or a conservative, the President treats capitalist interests as representative of the interests of all Americans. He will describe the overseas investments of giant corporations as *"United States* investments abroad," part of *"America's* interests in the world," to be defended at all costs—or certainly at great cost. He will speak of "our" oil in the Middle East and "our" markets in Latin America and "our" raw materials in Southeast Asia (to be defended by our sons) when what he is referring to are the holdings of a small but powerful segment of the population. Presidents have presented their multibillion-dollar spending programs on behalf of private industry as necessary for *"America's* growing needs" and have greeted the expansion of big business and big profits as manifestations of "a healthy *national* economy" and as good for the *"national interest."*

(Parenthetically, it should be noted that governors, mayors and Congressmen similarly equate the interests of the business community with the interests of the entire community. The billionaire former governor of New York, Nelson Rockefeller, called a "liberal" Republican by some, considers "economic growth—a continuing expansion of the private economy— to be the indispensable ingredient of all progress."[1] In a span of eleven years, Rockefeller imposed a sales tax on the consumer, then increased it, quadrupled the cigarette tax, tripled the gasoline tax, and *lowered* the minimum income below which working people are free of state income tax. The business community fared better. As Rockefeller boasted in a *Fortune* magazine advertisement inviting industries to New York: "Personal property of manufacturers is completely exempt from taxation in New York. . . . During the past eleven years, there has not been one single new business tax in New York."[2])

As authoritative figures whose opinions are widely publicized and positively received, Presidents have played an active role indoctrinating the American people into the ideology of the politico-economic establishment. Every modern President has

1. Quoted in an editorial in *Ramparts*, May 1970, p. 4.
2. *Ibid.*

had occasion to warn the citizenry of the wiles of radicalism, the leveling regimentations of socialism and the tyrannies of communism. Presidents have publicly praised businessmen for their allegedly great contributions to American life. "You men . . . are the leaders of this community," President Lyndon Johnson once announced to a group of corporation heads, "and through your industries the leaders of the United States. . . ." This country, Johnson continued, was built on "the free enterprise system [which] is made up of really four important segments," specifically "the government," "the capitalist," "the manager," and "the worker"—all operating together in prosperous partnership.[3]

In the last century all Presidents have brought businessmen into key administrative posts and have relied heavily on the judgments of corporate leaders. Many Presidents themselves enter the White House after an extended period of professional and personal ties with banking and business firms. Since World War II, most of the men who have run as presidential candidates on the Democratic and Republican tickets have been millionaires either at the time they first campaigned for the office or by the time they departed from it.

Presidents have made a show of concern for public causes, using slogans and images intended to enhance their popular appeal; thus Teddy Roosevelt had his "Square Deal," Woodrow Wilson his "New Freedom," Franklin Roosevelt his "New Deal," Harry Truman his "Fair Deal," John Kennedy his "New Frontier," and Lyndon Johnson his "Great Society." Behind the fine sounding labels, one discovers much the same record of service to the powerful and neglect of the needy. Consider John Kennedy, a President widely celebrated for his devotion to the underdog and his desire to "get America moving." In foreign affairs, Kennedy spoke of a new era of good will, international peace and self-determination for all peoples, yet he invaded Cuba after Castro nationalized U.S. corporate holdings. He delivered an ultimatum during the Cuban missile crisis which brought us to the brink of nuclear war. He drastically increased military expenditures, instituted counterinsurgency programs throughout the Third World, and sent troops into Vietnam. Kennedy set up aid programs in underdeveloped nations that benefited American investors and very few others. He en-

3. The speech is from the *Public Papers of the Presidents, Lyndon B. Johnson, 1963–1964*, vol. 2, pp. 1, 147–151, reprinted in Marvin Gettleman and David Mermelstein (eds.), *The Failure of American Liberalism* (New York: Vintage, 1971), pp. 124–128.

visioned major land reforms in these countries—supposedly to be carried out voluntarily by the landlords and the corporations —yet he sent vast quantities of arms to bolster the reactionary generals who ruled most of the "Free World." In all, his foreign policy was dedicated to ensuring the predominance of multinational corporations and pursuing a militaristic, anti-Communist cold war.

In domestic matters Kennedy presented himself as a champion of civil rights, yet he did little to create new job opportunities for Black people; he refrained from taking legal action to support antidiscrimination cases in housing; he appointed conservative, racist judges in the South; and in the face of repeated atrocities against civil rights organizers in that region, his Justice Department was unable to bring a single murderer or arsonist to justice—although it did successfully prosecute eight civil rights workers in Albany, Georgia, on charges of perjury and obstructing justice, leading to sentences ranging up to five years.

Kennedy talked as if he were the special friend of the working people. Yet he imposed wage restraints on unions at a time when the buying power of many wage earners was stagnant or declining; he strongly opposed introduction of the 35-hour week, accepted a 5.5 percent unemployment rate as normal, instituted regressive income tax programs, and pursued deficit spending policies that carried business profit rates to all-time highs without reducing unemployment. Kennedy discovered that millions of Americans still lived below the poverty level, but he never initiated a comprehensive program to deal with poverty, nor with the crises in transportation, housing and health care. Bernard Nossiter notes that the image of John Kennedy as anti-business was an undeserved one: "In fact, in every significant area—wage policy, tax policy, international trade and finance, federal spending—the president showed a keen understanding and ready response to the essential corporate program."[4]

Through his youth, vigor, intelligence and public rhetoric Kennedy gave every appearance of being the liberal activist; actually, he chose a course of "pragmatic politics," working cautiously within the special-interest system instead of attempting to challenge or change it. He did nothing to mobilize new political strengths and mass movements among workers, Blacks, the young and the poor. If anything, he tended to distrust and

4. Bernard Nossiter, *The Mythmakers* (Boston: Beacon Press, 1964), p. 40.

discourage popular activism. He even opposed the peaceful and moderate civil rights March on Washington in 1963, going so far as to invite various Black leaders to the White House to urge them, without success, to call it off.[5]

Conservative Presidents like Richard Nixon have manifested the same tendency to *talk* for the people and *work* for the corporate elites. In January 1970, President Nixon pledged an all-out effort for conservation, but a month later he threw his weight behind the Timber Supply bill, which opened new national forest lands for commercial exploitation, and after that he vetoed the water pollution bill that passed Congress by a nearly unanimous vote. In March 1973, Nixon spoke of his dedication to the returning Vietnam veteran, asserting that "in every area of Government concern, we are now doing more than we have ever done" to assist the veteran and reintegrate him into civilian life. Yet just the month before, he had proposed cuts in benefits to disabled Vietnam veterans. In 1971, through his White House Conference on Aging, Nixon gave lip service to "the plight of the elderly," yet in 1972 he opposed the 20 percent increase in Social Security retirement benefits voted by Congress. The following year he increased Medicare costs and stopped housing construction for the elderly.[6] Nixon and administration spokesmen like former Vice-President Agnew and Roy Ash, Director of the Office of Management and Budget, repeatedly claimed during 1972 that the administration had reduced the rate of inflation, turned back the tide of unemployment and curbed federal spending. In fact, (a) inflation was nearly twice as bad in 1973 as when Nixon first took office, and the rate of inflation was higher in March-April 1973 than at any time in the previous twenty-two years; (b) unemployment increased under Nixon from 3.3 percent to 5.1 percent by 1973, with increasing numbers forced to work part-time;[7] (c) as noted earlier, federal deficit spending under the Nixon administration was higher than under any other peacetime President (and most

5. My discussion of Kennedy draws heavily from the excellent article by Ian McMahan, "The Kennedy Myth," *New Politics*, 3, Winter 1964, pp. 40–48. For a treatment of the disparity between Lyndon Johnson's liberal rhetoric and his conservative policies, see Gettleman and Mermelstein, *The Failure of American Liberalism;* consider also Robert Sherrill, *The Accidental President* (New York: Grossman, 1967), Chapters 3, 5, 6 and *passim*.

6. See "Elderly Protest on Capitol Steps," *New York Times*, June 8, 1973.

7. The 5.1 percent is an official figure which counts only those who are collecting unemployment insurance or are registered with an employment agency as seeking a job. It does not include the many who have given up looking,

wartime Presidents), amounting to $73.8 billion by 1973 and expected to exceed $100 billion before Nixon's second term was over.

The Pressure Politician

Like other politicians, the men who run for President must procure vast sums from the rich and the corporate elites in order to pay their campaign costs. Big contributors disclaim any intention of trying to buy influence and favors with their gifts, insisting that they give freely because they "believe" in the candidate and think he will make the best President for America—certainly the best that money can buy. They believe he will pursue policies that are the most beneficial to the national interest. That they view the national interest from the elevated positions they occupy in the social structure and that it is therefore often indistinguishable from their own financial interests does not make their support hypocritical but all the more sincere. The contribution is not necessarily for a better personal deal but for a better America —this image encompasses the sum of the rich contributor's class experiences and life values.

If it should happen, however, that the man who is elected (or re-elected) President wishes to express his gratitude by performing a favor for a big donor, the donor usually accepts the favor without fear that he will thereby sully the selfless motives that originally inspired the contribution. Furthermore, if at any time in the four years after the election the rich contributor should find himself or his firm burdened by a problem that only the White House can handle, he sees no reason why he shouldn't be allowed to exercise his democratic rights like any other citizen and ask his elected representative, who in this case happens to be his friend, the President of the United States, for a little help. Such requests are a common practice.

Large donors to President Nixon's campaign, including certain insurance moguls, dairymen, bankers, carpet manufacturers, coal mine owners, railroad tycoons, hamburger

nor a good many youth just entering the job market and unable to find work, nor the many millions who are underemployed or irregularly employed, nor the many women who look for jobs but who, being "housewives," are not counted as job seekers, nor the many others unknown to officialdom. Some nongovernmental estimates of unemployment run as high as 10 and 12 percent.

restaurant-chain owners and managers of giant conglomerates like ITT, benefited many times over from direct White House intercessions on their behalf. In the case of ITT, it was charged that the Nixon administration helped settle a multibillion-dollar antitrust suit against that corporation in return for a promised $400,000 donation.[8] Nixon's former White House counsel, John W. Dean, testified before a congressional committee in June 1973 that on occasion the President requested the Internal Revenue Service to stop auditing the incomes of certain close friends.[9]

Some big contributors are awarded ambassadorships. Every four years the White House "auctions off its embassies in Western Europe and in a few other agreeable areas to the highest bidders. The cash goes not to the United States Treasury but to the Republicans or Democrats, whichever party is in power."[10] Arthur K. Watson donated $371,000 to various Nixon campaigns and was appointed ambassador to France in 1970. To become ambassador to Austria in 1968, John Humes gave $43,000; he renewed his tenure in 1972 with another $103,500. The embassy in cold, snowy Finland went to John Krehbiel for the cut-rate price of $5,500 in 1968 and $12,500 four years later, while beautiful sunny Jamaica went to Vincent de Roulet for $44,500 in 1968 and $32,000 in 1972. Ruth Farkas contributed $300,000 to Nixon's campaign in 1972 and was awarded the embassy in Luxembourg, an overpriced bid.

Sometimes money isn't everything. Chicago insurance man W. Clement Stone contributed more than $1 million to the 1972 Nixon campaign and indicated that he would be "honored" to get the embassy in London, but that choice post remained in the hands of millionaire Walter Annenberg, who renewed his lease with a mere $254,000. All the aforementioned persons had

8. White House involvement in the ITT affair was publicly confirmed in testimony given to a congressional committee by Charles Colson, former Special Counsel to the White House. See *New York Times*, June 15, 1973; see also Anthony Sampson, *The Sovereign State of I.T.T.* (New York: Stein and Day, 1973). For other evidence of White House efforts on behalf of large contributors see James Ridgeway, "Republican Campaign Contributions (4), 'We Deserve a Break Today,' " *Village Voice*, October 20, 1972, pp. 13 ff.; Ben A. Franklin, "Milk Aide Says a Lawyer for Nixon Sought Funds," *New York Times*, January 11, 1973: and the statement published by the Democratic party: "The Nixon Administration Peddles Special Favors to the Super-Rich," *New York Times*, October 25, 1972.

9. *New York Times*, June 21, 1973; also June 22, 1973, for other reports of intervention on behalf of White House friends.

10. *New York Times* editorial, April 4, 1973.

several things in common: they were rich; they believed in Richard Nixon; and they had no previous diplomatic qualifications or experience.

At times, Presidents, like other politicians, use their public office not only to help their friends but to help themselves. In 1973 it was reported that official audits by the General Services Administration revealed that $10 million of the taxpayer's money was spent on improvement and maintenance of President Nixon's private homes in San Clemente and Key Biscayne. Confronted with the GSA audit, the White House said that the entire amount had been spent for "security purposes," presumably even the $100,000 for landscaping and roofing and other sums spent on home furnishings, general repairs, beach erosion, a swimming pool heater, and golf carts. Nearby homes in both places owned by some of President Nixon's millionaire friends also benefited.[11]

Some lobbyists make their fortunes by working with key Congressmen, but the most successful ones work out of the White House itself. Herbert Kalmbach, Nixon's former personal lawyer, while occupying no official post, was able to use his special line to the President as a means of helping his business clients. In return, he collected from them the campaign funds the President needed for re-election and handsome fees for himself. One businessman described Kalmbach as "the lawyer with the mostest in these parts" because of his well-known influence at the White House and his personal relationship with President Nixon, adding that "if you had business with Washington and you want a lawyer, you go to Herb but you can't talk with him for less than $10,000."[12]

On some occasions the President, like any good pressure politician, not only responds to special interests but actively performs as a lobbyist on their behalf. In early 1971 when the

11. *New York Times*, June 25, 1973. Nixon had maintained earlier that the public funds spent on his San Clemente home were only $39,000 instead of the $6 million reported by the GSA. It was subsequently disclosed that Vice-President Spiro Agnew's Maryland home, which was not even occupied by Agnew and his family, had benefited from $125,000 in public funds, including $39,000 for a redwood fence, $14,000 for a driveway and parking area and $3,000 to remodel a basement bathroom and paint the basement. Agnew had purchased the house for $190,000. Not long after, in October 1973, Agnew resigned from office because of pending charges of bribery, extortion and corruption involving deals carried out when he was Vice-President and governor of Maryland. Agnew was given three years probation and fined $10,000 for income-tax evasion; the other charges were dropped by the Justice Department.

12. Everett R. Holles, "Nixon's Lawyer No Longer: Herbert Warren Kalmbach," *New York Times*, May 2, 1973.

Senate passed a water pollution bill that would have imposed high pollution-control costs on industry, the President's staff descended upon Congress to voice its vigorous opposition. Trade representatives from all over the nation were called to the White House, informed of the situation and urged to get into the fight "in a big way" and get changes worked into the bill before its final passage. As Douglas Trussel, vice-president of the National Association of Manufacturers, said: "The notion that somehow industry 'got to' the administration and pushed them into [opposing the bill] is really the reverse of what happened. The administration took the initiative, and many executives were ignorant of what was going on."[13]

Presidents place business representatives in command of public agencies that are supposed to regulate their business activities. President Nixon's choice for Undersecretary of Agriculture, responsible for implementing the 1967 Meat Inspection Act, was Philip Campbell, a former state inspector with close ties to the meat industry, who had opposed passage of the Act and was against having the federal government enforce clean meat standards.[14] Within the Department of Interior, the Deputy Assistant Secretary for water and power development appointed by Nixon was a man who had previously served the U.S. Chamber of Commerce as a paid lobbyist against water pollution legislation.[15] In 1970 Nixon set up a 53-man National Industrial Pollution Control Conference (with salaries and expenses at $475,000 a year) to advise him on pollution reforms. All the members were businessmen from industries that, according to Senator Lee Metcalf, "contribute most to environmental pollution." Federal housing programs have been supervised by conservative businessmen who were openly hostile to low-income public housing. And the occupational safety program has been administered by business and government officials who were originally opposed to occupational safety legislation.

The success any group enjoys in winning the intervention of the President has less to do with the justice of its cause than with the position it occupies in the class structure. If a large group of migrant workers and a small group of aerospace executives both sought the President's assistance, it would not be too difficult to

13. Mark J. Green, James M. Fallows and David R. Zwick, *Who Runs Congress?* (New York: Bantam Books/Grossman, 1972), pp. 106–107.
14. *I. F. Stone's Weekly*, January 27, 1969.
15. Duane Lockard, *The Perverted Priorities of American Politics* (New York: Macmillan, 1971), p. 280.

predict which of them would be more likely to win it. Witness these events of April 1971:

(1) Some eighty thousand to ninety thousand migrant farm workers in Florida, out of work for much of the season because of crop failures and explicitly exempted from unemployment compensation, were left without any means of feeding themselves and their families. Welfare agencies supplied some surplus commodity foods as relief, but the foods were "almost pure starch, usually unpalatable, and cause diarrhea to children."[16] Faced with the prospect of seeing their children starve, the workers demonstrated in large numbers outside President Nixon's Key Biscayne vacation residence in Florida. The peaceful gathering was an attempt to attract public attention to their desperate plight and to get the White House to intercede. The workers succeeded in attracting only the attention of the police, who swiftly dispersed them, charging their lines with swinging clubs. The demonstration and the problems related to it were reported in a few small-circulation radical newspapers and ignored by most of the establishment news media.

There was no evidence that the farm workers' message ever intruded upon the President's attention although information about their condition did reach several lower-level federal agencies. Subsequent appeals to Washington by the workers brought no response. Eventually the Florida farm counties were declared disaster areas not because of the hunger and misery of the migrants but because of the crop losses sustained by the commercial farms. Since the migrant workers had no state residence, there was a question of whether they would qualify for relief. Most of the government emergency relief money ended in the hands of the big growers, who worked with state agencies in distributing it. The workers were "summarily left out of the decisions."[17]

(2) During the very week the farm workers were expressing their anguish and despair in Key Biscayne, leaders of the aerospace industry placed a few telephone calls to the right people in Washington and, without benefit of demonstration or agitation, were invited to meet quietly with President Nixon to discuss their companies' job problems. Later that same day the White House announced a $42-million authorization to the aerospace industry to assist 75,000 to 100,000 of its top adminis-

16. Tom Foltz, "Florida Farmworkers Face Disaster," *Guardian*, April 3, 1971, p. 4.
17. *Ibid*.

trators, scientists and technicians. The spending plan, an industry creation accepted by the government without prior study, provided $5 million for a "job search" program, $25 million for industry personnel retraining, $10 million to assist the companies in relocating personnel, $2 million for something called a "skill conversion fund," supposedly enabling the industry's scientists to "explore" ways of providing technical help for "traditional areas of the economy."[18]

Contrasting the treatment accorded the farm workers with that provided the aerospace industrialists, or big farm owners, or big dairymen, or representatives of General Electric, Standard Oil, U.S. Steel, ITT, General Motors, etc., we might ask: Is the President responding to a "national interest" or a "special interest" when he helps the giant firms? Much depends upon how the labels are applied. Those who believe the national interest necessitates taking every possible measure to maintain the profits and strength of the industrial and military establishment, of which the aerospace industry is a part, might say the President is not responding to a special interest in such instances but to the needs of national security. Certainly almost every President in modern times might have agreed and acted accordingly. Industry is said to be the muscle and sinews of the nation. In contrast, a regional group of farm workers represents a rather marginal interest. Without making light of the suffering of the migrants, it is enough to say that a President's first responsibility is to tend to the crucial levers of our industrial economy. In fact, the argument goes, when workers act to disrupt and weaken the sinews of industry, as have striking coal miners, railroad operators and steel workers, the President may see fit to deal summarily with them, especially during times of acute economic strife or "national emergency" or war—periods which encompass most of our history.

Other people would argue that the national interest is not served when giant industries continually receive favored treatment at the expense of the taxpayers, consumers and workers and to the lasting neglect of millions like the farm workers. That the favored corporations have holdings that are national and often multinational in scope does not mean they represent the interests of the nation's populace. The "national interest" or "public interest" should encompass the ordinary working public rather than just the big commercial farm owners, corporate elites

18. *New York Times*, April 2, 1971.

and their well-paid technicians and managers. Contrary to an established myth, the public monies distributed to these favored few do not "trickle down" to the mass of poor and other working people at the bottom—as the hungry farm workers would be the first to testify.

Whichever position one takes, it becomes clear that there is no *neutral* way of defining the "national interest" or the "public interest." Whichever policy the President pursues, he is helping some class interests more than others, and it is a matter of historical record that Presidents, whether Democrats or Republicans, liberals or conservatives, have rather consistently chosen a definition of the national interest that well serves the giant conglomerates. It is also clear, whether we consider it essential or deplorable, that the President, as the most powerful officeholder in the land, is most readily available to the most powerful interests in the land and rather inaccessible to us lesser mortals.

The President versus Congress: Who Has the Power?

Since the turn of the century, the burdens of government have grown enormously at the municipal, state and federal levels and in the executive, legislative and judicial branches. But as industrial capitalism has expanded at home and abroad, the task of servicing and protecting its vast interests and dealing with the massively dislocative problems it has caused has fallen disproportionately on that level of government which is national and international in scope—the federal—and on that branch which is suited for carrying out the necessary technical, organizational and military tasks—the executive. The powers of the executive have increased so much that today there is no such thing as a "weak, Buchanan-type" of President, for even Eisenhower, who preferred to exercise as little initiative as possible in most affairs, found himself proposing huge budgets and participating in decisions of far greater scope than anything handled by a "strong, Teddy Roosevelt-type" of President a half century before.

The growth of the presidency has been so great as to have brought a *relative* decline in the powers of Congress (even though the scope of legislative activity itself has greatly increased over the years). This is especially true in international affairs. Congressional influence over foreign policy has been exercised largely by withholding funds, passing resolutions, ratifying treaties, confirming ambassadors and other such indirect means; but in recent times Presidents increasingly have acted on their own, making covert military commitments, ignoring legislative amendments in international matters, circumventing the Senate's power to ratify treaties by resorting to "executive agreements," placing White House policy-makers beyond the reach of congressional interrogation by claiming "executive privilege" for them, and in other ways bypassing Congress or confronting it with *faits accomplis.*

The legislative branch is often no better informed than the public it represents. For a number of years Congress unknowingly funded CIA operations in Laos and Thailand that were in violation of congressional prohibitions. And most of the members of the Senate who were questioned by Senator Proxmire had never heard of the automated battlefield program they had voted secret appropriations for.[19] A report from two House Foreign Affairs subcommittees complained of the White House's habits of secrecy and deviancy when dealing with Congress and the "unwillingness of the executive branch to acknowledge major decisions and to subject them to public scrutiny and discussion."[20]

In many instances, whether in foreign or domestic matters, it is not that the President acts without Congress but that he commands levers of power which leave the legislature no option but to move in a direction predetermined by him. The executive's control of crucial information, its system of management and budgeting and its vast network of specialized administrators and staff workers enables it to play a greater role in shaping the legislative agenda than the understaffed, overworked and often ill-informed legislators. In recent years approximately 80 percent of the major laws enacted have originated in the executive branch. Commanding the kind of media exposure that most politicians can only dream of, the President is able to direct attention to his program, be it for defense spending, taxes, wage controls, foreign trade, oil imports or international conflicts; and once he succeeds in defining his program as crucial to

19. Paul Dickson and John Rothchild, "The Electronic Battlefield: Wiring Down the War," *Washington Monthly*, May 1971, pp. 6–14. If the Pentagon Papers reveal anything it is the secretive, unaccountable nature of executive policy. See the latter portion of Richard J. Barnet's *Roots of War* (New York: Atheneum, 1972) for an account of the ways public opinion is manipulated by officialdom; also John C. Donovan, *The Cold Warriors: A Policy Elite* (Lexington, Mass.: D.C. Heath, 1973).

20. The subcommittees' statement is quoted in Graham Hovey, "Making Foreign Policy," *New York Times*, January 22, 1973, p. 31.

the "national interest" and himself as the key purveyor of that interest, Congress usually is left with little choice but to vote the necessary funds and enabling powers, contenting itself with making marginal modifications and inserting special amendments for special friends of its own. This is particularly true as long as the President is not attempting anything of a radically deviant nature but much less true if he is hoping to initiate a program oriented toward social change, especially of a seemingly progressive kind.

One recalls that liberals frequently complained about the way Congress managed to thwart the desires of liberal Presidents like Truman and Kennedy. They concluded from this that Congress had too much power and the President needed more. But having witnessed a conservative President like Richard Nixon regularly effect his will over a Democratic Congress, some of these same liberals now conclude that the President has too much power and Congress not enough. Actually, there is something more to these respective complaints than partisan inconsistency. In the first situation liberals are talking about the President's insufficient ability to effect measures that might benefit the many millions toward the bottom of the social ladder. And in the second instance liberals are talking about the President's seemingly limitless ability to make overseas military commitments and to thwart social welfare legislation at home. What underlies the ostensibly inconsistent liberal complaint is the fact that *the relative powers of the executive and legislative branches depend in part on the interests being served,* and that regardless of who is in what office, the political system operates more efficiently to realize conservative goals than reformist ones, both the executive and legislative branches being more responsive to the corporate powers than to economically deprived social groups. Furthermore, as the Founding Fathers intended, the system of separation of powers and checks and balances is designed to give the high ground to those who would resist social change, be they Presidents or Congressmen. Neither the executive nor the legislature can single-handedly initiate reform, which means that conservatives need to control only one or the other branch to thwart domestic actions (or in the case of Congress, key committees in one or the other house) while liberals must control both branches.

Small wonder that conservative and liberal Presidents have different kinds of experiences with Congress. Since a conservative President generally wants very little from Congress in the way of liberal domestic legislation and, with a few well-placed allies in the legislature, can often squelch what little Congress attempts to produce in that direction, he is less beholden to that body than a liberal President. Should Congress insist upon passing bills that incur his displeasure, the conservative President need control only one third plus one of either the House or the Senate to sustain his vetoes. If bills are passed over his veto, he can still undermine legislative intent by delaying enforcement, impounding funds, reprogramming or freezing funds under various pretexts relating to timing, efficiency and other operational contingencies. The Supreme Court has long been aware that its decisions have the force of law only if other agencies of government choose to carry them out. In recent years Congress has been coming to the same realization, developing a new appreciation of the executive's power to command in a direct and palpable way the men, materials and programs needed for carrying out decisions.

Monies which Congress allocated for pollution control, education and the food-stamp program were impounded by President Nixon in 1972 with the explanation that the sums could not be spent until there was a proper executive "development of approved plans and specifications"—which did not seem forthcoming. The Office of Management and Budget, under the President's direction, does not publicize these impoundings until the following year, when the new budget is presented. The funds are then designated as "reserves" and lumped into general categories that prevent close analysis.[21] Also in 1972, Nixon vetoed twelve major social spending bills passed by Congress, while approving the fattest defense budget in history—close to $80 billion—thus demonstrating that a President of the minority party can successfully promote major programs ("defense") or destroy them ("human services"); in either case the goal is essentially conservative.

The techniques of veto, impoundment, decoy and delay used by a conservative President to dismantle or hamstring already weak domestic programs are of little help to a liberal President who might claim a genuine interest in widespread social change, for the immense social problems he faces cannot be solved by administrative sleight-of-hand. What minor efforts liberal Presidents do make in the field of "social reform" legislation are frequently thwarted or greatly diluted by entrenched

21. See "Expendables," *New Republic*, December 2, 1972, p. 9.

conservative powers in Congress. It is in these confrontations that the Congress gives every appearance of being able to frustrate presidential initiatives.

Change from the Top?

The ability of even a well-intentioned executive to generate policies for the benefit of unorganized and relatively powerless constituents is, to say the least, quite limited. Not only Presidents but executive heads at other levels of government, mayors and governors, have complained of the limited opportunities available to them when attempting to move in new directions. The Black mayor of Gary, Indiana, Richard Hatcher, one of the more dedicated and socially conscious persons to achieve public office, offered this observation:

I am mayor of a city of roughly 90,000 Black people but we do not control the possibilities of jobs for them, or money for their schools, or state-funded social services. These things are in the hands of the U.S. Steel Corporation, and the County Department of Welfare, the State of Indiana. . . . For not a moment do I fool myself that Black political control of Gary or of Cleveland or of any other city in and of itself can solve the problems of the wretched of this nation. The resources are not available to the cities to do the job that needs doing.[22]

Hatcher's statement is not unique. "The speeches of mayors and governors," writes Richard Goodwin, "are filled with exculpatory claims that the problems are too big, that there is not enough power or enough money to cope with them, and our commentators sympathize, readily agreeing that this city or that state is really ungovernable."[23]

When Presidents, governors and mayors contend that the problems of social change they confront are of a magnitude far greater than the resources they command, we can suspect them of telling the truth. Most of the resources are preempted by vested interests. The executive leader who begins his term with the promise of getting things moving is less likely to change the political-corporate-class system than be absorbed by it. Once in office, he finds himself staggered by the vast array of en-

22. From a speech delivered by Hatcher to an NAACP meeting, reprinted in the *Old Mole* (Boston), October 5, 1968.
23. Richard Goodwin, "Reflections: Sources of the Public Unhappiness," *New Yorker*, January 4, 1969, p. 41.

trenched powers working within and without government. He is confronted with a recalcitrant legislature and an intractable bureaucracy. He is constantly distracted by issues and operational problems that seem to take him from his intended course, and he is unable to move in certain directions without incurring the hostility of those who control the economy and its institutional auxiliaries. So he begins to talk about being "realistic" and working with what is at hand, now tacking against the wind, now taking one step back in the often unrealized hope of taking two steps forward, until his public begins to complain that his administration bears a dismaying resemblance to the less dynamic, less energetic ones that came before. In the hope of maintaining his efficacy, he begins to settle for the *appearance* of efficacy, until appearances are all he is left struggling with. It is this tugging and hauling and whirling about in a tight circle of options and ploys that is celebrated by some as "the give-and-take of democratic group-interest politics." To less enchanted observers the failure of reform-minded leaders to deliver on their promises is another demonstration of the impossibility of working for major changes within a politico-economic system that is structured to resist change.

The Politics of Bureaucracy

15

AS EVERYONE COMPLAINS, BUREAUC-racy is beset by inertia, evasion and unac-countability, but there are reasons why bureaucrats behave the way they do, and many of these reasons are profoundly political, being less a peculiarity of bureaucrats than a reflec-tion of the wider system of power and interest in which they operate.

Government by Secrecy and Deception

The first line of defense for any bureaucracy, Max Weber once wrote, is the withholding of information. Actually, it is the first line of defense of any person in authority who con-siders an informed citizenry to be a trouble-some thing and who wishes to keep himself as much beyond criticism as possible. Officials who lie or who resort to secrecy do so not only because they want to maintain a free hand in the pursuit of their interests (or the interests they serve) but because they distrust the public's ability to judge correctly. These two sentiments strengthen each other, as when of-ficeholders do their best to keep the public ignorant and then use this ignorance as justifi-cation for not inviting public criticism.

Chief executives have repeatedly misled Congress and the public about U.S. overseas interventions and then claimed a special knowledge or expertise in foreign affairs. Thus the Eisenhower administration lied about the role it played in overthrowing a democratic reform government in Guatemala. It lied about its intervention in the Congo against Lumumba, and about the hand it took in the overthrow of Mossadegh in Iran, and about its part in the abortive coup against Sukarno in Indonesia in 1958. It lied about the CIA's use of U-2 spy planes over the Soviet Union until the Russians produced a live American U-2 pilot who had been shot down over their territory. The Kennedy administration lied about American involvement in the Bay of Pigs invasion of Cuba, and it lied about its early involvement in the Portuguese colonial war in Africa and about the extent of our intervention in Vietnam. The Johnson administration lied about its role in the successful overthrow of Sukarno in 1965 and the subsequent bloodbath in Indonesia. It lied repeatedly about growing U.S. involvement in Indochina and about the nature of our intervention in the Dominican Republic and much of Latin America. The Nixon administration lied about attempts to subvert the Chilean election of a Marxist president. It lied about the presence of American military personnel in Laos and Cambodia and the role they played. And it repeatedly lied to keep secret some 3,630 B-52 raids that took place in Cambodia in 1969–1970.

The White House and the various executive departments and agencies frequently cooperate more closely with private business than with Congress, especially when it comes to keeping things secret. Government regulation of prices charged by utilities and gas companies and government leasing of offshore drilling tracts to oil companies are based on data supplied by the interested corporations; this information is not made available to Congress or to the public. The FAA refuses to make public its reports on airline accidents and mechanical defects, distributing them only to the airline industry. The Social Security Administration has declined to publicize its report on Medicare operations and the way Blue Cross has carried out the program, despite growing public criticism of rising costs and curtailed benefits. And in the Departments of Agriculture, Interior, Commerce and, of course, Defense, the doings of government and industry frequently are known only to select groups of bureaucrats and corporate leaders, leaving the rest of us to guess whether these policies are economically or socially beneficial.[1]

The government has repeatedly repressed information concerning health and safety problems. As early as 1954 the Food and Drug Administration was warned that the cyclamates put in

1. James Ridgeway, "How Government and Industry Keep Secrets from the People," New Republic, August 21 and 28, 1971, pp. 17–19.

many drinks and foods were linked to cancer. Yet five years later the FDA listed the cyclamates as safe additives, and it was not until 1969, after repeated studies and warnings, that it removed them from beverages (it still allows their use in certain foods). In order not to arouse public anxieties, the Atomic Energy Commission has repeatedly suppressed information about the highly hazardous features of nuclear reactors. Although a study commissioned by the Department of Health, Education and Welfare showed that herbicides used in heavy amounts as defoliants in Vietnam and as weed killer in the United States produced birth deformities at low exposure levels, for three years this information was suppressed. Meanwhile one eighth of the acreage in South Vietnam was sprayed with these chemicals, and a drastic increase in the number of deformed births was reported. Investigations into these and other such incidents caused two Stanford University scientists to issue a report which concluded:

We believe, as a result of our studies, that . . . the executive decision-making process too often sacrifices the safety and welfare of the public to the short-term interests of the government bureaucracy and the large industrial interest to which it has become allied. . . . In these cases, where the facts and the best expert advice did not support the current administration policy, the primary interest of the Executive in the facts was to suppress them—even while stressing in public that its policies had a sound technical foundation.[2]

The growing tendency of officials to withhold critical information does not prevent the government from spending millions in publicity to justify its military, aeronautics, space, highway, atomic energy and agricultural programs. While the mass of voters have little opportunity to convey their feelings to those who govern, they themselves remain the object of a continual barrage of propaganda from official sources. Of the many agencies engaged in propagandizing the public, none is more active than the Pentagon.[3] The armed services currently compose the

2. Portions of the Stanford report are summarized and quoted in Bernard H. Gould, "Government Suppressed Scientists' Warnings of Dangers to the Health and Safety of Public," *National Enquirer*, February 21, 1971. The report's authors are Dr. Frank von Hippel and Dr. Joel Primack.
3. See J. William Fulbright, *The Pentagon Propaganda Machine* (New York: Vintage, 1971); Sidney Lens gives a description of the public relations efforts of the Pentagon in his *The Military-Industrial Complex* (Philadelphia: United Church Press, 1970). An interesting account of the propaganda techniques used by NASA to sell the $30-billion space shuttle and space station programs can be found in Les Aspin, "The Space Shuttle: Who Needs It?" *Washington Monthly*, September 1972, pp. 18–22.

strongest lobby in Washington, exerting more influence over Congress than that body exerts over the Defense Department.

That it happens to be a federal offense to use the taxpayers' money to propagandize the taxpayers seems not to have deterred the military.[4] The Pentagon spends more than $30 million a year on propaganda, including exhibitions, films, books, armed services magazines and brochures, recruitment tours to colleges and high schools and a flood of press releases which, publicized as "news reports" and "news events" in thousands of newspapers and magazines and on radio and televison shows, propagate the military's view of the world without identifying the military as their source.

The Central Intelligence Agency is another government unit actively propagandizing its particular view of the world among the American people, mostly through secretly funded "front" organizations. The CIA, supposedly designed to function as the government's central counterinsurgency and espionage unit throughout the world, has clandestinely infiltrated student, labor, scientific and academic groups, secretly financed the writings of "independent" scholars and subsidized publishing houses and periodicals (e.g., *Encounter*). CIA agents were staff members of the Michigan State University research programs for the early U.S. ventures in Vietnam. The Center for International Studies at MIT was financed in part by the CIA. And, more recently, numerous local police departments around the country have received training in surveillance, detection and counterinsurgency from the CIA. All this despite a congressional ban on CIA activities in domestic affairs.[5] Other secret intelligence units like the Defense Intelligence Agency and the National Security Agency, both in the Pentagon, also engage in clandestine operations within this country. The NSA was created by a still-classified presidential directive in 1952. It has more personnel and twice the budget of the CIA but little is known about it.

Bureaucratic Action and Inaction

The rulings of bureaucratic agencies are published daily in the

4. Fred C. Cook, "The Juggernaut," *Nation*, October 28, 1961, p. 286; also Lens, *The Military-Industrial Complex*, Chapter Five.

5. David Wise and Thomas B. Ross, *The Invisible Government* (New York: Random House, 1964). A book which collects a great deal of evidence on government secrecy, duplicity and deception is David Wise, *The Politics of Lying* (New York: Random House, 1973).

Federal Register, a volume as imposing in size as the *Congressional Record* itself. In their scope and effect, many of these rulings are as significant as major pieces of legislation, and in the absence of precise guidelines from Congress, they often take the place of legislation. During a three-month period in 1972, for instance, without a single law being passed and without an iota of public debate, the Nixon-appointed Price Commission approved more than $2 billion in rate increases for 110 telephone, gas and electric companies, thereby imposing upon the public by administrative fiat an expenditure far greater than what is contained in most of the bills passed by Congress.[6] Even when specific legislation does exist, it usually allows for much leeway in application. Which laws are applied fully and which are ignored, what interpretations are made to suit what interests, what supplementary regulations are formulated—these matters, of keen concern to lobbyists, are almost unknown to the general public. To treat public administration as a "neutral" "nonpartisan" function, then, is grossly misleading. *The political process does not end with the passage of a bill but continues with equal or even greater intensity at the administrative level, albeit in more covert fashion.*[7]

Those people who bemoan the "mess" and "inaction" within municipal, state and federal administrations and who insist that things don't get done because that's simply the nature of the bureaucratic beast, seem to forget that only certain kinds of things don't get done—other things get done all too well. A law establishing a "community development" program for the ghetto poor, passed by a reluctant and distrustful Congress in response to the urgings of a few liberal spokesmen and the pressure of demonstrations and urban riots, is formally and legally the same as a law enacted to develop a multibillion-dollar, high-profit weapons system, the latter supported by giant industrial contractors, well-placed persons within the military, scientific and university establishments and numerous interested Congressmen whose patriotism is matched only by their desire to bring

6. See the statement by Senator Lee Metcalf reported in *Ramparts*, November 1972, p. 24.

7. The myth of administrative "neutrality" is encouraged by such things as the Hatch Act, a law prohibiting political activities by federal employees, presumably to preserve them from corrupt or biased influence. The act accomplishes no such thing. What it does is prevent millions of Americans from organizing in the defense of their own beliefs and interests, while leaving them fully exposed to the politics of bureaucracy. The constitutionality of the Act was upheld by the Supreme Court in 1973 by a 6–3 decision, in *U.S. Civil Service Commission* v. *National Association of Letter Carriers.*

the defense bacon home to their districts and keep their campaign coffers filled by appreciative donors. If anything, the weapons program has many more technical problems and is of vastly greater administrative complexity than the smaller, modestly funded ghetto program. Yet it is the latter that is more likely to suffer from inaction and ineffectiveness, the important difference between the two programs being not bureaucratic but political. The effectiveness of the law depends on the power of the groups supporting it. Laws that serve powerful interests are likely to enjoy a vigorous life while laws that have only the powerless to nurture them are often stillborn.

With the right political support bureacracies are capable of carrying out policies of momentous and far-reaching scope. "The feat of landing men on the moon," Duane Lockard reminds us, "was not only a scientific achievement but a bureacratic one as well."[8] The same might be said of the Vietnam war, the entire defense program, the U.S. counterinsurgency effort in Latin America, the exploits of the Internal Revenue Service, the harbors and rivers construction programs and the farm, highway and housing programs. These endeavors represent the mobilization and coordination of stupendous amounts of energy, skill and material resources by complex, centralized systems of command—i.e., bureaucracies. What is impressive about the federal housing program, for instance, is not how little has been done but how much, yet with so little benefit to low-income people: how many public agencies established, billions spent, millions of work hours expended, millions of tons of materials utilized, and hundreds of thousands of structures built, subsidized and mortgaged at such profit to realty investors, speculators, contractors, manufacturers, big merchants, banks and public officials and at such cost to the taxpayers—a stupendous bureaucratic effort. Bureaucracy's failure to serve the various sectors of the unorganized and needy public has led some observers to the mistaken notion that it serves no one. But as we have seen in previous chapters, for some groups the government has been anything but idle.[9]

The same can be said of Congress. As already noted, the complaint that Congress can't get things done is incorrect. While

8. Duane Lockard, *The Perverted Priorities of American Politics* (New York: Macmillan, 1971), p. 282.
9. See Orion F. White, Jr., "The Dialectical Organization: An Alternative to Bureaucracy," *Public Administration Review*, 19, January–February 1969, pp. 32–41.

unable to accomplish certain things, especially in regard to low-income housing, hunger, medical care, unemployment and mass transportation, it is capable of extraordinary achievements. The space, defense, highway, agricultural and tax programs are not only bureaucratic feats, they are legislative ones. The question is not, "Why can't administrators and legislators act?" but "Why are they able to act so forcefully and successfully in some ways and not at all in other ways?" The first question invites us to throw up our hands in befuddlement; the second requires that we investigate the realities of power and interest.

Why are reform-minded administrative bodies rarely able to operate with any effectiveness? Consider the fate of the agency, bureau or commission set up to regulate some area of industry on behalf of consumers and workers. In its youth, it may possess a zeal for reform, but before long the public concern that gave it impetus begins to fade. The business-owned newspapers and other news media either turn their attention to more topical events and personalities or present an unsympathetic and superficial picture of the agency's doings. The President, if he was originally sympathetic to the agency's mission, is now occupied with more pressing matters, as are its few articulate but not very influential friends in Congress. But the industry that is supposed to be brought under control remains keenly interested and by now is well alerted and ready to oppose government intrusions. First, it may decide to challenge the agency's jurisdiction or even the legality of its existence in court, thus preventing any serious regulatory actions until a legal determination is made.[10] If the agency survives this attack, there begins a series of encounters between its investigators and representatives from the industry. Possessing a superior knowledge of its own internal affairs, the industry is able to counter the agency's moves with a barrage of arguments and technical information, not all truthful but sufficiently impressive to win the respectful attention of the agency's investigators. The investigators begin to develop a new appreciation of industry's side of the story and of the problems it faces in maintaining profitable operations. Indeed, for extended periods it is the only side administrators may be exposed to, and in time they begin to adopt industry's perspective. As Dolbeare and Edelman note:

10. See the discussion in Grant McConnell, *Private Power and American Democracy* (New York: Knopf, 1966), p. 288.

At the same time the consumers, being unorganized, can exert no such subtle but powerful psychological embrace around the administrative agency. On the contrary, the very existence and functioning of the agency are taken as signals that the consumer is being protected, for that is the reason the agency was established. The net effect, therefore, is that the business groups get much of what they want at the same time remaining relatively free from public resistance or protest.[11]

Administrators are immobilized not only by "bureaucratic in-fighting" but by the "out-fighting" that bears upon them from the wider politico-economic system. Given his desire to survive and advance, the bureaucrat's instinct is to equivocate in the face of controversial decisions, moving away from dangerous areas and toward positions favored by the strongest of the pressures working on him. With time, the reform-minded agency loses its crusading spirit and settles down to standard operations, increasingly serving the needs of the industry it is supposed to regulate. The more public-spirited staff members either grow weary of the struggle and make their peace with the corporations, or they leave, to be replaced by personnel who are "acceptable to, if not indeed the nominees of, the industry."[12] Frequently administrative personnel are drawn from the very industry they are charged with regulating, their business background being taken as proof of their "expertise"; they return to higher positions in the same industry after serving their terms in office. Likewise, many career administrators eventually leave government service to accept higher paying jobs in companies whose interests they favored while in office. This promise of a lucrative post with a private firm can exercise a considerable influence on the judgments of the ambitious public administrator.

Little Administrators and Big Businessmen

Most administrative bodies are directly integrated into the various departments of the executive branch and fall under the command of department heads and ultimately the President. But

11. Kenneth M. Dolbeare and Murray J. Edelman, *American Politics: Policies, Power and Change* (Lexington, Mass.: D. C. Heath, 1971), p. 326.

12. McConnell, *Private Power and American Democracy*, p. 288. For an interesting and well-edited selection of readings on the politics of bureaucracy see Francis E. Rourke (ed.), *Bureaucratic Power in National Politics* (Boston: Little, Brown, 1965).

the independent regulatory commissions operate outside the executive branch, making quasi-judicial rulings that can be appealed only to the courts.[13] Congress created the regulatory commissions to be independent of the normal administrative departments in the hope of keeping them free of the politics that permeated other executive bodies. The hope was an unrealistic one. For all the reasons discussed in this chapter, they are no more independent of special influences and they perform much the same as the regular departmental agencies—the niceties of structure counting for less than the realities of power and interest.

On those infrequent occasions when government agencies succeed in enforcing a regulation on behalf of the unorganized public, the accomplishment requires much time and effort and usually has only a highly marginal effect on the overall politico-economy. Consider the actions taken by the Federal Trade Commission against the manufacturers of Geritol, a vitamin and iron preparation that promised to give people energy by ridding them of something called "tired blood." In April 1959 the Commission staff began an investigation of Geritol's advertising claims. It was not until November 1962 that it issued a complaint to J.B. Williams Company, the manufacturers of Geritol, and the Parkson Advertising Company, and not until September 1965 that it issued a cease-and-desist order, almost six and a half years after the inception of the investigation. The Geritol manufacturers and advertisers appealed the ruling in federal court. Another two years went by before the court issued its decision upholding the Commission's order. Geritol advertisements that referred to tiredness now had to specify that "the great majority of tired people don't feel that way because of iron-poor blood and Geritol won't help them."

But the matter was far from settled. A year later, the FTC held public hearings and found that J.B. Williams Company and Parkson Advertising had failed to comply with the order. The

13. The major independent regulatory commissions are the Civil Aeronautics Board, the Federal Communications Commission, the Federal Power Commission, the Federal Trade Commission, the Interstate Commerce Commission, the National Labor Relations Board and the Securities and Exchange Commission. While the commissions report directly to Congress, their personnel are appointed by the President, with Senate confirmation. For a recent study see Louis Kohlmeier, *The Regulators: Watchdog Agencies and the Public Interest* (New York: Harper and Row, 1969). Kohlmeier finds that regulation has resulted in diminished competition, producer controlled markets, restricted consumer choice and higher prices. See also Morton Mintz and Jerry S. Cohen, *America, Inc.* (New York: Dial Press, 1971).

Commission entered into an exchange of correspondence and informal negotiations with the companies lasting until June 1969, at which time a majority of the Commission voted to allow the Geritol people to file a new compliance order within thirty days. The compliance order required that the word "power" be deleted from commercials which claimed that "Geritol builds iron power," along with all references to "prevention of tiredness" on Geritol labels.[14] After further delay, the Geritol manufacturers and advertisers did delete the offending word. But by 1972 Geritol televison commercials were showing remarkably youthful-looking mothers talking to their teenage daughters about how they managed to stay so young, energetic and lovely: it was Geritol that did it, for Geritol was the thing that supplemented a woman's "special iron needs." "And by the way," the mother cheerily would ask her post-pubescent daughter, "isn't it time *you* started taking Geritol?" Thus Geritol had graduated from fighting tired blood to retarding the aging process itself and helping women preserve their youth and beauty. If the FTC's efforts over a twelve-year period could produce only this, small wonder that critics remain skeptical about the government's ability to regulate business on behalf of the public interest.

If certain administrative bodies persist in making unfavorable rulings, businessmen appeal to their elected representatives, or to a higher administrative official within the bothersome agency's department, or, if they have the pull, to the President himself. In its youthful days after World War I, the FTC hunted bigger game than Geritol advertisements, but representatives of large corporations prevailed upon the President to replace "some of the commissioners by others more sympathetic with business practices: this resulted in the dismissal of many complaints which had been made against corporations."[15]

Frequently members of Congress demand to know why an agency is bothering their constituents. Administrators who are more interested in building congressional support than making congressional enemies are likely to apply the law in ways that satisfy influential legislators. "If the bureaucrats are to escape criticism, unfavorable publicity, or a cut in their appropriations, they must be discreet in their relations with the legislative

14. *New York Times*, July 5, 1969.
15. Edwin Sutherland, *White Collar Crime* (New York: Holt, Rinehart and Winston, 1949), p. 232.

body."[16] Some administrative bodies, like the Army Corps of Engineers, so successfully cultivate support among powerful Congressmen and big business clientele as to become relatively free of supervisory control from department heads or the White House. "Fierce rivalries for funds and functions go on ceaselessly among the departments and between the agencies," reports Cater. "A cunning bureau chief learns to negotiate alliances on Capitol Hill [Congress] that bypass the central authority of the White House."[17] In the executive branch, as in Congress, the fragmentation of power is hardly indicative of its democratization. Rather it represents little more than a distribution among entrenched special interests.

Frequently executive leaders and key Congressmen work together to squelch a troublesome agency. The General Accounting Office, created by Congress to check on how government monies are used, did a series of studies on profiteering and waste in the war industries in the late 1950s. The probes, initiated by the newly appointed Comptroller General, Joseph Campbell, soon incurred the displeasure of the Pentagon and the big defense contractors, who eventually prevailed upon the chairman of the House Government Operations Committee, Chet Holifield, to hold hearings on the GAO. Holifield, like other influential senior members of Congress, had frequently been the recipient of favors from the executive and could be counted on for support. In the hearings, he pointedly informed the GAO of "the great concern that has been shown in industry circles, and, recently, in the Department of Defense over the difficult and sometimes awkward situations created by the GAO audit reports." By the end of the investigation, the GAO had agreed to stop naming specific companies in its reports and to start making a greater effort to be "constructive."[18] The GAO now operates in more circumspect ways: in its recent study of defense contractors, it revealed that seventy-seven weapons systems would cost $28.7 billion more than estimated and that the average profit rate was a colossal 56 percent, but this time the GAO sent the report to defense companies before releasing it and then incorporated

16. E. Pendleton Herring, "The Balance of Social Forces in the Administration of the Food and Drug Law," *Social Forces*, 13, March 1935, p. 364.

17. Douglass Cater, *Power in Washington* (New York: Random House, 1964), pp. 10–11.

18. This account is taken from Mark J. Green, James M. Fallows and David R. Zwick, *Who Runs Congress?* (New York: Bantam Books/Grossman, 1972), p. 127, including Holifield's comment.

many of the corporations' alibis into the report and toned down its own charges.[19]

The way the GAO directs its efforts says something about the comparative power of administrative bodies. In 1969 it had only five or six employees looking into the nearly $75-billion Pentagon military budget but more than two hundred investigating the much smaller poverty program. The same pattern held true throughout the executive branch. More than half a billion dollars is spent yearly to police the Aid to Families with Dependent Children program (popularly known as "welfare") but no equivalent sums have been provided to check the multibillion-dollar government subsidies granted to agribusiness, airlines, shipping companies and other welfare recipients of the business world.

Administrators who are not sufficiently understanding of the needs of industry do not enjoy a high survival rate. Witness the case of John O'Leary, a career government administrator who was appointed director of the Bureau of the Mines by Lyndon Johnson in 1968, not long before Johnson departed from the White House. Almost immediately after O'Leary's appointment, an underground explosion took the lives of seventy-eight miners in Farmington, West Virginia. Various press reports began appearing, along with protests from public-interest groups, concerning the unsafe conditions in the mines and the failure of the Bureau of the Mines to enforce federal regulations. Former Secretary of the Interior Stewart Udall called the Bureau "timorous and almost apologetic" in its regulation of the mining industry. To the surprise of everyone and to the horror of the mine owners, the newly appointed O'Leary agreed. He startled the old-line staff at the Bureau by insisting that they "represent the public interest rather than the industry alone."[20] He ordered the Bureau's three hundred mine inspectors to make unannounced spot checks of safety conditions, a step involving an element of surprise that federal inspectors had rarely tried before, although directed to do so by legislation. In December 1968 the Bureau made six hundred spot checks, almost four times the number for the entire previous year. With the power to close mines only on evidence of "imminent disaster" or "unwarrantable disregard" of previously reported safety violations, O'Leary's men still managed to order workers out of more than two hundred unsafe mines. Various mines began taking neglected,

19. *Ibid.*, p. 128.
20. *New York Times*, February 17, 1969.

elementary steps toward safer conditions. Despite these moves, O'Leary noted, forty-two more miners died in the sixty-three work days after the Farmington disaster. He urged his inspectors to still greater efforts and publicly charged in blunt terms that the coal mining industry was "designed for production economy and not for human economy, and there's going to have to be a change of attitudes on that."[21]

The change came—but it was not the one hoped for. The mine owners voiced their strong opposition to the Bureau's troublesome new policies and made known to the White House their desire to be rid of O'Leary. In February 1969, having been in office only twenty-six days, the Nixon administration, through the Secretary of Interior, announced that the Bureau's director was to be replaced forthwith. O'Leary had lasted four months. His successor reestablished more cooperative relations with the mine owners, making personal appearances at corporate gatherings, riding in company planes and avoiding any "get tough" policies.[22]

People like O'Leary are the exception. The picture of administrators chaffing at the bit or beaten into submission by forces stronger than they is somewhat misleading. In most instances, public bureaucrats are vigorous promoters of the private industries. Upon hearing the newly appointed chairman of the Civil Aeronautics Board begin a press conference with: "We of the aviation community . . . ," Murray Kempton was moved to comment:

Now the Chairman of the Civil Aeronautics Board is commissioned to regulate the aircraft industry; anywhere else but in Washington, it would be curious to encounter a judge whose first remarks upon assuming the robe were an expression of identification with the community of defendants. What is peculiar to the city is that it almost never suggests to us the sense of the nation as a community but continually sets before us its image of a conglomeration of licensed franchise holders.[23]

As part of this "conglomeration," the Civil Aeronautics Board

21. *Ibid.* See also "Mine Safety Case Hit," *Christian Science Monitor*, April 8, 1970.
22. Jack Anderson, "Mine Officials Got Free Air Travel," *Times-Union* (Albany), June 17, 1973. The Bureau's deputy director accepted various gratuities including free football tickets and plane rides from firms under the Bureau's jurisdiction, Anderson reports.
23. Murray Kempton, "A Letter from the Wasteland," *New York Review of Books*, October 23, 1969, p. 8.

and the Federal Aviation Administration tend to the wants of the airline industry; the Highway Safety Bureau and the entire Department of Transportation defer to the oil-highway-automotive combine; the Agriculture Department promotes the policies and products of giant farming corporations; the Interstate Commerce Commission continues its long devotion to the trucking and railroad companies; the Federal Communications Commission serves the monopolistic interests of the telephone and telegraph companies and the media networks; the Securities and Exchange Commission regulates the stock market mostly for the benefit of the large investors and to the detriment of small ones; the Federal Reserve Board continues to be run by and for the large banks—setting the value of the dollar, setting the interest rate, funding lobbyists, and refusing to have Congress audit its books; the Federal Power Commission pursues a permissive policy on behalf of the private utilities; the Army Corps of Engineers continues to mutilate the natural environment on behalf of agricultural corporations, utilities, and land developers; various bureaus within the Department of Interior serve the oil, mining and timber companies;[24] and one need not speculate on the many billions distributed every year by the Department of Defense to pay the bloated profits and cost overruns of favored manufacturers.[25]

Public Authority in Private Hands

The ultimate submergence of public power to private interest comes when government gives, along with its funds and services,

24. There is an ample literature documenting how administrative bodies serve the interests of the industries they are supposed to regulate. See Kohlmeier, *The Regulators*; Anthony Lewis, "To Regulate the Regulators," *New York Times Magazine*, February 22, 1959; Bernard Schwartz, *The Professor and the Commissions* (New York: Knopf, 1958); Walter S. Adams and Horace Gray, *Monopoly in America* (New York: Macmillan, 1955); The Ralph Nader Study Group Report, *The Interstate Commerce Omission: The Public Interest and the ICC* (New York: Grossman, 1970), Robert C. Fellmeth, project director; James Ridgeway, "The Antipopulists," *Ramparts*, December 1971, pp. 6–8; Richard Ney, *The Wall Street Jungle* (New York: Grove Press, 1970); William O. Douglas, "The Corps of Engineers; The Public Be Damned," *Playboy*, July 1969, reprinted in Walt Anderson (ed.), *Politics and Environment* (Pacific Palisades, Calif.: Goodyear, 1970), pp. 268–284; Arthur Maass, *Muddy Waters* (Cambridge, Mass.: Harvard University Press, 1951); Ross Macdonald, "Life with the Blob," in Anderson, *Politics and Environment*, pp. 130–31.
25. See the section in Chapter Six entitled "The Pentagon: Billions for Big Brother."

its very *authority* to business. Grant McConnell has documented how state authority is taken over by private groups in such areas as agriculture, land and water usage, medicine, industry and trade.[26] Thus Western ranches not only enjoy the use of federal land and water resources; they also have been granted the public authority that goes along with the task of administering such subsidies. Control of land and water usage has been handed over to local "home-rule" boards dominated by the large ranchers, who thereby successfully transform their economic power "into a working approximation of publicly sanctioned authority."[27] Large agricultural producers exercise a similar formal authority in the administration of farm programs. Citing the wheat-cotton bill of 1964, Theodore Lowi commented: "Agriculture has become neither public nor private enterprise. It is a system of self-government in which each leading farm interest controls a segment of agriculture through a delegation of national sovereignty. Agriculture has emerged as a largely self-governing federal estate within the Federal structure of the United States," enjoying a power that has extended "through a line unbroken by personality or party in the White House."[28]

One congressional committee, investigating relations between government and industry, complained of "a virtual abdication of administrative responsibility on the part of the Government officials in charge of the Department of Commerce in that their actions in many instances are but the automatic approval of decisions already made outside the Government in business and industry."[29] In almost every significant line of industry, advisory committees staffed by representatives of leading firms work closely with government agencies, making most of the important recommendations. In trying to assess their roles it is "difficult to determine where the distinction between advice and the making of policy lies."[30] There are 3200 committees and boards advising the executive branch and Congress, costing the government $65 million a year to finance. The most influential are composed exclusively of big businessmen and deal with banking, chemi-

26. See McConnell, *Private Power and American Democracy*. Another interesting work that picks up on McConnell's analysis and offers some additional evidence is Theodore Lowi, *The End of Liberalism* (New York: W. W. Norton, 1969).
27. McConnell, *Private Power and American Democracy*, p. 210.
28. Lowi, *The End of Liberalism*, pp. 103–104.
29. From a congressional report cited in McConnell, *Private Power and American Democracy*, p. 271.
30. McConnell, *Private Power and American Democracy*, p. 275.

cals, communications, pollution control, safety, trade, meat packing, commercial farming, natural gas, oil, utilities, railroads,
taxation and other such subjects. They meet regularly with
administrative leaders to formulate policies. Their many reports
become the basis for major administrative actions and new
legislation. These business advisers have unparalleled occasion
to monopolize informational inputs, defining "industry's needs"
from the vantage point of their own interests and with the
coercive power of the state backing their decisions. In this way
they secure advantages over smaller competitors, workers and
consumers of a kind less easily gained in open competition.

The advisory committees are expert in frustrating attempts at
enforcing laws that are not to their tastes. When the government
first began to gather information for legislation on water pollution, it consulted the Advisory Council on Federal Reports, a
private body which describes itself as the official business
consultant to the Budget Bureau; it also considers itself responsible only to the business community.[31] The Advisory Council,
in cooperation with the Budget Bureau, set up a committee on
pollution which included representatives of DuPont, the Manufacturing Chemists Association and the American Paper Institute. The committee opposed the basic policy advocated by
Congress, which was to set up an inventory on water pollutants.
In deference to industry's wishes the government decided that
the inventory would be provided by companies only on a
voluntary basis, in effect approving industry's claim that the
poisons and chemical wastes it unleashed into the public waters
were a trade secret and a property right. Throughout all this, as
Robert Dietsch observed, "Nobody thought of consulting environmental and conservation organizations, nobody thought of
insisting that consumer representatives take part in discussions
or even that meetings should be public."[32] The meetings of these
business advisory committees are not open to the press or public.

The advisory committees have flourished under Democratic
as well as Republican administrations. The Business Advisory
Council was set up during Franklin Roosevelt's reign; the
National Petroleum Council was established under Truman; and
the Pentagon's Industry Advisory Council, "through which the
nation's top defense contractors tone down General Accounting
Office reports on excess profits and urge the FBI to share with

31. Robert W. Dietsch, "The Invisible Bureaucracy," *New Republic*, February
20, 1971, p. 19.
32. *Ibid.*

industry its files on restive students,"[33] was established by the Kennedy administration. The Nixon administration, while cutting back on employment in some administrative agencies and bypassing the legislature with increasing frequency, extended the size and powers of the "business advisory branch of government" so as better to transform "industry wishes into government writ."[34]

In many state and municipal governments, as in the federal government, private business associations, dominated by the biggest firms in the area, are accorded the power to nominate their own personnel to licensing boards, production boards and other administrative bodies. The transfer of public authority to private hands frequently comes at the initiative of large companies. But sometimes the government itself will make the first overtures, organizing private associations, and then handing them the powers of the state, thereby supposedly moving toward "voluntaristic" and "decentralized" forms of policy making. In fact, these measures merely transfer public power to favored producers who can more readily control their markets without being held democratically accountable by the public for the sovereign authority they exercise. The public official who invites the big manufacturing associations to take over the decision-making problems in important areas of the political economy, as McConnell points out, "has successfully maintained his formal position and has cleared his desk of immediate work and trouble. Nevertheless, by his action he will have materially diminished his office and will over time discover that he has incurred a permanent debt to the group he has helped conjure into being and has endowed with authority."[35]

There exists, then, unbeknownst to most Americans, a large number of decision-makers who are with the government but not quite within it, who exercise public authority without having to answer to the public and who determine official policy while considering their first interest and obligation to be their private businesses. They belong to what I would call the "public-private authority." Included in this category are the various quasi-public corporations, institutions, foundations, boards, councils and associations, such as the Hudson Institute, the Federal Reserve

33. Vic Reinemer, "Corporate Government in Action," *Progressive*, November 1971, p. 30.
34. *Ibid.*, p. 29.
35. McConnell, *Private Power and American Democracy*, p. 163.

Board, the Business Council and the Port Authority of New York, which make private policies that have all the force of public law. Consider the last-mentioned: the Port Authority is a "public corporation" created by interstate compact for the purpose of running the bridges and tunnels between New York and New Jersey and the various metropolitan airports. Its bonds, like those of federal, state and municipal governments, are sold to large financial and corporate institutions and very rich individuals. It acts with "public" authority on most matters, but an authority answerable to none of the governing bodies in the region—not to the mayors, nor the city councils, nor the state legislators, nor the governors of New York and New Jersey, nor the U.S. Congress.[36] The Port Authority can condemn property and construct tax-exempt developments like the World Trade Center, from which it can lease space for shops, restaurants and offices. The profits from its commercial ventures ($12 million annually from the JFK Airport restaurants alone) are distributed as *tax-free returns to private investors.* Hundreds of millions in surpluses which could be used to salvage New York's decaying mass-transit system are kept in reserve by the Port Authority, "not for the people of New York City, but for bondholders. Thus does public authority and private power come together in a massive fusion of wealth that leaves the ordinary taxpaying New Yorkers as its victim."[37]

The public-private authority extends into overseas areas, an expansion that has been highly costly in lives and taxes. In many international affairs it is difficult to tell the difference between governmental and corporate efforts. When the Peruvian generals nationalized the holdings of private oil companies, the President sent a special envoy to protest the move and negotiate for reacquisition. When the Chilean government nationalized the copper mines that were owned by private U.S. corporations, the White House warned: "Countries that expropriate *our assets* will be on notice that this will generate a fresh policy review at very high levels of government." The U.S. Information Agency pub-

36. See the discussion in Jack Newfield and Jeff Greenfield, "Them That Has Keep: Taxes," *Ramparts*, April 1972, pp. 35, 61–62.
37. *Ibid.*, p. 61. When the Port Authority had trouble renting space in its ugly World Trade Center buildings, a predicament that could have meant difficulties for its bondholders, Governor Rockefeller came to the rescue by renting fifty-eight floors of the Center for New York State offices. One of the financial institutions with holdings in the Port Authority is the Chase Manhattan Bank, whose chief executive and biggest stockholder is Nelson Rockefeller's brother, David.

lishes, at the taxpayers' expense, pamphlets extolling the benefits of private oil exploration for distribution in Ecuador. Agents of ITT and the CIA consider ways of preventing a democratically elected, socialist-minded government from taking office in Chile.[38] And when a reform-minded government in Guatemala begins to nationalize some of the immense land holdings of the United Fruit Company, the U.S. government actively intercedes and helps overthrow it.[39] Here, too, the corporations do not merely benefit from public policy; they often *make* policy, selecting the key officials, using public funds or channeling funds of their own through public agents, directing World Bank loans and foreign aid investments, offering recommendations that are treated as policy guidelines—in sum, pursuing their interests abroad with all the formal authority and might of the United States government behind them.

The corporate interests exert an influence that cuts across particular administrative departments. Within a government whose power is highly fragmented, they form cohesive, though sometimes overlapping, blocs around major producer interests like oil, steel, banking, drugs and medicines, transportation and armaments; these blocs are composed of bureaucrats at all levels, regulatory commissioners, senior Congressmen, lobbyists, newspaper publishers, trade associations and business firms, operating with all the autonomy and unaccountability of princely states within the American polity.

Government "Meddling"

If government is capitalism's provider and protector at home and abroad, and if government and business are so intermingled as to be often indistinguishable, then why are businessmen so critical of "government meddling in the economy"? There are a number of explanations. First, as previously noted, businessmen are not opposed to government activity as long as it is favorable to them. Since the beginning of the Republic government activity in the economy often has been at the behest of leading producers. "Whether we like it or not, the federal government is a partner in

38. See Tad Szulc, "I.T.T.: A Private Little Foreign Policy," *New York Times*, March 26, 1972.

39. For an account of U.S. intervention in Guatemala see John Gerassi, *The Great Fear in Latin America*, rev. ed. (New York: Collier-Macmillan, 1965), pp. 180–186.

every business in the country," announced Lammot duPont Copeland, president of DuPont Chemicals. "As businessmen we need the understanding and cooperation of government in our effort to throw the economic machine into high gear."[40] When business leaders do denounce government "meddling" they are usually referring to those infrequent occasions when public agencies attempt to impose environmental protections, antitrust laws or worker and consumer safety regulations. When business criticizes "excessive government spending" they have in mind those modest programs which appear to benefit lower-class people. The business community has always been fearful that government might become unduly responsive to popular sentiments, arousing mass expectations and eventually succumbing to demands that could seriously challenge the ongoing allocations of income and wealth and perhaps even upset the class structure. The most common business criticism is not against existing arrangements of government, most of which have served industry well, but against government activities that might mobilize new constituencies, introducing unsettling elements into policy areas now firmly under control of entrenched business groups. As McConnell explains:

The avowed hostility of business toward government may or may not be genuine. It is genuine where governmental action seems to threaten the autonomy and the system of rule established by a unit of business; it is false where a government agency is responsible purely to that unit. Hence, the railroad industry is largely content with regulation by the Interstate Commerce Commission, the securities trade is pleased to see extension of Securities and Exchange Commission policy, and the oil industry is happy to cooperate in the operation of the National Petroleum Council. Few industries or businesses, however, approve of any aggressive operation by the Anti-Trust Division, although this agency is the true protector of the avowed ideology.[41]

Second, criticisms of government officials are a means of bringing them closer into line with industry's desires. Despite the controls exercised in the selection and advancement process, some public servants forget their commitment to the business community and entertain notions intended to favor a wider constituency. Pressure must be brought upon them to remind

40. Quoted in David Bazelon, "Big Business and the Democrats," in Marvin Gettleman and David Mermelstein (eds.), *The Failure of American Liberalism* (New York: Vintage, 1971), pp. 145–146.
41. McConnell, *Private Power and American Democracy*, p. 295.

them of the vulnerabilities of their agencies and their careers. Third, many of the complaints lodged against government are from those firms least favored by government policies. Business is not without its interior divisions: policies frequently benefit the bigger, wealthier firms at the expense of smaller ones. The howls of pain emanating from these weaker competitors are more likely to be heard by us than the quiet satisfaction of the giant victors.

Finally, I would suggest that much of the verbal opposition to government is an ideological expression, a manifestation of the businessman's adherence to the business creed, his belief in the virtues of rugged individualism, private enterprise and private competition.[42] That he might violate this creed in his own corporate affairs does not mean his devotion to it is consciously hypocritical. One should not underestimate the human capacity to indulge in selective perceptions and rationales. These rationales are no less sincerely felt because they are self-serving; quite the contrary, it is a creed's very congruity with a favorable self-image and self-interest that makes it so compelling. The remarkable thing about many businessmen, including those who have benefited in almost every way from government contracts, subsidies and tax laws, is that they *believe* the advantages they enjoy are the result of their own self-reliance and their own efforts and talents in a highly competitive "private" market. They believe that everyone *except* them goes running to the government for a handout.

42. See Francis X. Sutton et al., *The American Business Creed* (New York: Schocken Books, 1962).

Nine Men and the Constitution

16

ALL THREE BRANCHES OF GOVERN-
ment are sworn to defend and uphold the
Constitution, but the Supreme Court, in pursuance of that responsibility, has the power of
reviewing the constitutionality of the actions
of the other two branches and having its judgments treated as the final word, at least in
regard to cases brought before it by others.
While there is nothing in Article III of the
Constitution that gives the Court this power,
the proceedings of the Constitutional Convention reveal that many of the delegates clearly
expected the federal judiciary to declare null
and void laws it deemed inconsistent with the
Constitution.[1] Of even greater significance
than its constitutional adjudications is the
Court's power to interpret the intent and scope
of various laws as they are applied in actual
situations. This power of review is also limited
to cases brought to the Court. Our main concern here is with trying to understand the
political role the Court has played over the
years.

Who Judges?

Some Americans like to think of their Constitution as a vital force, having almost an
animation of its own. At the same time they
expect Supreme Court Justices to be above the
normal prejudices of sentient persons. Thus

1. Max Farrand, *The Framing of the Constitution of the
United States* (New Haven: Yale University Press, 1913),
pp. 156–157.

they envision "a living Constitution" and an insentient Court. But a moment's reflection should remind us that it is the other way around. The Supreme Court is deeply engaged in the political process. If the Constitution is, as they say, an "elastic instrument," then most of the stretching has been done by the nine men who sit on the Court, and the directions in which they pull are largely determined by their own policy predilections.

There have been Supreme Court Justices who have insisted otherwise, contending that the Court is involved in judgments that allow little room for personal prejudice. Justice Roberts provided the classic utterance of this viewpoint:

When an act of Congress is appropriately challenged in the Courts as not conforming to the constitutional mandate the judiciary branch of the government has only one duty—to lay the Article of the Constitution which is invoked beside the statute which is challenged and to decide whether the latter squares with the former. All that the Court does, or can do, is to announce its considered judgment upon the question.[2]

This image of the Constitution as a measuring stick and the Justice as measurer has been challenged by critics of the Court and even by some Justices. No less a member than Chief Justice Hughes pointedly observed, "We are under a constitution but the constitution is what the judges say it is."[3] And Justice Oliver Wendell Holmes once reminded his colleagues that "the provisions of the Constitution are not mathematical formulas having their essence in their form. . . ."[4]

By class background, professional training and political selection, Supreme Court Justices over the generations have usually been inclined to identify with the landed interests rather than the landless, the slave owners rather than the slaves, the industrialists rather than the workers, the exponents of Herbert Spencer rather than the proponents of Karl Marx, the established social elites rather than unemployed Blacks, underpaid migrants or illiterate immigrants. Almost all Justices have been from well-to-do backgrounds and none has been known to harbor anything that might resemble a radical or a socialist thought —with the possible present-day exception of Justice William O.

2. *United States* v. *Butler*, 297 U.S. 1 (1936).
3. Dexter Perkins, *Charles Evans Hughes* (Boston: Little, Brown, 1956), p. 16.
4. *Gompers* v. *United States*, 233 U.S. 610 (1914).

Douglas.[5] Approximately a century ago Justice Miller, a Lincoln appointee to the Court, made note of the class biases of the judiciary:

It is vain to contend with judges who have been at the bar, the advocates for forty years of railroad companies, and all the forms of associated capital, when they are called upon to decide cases where such interests are in contest. All their training, all their feelings are from the start in favor of those who need no such influence.[6]

Nor is the situation much different today. One study shows that the men who enjoy life-tenure positions on federal courts, whether appointed by Democratic or by Republican Presidents, are drawn preponderantly from highly privileged Ivy League and private-school backgrounds.[7] Joel Grossman finds that the American Bar Association's quasi-official Federal Judiciary Committee, whose task is to pass on the qualifications of prospective judges, favors those whose orientation is strongly conservative and supportive of corporate interests.[8] Few mavericks, reformers or populists ever come close to appointment to the federal bench. As one U.S. District Court judge puts it: "Who are we, after all? The average judge, if he ever was a youth, is no longer. If he was ever a firebrand, he is not discernibly an ember now. If he ever wanted to lick the Establishment, he has long since joined it."[9]

The Supremely Political Court

There is an old saying that the devil himself can quote the Bible for his own purposes. The Constitution is not unlike the Bible in this respect, and over the generations Supreme Court Justices

5. Douglas would hardly qualify as a proponent of socialism, but he has manifested a sympathy for the substance of some radical protests that is unusual for the personages who have sat on the High Bench.
6. Quoted in Felix Frankfurter, *Mr. Justice Holmes and the Supreme Court* (New York: Atheneum, 1965), p. 54.
7. Sheldon Goldman, "Johnson and Nixon Appointees to the Lower Federal Courts: Some Socio-Political Perspectives," *Journal of Politics*, 34, August 1972, pp. 934–942.
8. See Joel B. Grossman, *Lawyers and Judges: The ABA and the Politics of Judicial Selection* (New York: Wiley, 1965).
9. Marvin E. Frankel, "An Opinion by One of Those Softheaded Judges," *New York Times Magazine*, May 13, 1973, p. 41.

have shown an infernal agility in finding constitutional justifications for the continuation of almost every inequity and iniquity, be it slavery or segregation, child labor or the sixteen-hour day, state sedition laws or federal assaults on the First Amendment. Consider the Court's decisions in the area of political economy. Justice Felix Frankfurter once observed:

The raw material of modern government is business. Taxation, utility regulation, agricultural control, labor relations, housing, banking and finance, control of the security market—all our major domestic issues —are phases of a single central problem, namely, the interplay of economic enterprise and government. These are the issues which for more than a generation have dominated the calendar of the Court.[10]

Throughout most of the late nineteenth century and well into the twentieth, the Court was a bastion of conservative economics. Whether the government was judged to be improperly interfering with the economy depended less on the actual range of its activity than on which social groups benefited. If the federal government wanted to establish national banks, or give away half the country to private speculators, or subsidize industries, or set up commissions and boards that fixed prices and interest rates on behalf of giant manufacturers, railroads and banks, or send Marines to secure corporate investments in Central America, such activities were as perfectly acceptable to the majority of the Court as to the majority of the business community. But if the federal or state governments sought to limit work-day hours, or outlaw child labor, or establish minimum wages, or guarantee the rights of collective bargaining, or in other ways impose some kind of limitation on the privileges of the business community, then the Court ruled that government could not tamper with the natural processes of the private market nor interfere with the principle of laissez-faire by depriving owner and worker of "liberty of contract" and "substantive due process."[11]

The concept of substantive due process illustrates as well as any other judicial doctrine the way the Court manufactures new constitutional meanings under the guise of interpreting old ones.

10. Frankfurter, *Mr. Justice Holmes* p. 41. Frankfurter made this comment in 1938, a year before he was appointed to the Court.
11. See for instance *Allgeyer* v. *Louisiana*, 165 U.S. 578 (1897); *Lochner* v. *New York*, 198 U.S. 45 (1905); and *Adair* v. *United States*, 208 U.S. 161 (1908).

Inherent in the notion of constitutionalism is the understanding that government, even when exercising its legitimate powers, must respect the rights of individuals by adhering to certain procedures and concepts of fair play. This adherence is what became known as "due process." The Fifth Amendment prohibits the federal government from depriving any person "of life, liberty, or property, without due process of law," and the Fourteenth Amendment places a similar prohibition on the state governments. Hence, law officers have the duty to apprehend criminals but they must observe the rights of a suspect to know the charges, have benefit of counsel, and be given an impartial, public trial. In actuality, as we saw in Chapter Eight, due process is violated daily in our law enforcement system, especially in the treatment extended to poor people, racial minorities and political dissenters.[12] Nevertheless, the right to due process is one of the more noble concepts of the present constitutional system and remains a standard to which no one can afford to be indifferent. But the due process concept sometimes has been applied by the Supreme Court in rather ignoble ways.

By about 1890 the Court, after years of pressure from corporate lawyers and American Bar Association spokesmen, decided that due process referred not only to procedural matters but to the substance of the legislation—that is, not only to the way the law had been made and applied but to its very content.[13] Having determined that there was such a thing as "substantive due process," which in an earlier day might have been considered a contradiction in terms, the Court then could review every kind of legislation passed by the states which business plaintiffs brought before it. When Congress enacted social welfare legislation outlawing child labor, the Court would find it to be a violation of substantive due process under the Fifth Amendment and an unconstitutional usurpation of the reserved powers of the states under the Tenth Amendment.[14] When the states passed social welfare legislation, the Court would find it in violation of substantive due process under the Fourteenth

12. See Chapter Eight.
13. The pressures of business lawyers and the Bar Association are described in Arthur A. North, S. J., *The Supreme Court, Judicial Process and Judicial Politics* (New York: Appleton-Century-Crofts, 1966), pp. 40–43.
14. See *Hammer* v. *Dagenhart*, 247 U.S. 251 (1918). The Tenth Amendment reads: "The powers not delegated to the United States by this Constitution, nor prohibited by it to the States, are reserved to the States respectively or to the people."

Amendment. In 1936, in an almost breathtaking display of judicial legerdemain, the Court struck down certain codes of the National Industrial Recovery Act, arguing among other things that the regulation of such matters fell beyond Congress' power under the commerce clause and were part of the reserved powers of the states under the Tenth Amendment.[15] During the same term, the same Court struck down an attempt by New York State to legislate on minimum wages because this violated due process under the Fourteenth Amendment.[16] Thus while prohibiting Congress from supposedly encroaching on the reserved powers of the states, the Court prevented the states from using their reserved powers.

The Fourteenth Amendment, adopted in 1868 ostensibly to establish full citizenship for Blacks, states that "No State shall make or enforce any law which shall abridge the privileges or immunities of citizens of the United States; nor shall any State deprive any person of life, liberty, or property, without due process of law; nor deny to any person within its jurisdiction the equal protection of the laws." The Court decided that the word "person" included corporations and that the Fourteenth Amendment was intended not only to uphold the civil rights of Blacks—which it seldom did—but to protect business conglomerations from the vexatious regulations of the states. Perhaps encouraged by the loose construction given to the word "person" or more likely convinced that they really were persons despite the treatment accorded them by a male-dominated society, spokeswomen for the feminist movement began to argue that the Fourteenth Amendment and the Fifth Amendment applied to women and that the voting restrictions imposed on them by state and federal government should be abolished. A test case reached the Supreme Court in 1894 and the Justices decided that they could not give such a daring reading to the Constitution.[17] The Court seemingly had made up its mind that "privileges and immunities of citizens" and "equal protection of the laws" applied only to stockholders, corporate directors and banks, and to women and Blacks not at all.

By the late 1930s the Court was sufficiently reconstructed with new members to allow government to break out of the

15. *Carter* v. *Carter Coal Co.*, 298 U.S. 238 (1936).
16. *Morehead* v. *New York*, 298 U.S. 587 (1936).
17. *Minor* v. *Happersett*, 88 U.S. 162 (1894).

straitjacket imposed on "reform" legislation.[18] It is highly doubtful that New Deal legislation had all the salutary reforming effects that liberals claimed and conservatives feared (a matter discussed at length in Chapter Five), but it does seem that from about 1937 onward, the Court became unwilling to impose an ultraconservative, laissez-faire interpretation on legislation and gave the modern capitalist state pretty much of a free hand in servicing, manipulating and rationalizing the corporate economy.

Not only did the Court abandon its "Catch-22" use of the Tenth and Fourteenth Amendments and substantive due process; it also discarded its obstructionist role in regard to Congress' power to regulate interstate commerce. In 1935, in the *Schechter Poultry* case,[19] the Court ruled that Congress could not regulate the wages and hours of employees in a poultry slaughterhouse because, although 96 percent of the chickens came through interstate commerce, the slaughterhouse itself was not "in" interstate commerce since "the poultry had come to a permanent rest within the state" and was not part of "any further transaction in interstate commerce and was not destined for transportation to other states." Here the Court seemed to be defining *commerce* not as "trade" or "business" but exclusively as "shipment" or "transportation." If the Court's reasoning was not clear, its intent and effect were: keep Congress from regulating work hours. By 1942 the Court had retreated from this restrictive view of the commerce power so as to allow Congress to regulate any business activity within a state that might affect interstate commerce, and even nonbusiness production activities that came nowhere near interstate shipment, including the production of wheat intended for consumption on the very farm where it was planted, it being ruled in *Wickard* v. *Filburn*[20] that, while never entering the market, the wheat would "have a substantial influence on price and market conditions" and therefore on Congress' ability to control the market, boost prices and reactivate commerce.

18. Actually the Hughes Court voted down much of the New Deal program by 5–4 majorities until 1937, when Justice Roberts stopped voting with the conservatives and began voting with the liberals in the aftermath of Roosevelt's attempt to pack the Court by expanding its membership. From then on, New Deal laws challenged in the Court were usually *upheld* by 5–4 decisions. It was known as "the switch in time that saved nine." No one knows for certain what induced Roberts to change his mind; perhaps Roberts himself didn't.

19. *Schechter Poultry Corp.* v. *United States*, 295 U.S. 495 (1935).

20. 317 U.S. 111 (1942).

Nibbling Away at the First Amendment

While opposing restraints on economic power, the Court seldom opposed restraints on free speech. The same conservatism that feared experimentation in economics also feared expression of the heretical and radical ideas which espoused such changes.[21] The First Amendment says "Congress shall make no law . . . abridging the freedom of speech, or of the press." This would seem to leave little room for doubt as to the freedom of *all* speech.[22] Yet ever since the Alien and Sedition Acts of 1798, Congress and the state legislatures have found repeated occasion to pass laws penalizing the expression of heretical ideas. Over the years many who expressed opposition to government policy and to the established politico-economic system were deemed guilty of "subversion" or "sedition."[23] During the First World War, Congress passed the Espionage Act, under which almost two thousand successful prosecutions were carried out against persons, usually socialists, who expressed opposition to the war. One William Powell, who in private conversation in a relative's home voiced his dissatisfaction with U.S. policy and with the President and opined that the conflict in Europe was a rich man's war, was convicted, fined $5,000 and sentenced to twenty years in prison.[24] Far from acting as a bulwark of the Constitution against the political oppressors of the day, the federal judiciary showed itself second to none in its persecutory fervor. Under the Espionage Act and related laws, the judges sentenced some twenty-four persons to twenty years; six persons received fifteen years, and eleven got ten years; others received lighter sentences.

The Supreme Court's attitude toward the First Amendment was best expressed by Justice Holmes in the *Schenck* case. Schenck was charged with attempting to cause insubordination among U.S. military forces and obstructing recruitment, both

21. See Frankfurter's comments in *Mr. Justice Holmes*, p. 85.
22. Even the staunchest proponents of free speech allow that libel and slander might be restricted by law, although here, too, such speech when directed against public figures has been treated as protected under the First Amendment. See *New York Times Co.* v. *Sullivan*, 376 U.S. 254 (1964) and *Time, Inc.* v. *Hill* 385 U.S. 374 (1967).
23. *Sedition* is defined in Webster's Dictionary as "excitement of discontent against the government or resistance to lawful authority."
24. Hearings before a Subcommittee of the Senate Judiciary Committee, *Amnesty and Pardon for Political Prisoners* (Washington, D.C.: Government Printing Office, 1927), p. 54. See also Charles Goodell, *Political Prisoners in America* (New York: Random House, 1973), Chapter Four.

violations of the Espionage Act of 1917. What he had done was distribute a leaflet that condemned the war as a wrong against humanity perpetrated by Wall Street; it also urged people to exercise their right to oppose the draft but confined itself to advocating peaceful measures such as a petition for the repeal of the draft law. The leaflet was sent, Holmes observed, with the intention of influencing persons to obstruct the draft. The function of speech, especially of political advocacy, is to induce actions. In ordinary times such speech is amply protected by the First Amendment, but "the question in every case," Holmes reasoned, "is whether the words used are used in such circumstances and are of such a nature as to create a clear and present danger that they will bring about the substantive evils that Congress has a right to prevent."[25] Holmes never established why obstruction of the draft was a substantive evil except to assume without benefit of argument or evidence that prosecution of the war was a substantive good (the very idea that Schenck was trying to debate and challenge) and that therefore actions that hampered the war effort were evil and Congress could stop them.

Free speech, Holmes argued, "does not protect a man in falsely shouting fire in a crowded theatre and causing a panic." Maybe not, but the analogy is a farfetched one: Schenck was not in a theater but was seeking a forum in order to voice political ideas and urge peaceful nonviolent opposition to policies that Holmes treated as being above challenge. "When a nation is at war," Holmes continued, "many things that might be said in time of peace are such a hindrance to its efforts that their utterance will not be endured so long as men fight and that no Court could regard them as protected by any constitutional right." Behind the tempered prose Holmes was summoning the same argument paraded by every ruler who has sought to abrogate a people's freedom: these are not normal times; there is a grave menace within or just outside our gates; extraordinary measures are necessary and the democratic rules must be suspended for our own good and our nation's security.

At no time was it established that Schenck had actually obstructed anything. He was convicted of *conspiracy* to obstruct.[26] The allegedly wrongful *intent* of his action, regardless

25. *Schenck* v. *United States*, 249 U.S. 47 (1919); also Holmes' decision in *Debs* v. *United States*, 249 U.S. 211 (1919).

26. Under the law, "conspiracy" is said to be an agreement by two or more people to commit an unlawful act, or to commit a lawful act by unlawful means. In some cases, it has been argued by prosecutors and some judges that like-

of its success, constituted sufficient reason to declare his leaflet a clear and present danger to the survival of the Republic.

Of the Supreme Court Justices of his day, Holmes was considered one of the more liberal. And in subsequent cases he did place himself against the Court's majority and on the side of the First Amendment, earning himself the title of the Great Dissenter. Thus in *Abrams* v. *United States* he saw no "imminent" and "immediate" danger in the five young Russian aliens who distributed a leaflet opposing U.S. armed intervention in the Soviet Union in 1918.[27] Again, in the *Gitlow* case, Holmes saw no clear and present danger in the publication of a manifesto that urged revolution, but once more his colleagues differed with him. Writing for the majority, Justice Sanford explained:

A single revolutionary spark may kindle a fire that, smouldering for a time, may burst into a sweeping and destructive conflagration. It cannot be said that the State is acting arbitrarily or unreasonably when in the exercise of its judgment as to the measures necessary to protect the public peace and safety, it seeks to extinguish the spark without waiting until it has enkindled the flame or blazed into the conflagration.[28]

This fire department approach to the First Amendment enabled the Court to see smoke anywhere and anytime, not only during war but during peace, not only in some impending action but in a philosophical idea. More than once the Court would treat the allegedly pernicious quality of an idea as certain evidence of its lethal efficacy and as justification for its suppression.

This was especially true if the purveyors of the idea were thought to be organized for revolutionary purposes. In 1940 Congress passed the Smith Act, making it a felony to teach and

mindedness or working for a common purpose, even without actual planning sessions or cooperative actions, is sufficient evidence of conspiracy. Thus, some of the Chicago Eight brought to trial for conspiracy to incite riot had not met each other until the time of the trial. The conspiracy doctrine has been described by Judge Learned Hand as the prosecutor's "darling"; it can make a crime out of the most amorphous political rally and out of the thoughts in people's heads even when these are expressed openly and promulgated by lawful means. For a discussion of the conspiracy doctrine, see Jessica Mitford, *The Trial of Dr. Spock* (New York: Knopf, 1969); also Thomas I. Emerson, *The System of Freedom of Expression* (New York: Vintage, 1971).

27. *Abrams* v. *United States*, 250 U.S. 616 (1919). Although most Americans —including, I suspect, most college students—are not aware of the fact, U.S. troops invaded the Soviet Union in the early years of that nation's existence as part of a larger multinational expeditionary force that sought to overthrow the newly established communist government.

28. *Gitlow* v. *New York*, 268 U.S. 652 (1925).

advocate the violent overthrow of the government. Soon after, a group of Trotskyist socialists were convicted under the act and sent to prison. Ten years later the Justice Department indicted the top leadership of the Communist party on charges of conspiring to organize to teach and advocate the violent overthrow of the government, specifically by forming the Communist party and teaching its members the ideas of Marxism-Leninism. The defendants were convicted but took their case to the Supreme Court. In a 6–2 decision in *Dennis et al.* v. *United States*,[29] the Court upheld the Smith Act and the convictions.

A look at the Court's reasoning in this case shows how, during a time of red-baiting and witch-hunting, most Justices were able to bend the First Amendment one way or another:

(1) Chief Justice Vinson, with three other Justices concurring, reasoned that in the face of a Communist Menace the government need not wait until a putsch was about to be executed. There was no freedom under the Constitution for revolutionaries. Not only the clear and present quality of the danger but also its "gravity" and "probability" had to be taken into account.

(2) In a concurring opinion, Justice Frankfurter argued that free speech was not an absolute value but one of a number of competing values and that the priorities placed on these various interests were a question of public policy, a legislative matter best settled by the people's representatives in Congress. The Court was not a legislative body and should not place itself above the judgment of the Congress that had passed the Smith Act. Furthermore, "not every type of speech occupies the same position on the scale of values." The lewd and the libelous have no unqualified protection under the First Amendment, and certainly language that advocates violent overthrow of the government should rank low.

(3) Justice Jackson concurred, warning that the communists sought to infiltrate every institution in American life. "Through these placements in positions of power [the Communist party] seeks a leverage over society that will make up in power of coercion what it lacks in power of persuasion. The Communists have no scruples against sabotage, terrorism, assassination or

29. 341 U.S. 494 (1951). Only eight Justices participated; the ninth, Tom Clark, excused himself from the decision because he had been Attorney General at the time the case was being handled by the Justice Department. Clark participated in subsequent cases of a similar nature, of course, and took the side of the prosecution.

mob disorder. . . ." Clear and present danger was too ambiguous a rule to apply; suffice it to say that communists were part of a well-organized, nationwide conspiracy directed toward unlawful ends that enjoyed no protection under the Constitution.

(4) Dissenting from the majority view was Justice Black, who observed that the petitioners had not been charged with any overt acts nor even with saying anything about violent revolution. The indictment was that they had conspired to organize the Communist party and at some future time publish things which would teach and advocate violent revolution. A restriction at the present time was nothing but prior censorship and a violation of the First Amendment. In any case, the First Amendment did not permit us to sustain laws suppressing free speech on the basis of Congress' or our own notion of "reasonableness" but was designed to protect those very forms of expression we might find heretical. Safe and orthodox views rarely needed the protection of the Constitution.

(5) Also dissenting was Justice Douglas, who reminded the Court that no evidence was introduced at the Dennis trial demonstrating that the petitioners were teaching or even planning to teach the methods of terror and violence. What was being condemned was the teaching of the classic works of Marx, Engels and Lenin. If communist beliefs were to be defeated, let it be in the market place of ideas. The attack should be against the ideas and not against those who hold them. "Full and free discussion," Douglas concluded, "even of the ideas we hate encourages the testing of our own prejudices and preconceptions."

Six years after Dennis and the other top leaders of the Communist party were jailed, fourteen more party leaders were indicted and convicted under the same Smith Act. This time a majority of the Court made a distinction between "advocacy of abstract doctrine and advocacy directed at promoting unlawful action" and decided that the Smith Act had intended to outlaw only the latter.[30] Thus, without declaring the act unconstitutional, the Court overthrew the conviction, arguing that the law had not been applied correctly. Justice Black, concurring in the decision, did enter a "dissent in part," along with Justice Douglas, expressing the opinion that the Smith Act itself should be declared a violation of the First Amendment. "I believe," Black stated unequivocally, "that the First Amendment forbids Congress to

30. *Yates et al.* v. *United States*, 354 U.S. 298 (1957).

punish people for talking about public affairs, whether or not such discussion incites to action, legal or illegal."

Needless to say, Black's postulate remains the minority opinion among the directors, trustees and owners of our political and private institutions and even among many who fancy themselves to be civil libertarians. These latter argue that freedom of speech does not include the right to advocate revolution and dictatorship. Revolutionaries should not be allowed to take advantage of the very liberties they seek to destroy. Revolutionary advocacy constitutes an abuse of freedom by urging us to violate the democratic rules of the game.[31] Hence, the argument goes, in order to preserve our political freedom, we may find it necessary to deprive some people of theirs. Several rejoinders might be made in regard to this position.

First, as a point of historical fact, the threat of revolution in the United States has never been as real or harmful to "our liberties" as the measures allegedly taken to protect us from revolutionary ideas. History repeatedly demonstrates the expansive quality of repression: first, revolutionary advocacy is suppressed, then proponents of certain doctrines and theories, then "inciting" words, then "irresponsible" news reports and public utterances that are not "balanced" or "constructive," then any kind of dissent which those in power might find intolerable.

Second, the suppression is conducted by political elites who, in protecting us from what they consider "harmful" thoughts, deprive us of the opportunity of hearing and debating revolutionary advocates and make up our minds for us. An exchange is forbidden because the advocate has been silenced, jailed or whatever.[32]

Third, it is a debatable point whether socialist, communist and other radical revolutionaries are dedicated to the destruction of freedom. Most revolutionaries would argue that freedom is one of the things lacking in the *present* society. The millions who are crushed by poverty and hunger and the millions more who are stupified by the business-owned mass media are hardly as

31. For samples of this kind of thinking see the Vinson and Jackson opinions in the *Dennis* case briefly summarized above; also Sidney Hook, *Political Power and Personal Freedom* (New York: Criterion Books, 1959), and Frederick Bernays Wiener, " 'Freedom for the Thought That We Hate': Is It a Principle of the Constitution?" *American Bar Association Journal*, 37, March 1951.

32. The classic statement on this position is John Stuart Mill, *On Liberty*, published more than a century ago. See also Alexander Meiklejohn, *Free Speech and Its Relation to Self-Government* (New York: Harper and Brothers, 1948).

free as we might think. Revolutionaries argue that the construct-
ing of new social alternatives and new modes of communal
organization brings an *increase* in freedom, including freedom
from the tyranny of poverty and hunger, freedom to exercise
more power in making the decisions that govern one's work
conditions, education, community and life, freedom to experiment with new forms of social organization and production.
Admittedly some freedoms enjoyed today would be lost in a
revolutionary society—for instance, the freedom to exploit other
people and get rich off their labor, the freedom to squander
human and natural resources and treat the environment as a
sceptic tank, the freedom to monopolize information and use
technical and professional skills primarily for personal gain and
the freedom to exercise unaccountable, autocratic power. In
many countries throughout the world, successful social revolutionary movements have brought a net increase in the
freedom of individuals, revolutionaries point out, by advancing
the conditions necessary for the preservation of health and
human life, by providing jobs and education for the unemployed
and illiterate, by using economic resources for social development rather than for private corporate profit and by overthrowing
repressive reactionary regimes and ending foreign exploitation
and involving large sectors of the populace in the task of socialist
reconstruction. Revolutions have extended a number of real
freedoms without destroying those that never existed for the
common people. The repression in America is here and now,
while the hope for a better life lies ahead, the revolutionary
would argue. The argument can be debated, but not if it is
suppressed.

To repeat: the Supreme Court's record as a defender of our
political liberties is less than inspirational. Far from being a
bulwark against government suppression, it has usually gone
along with attempts by Congress and the states to strangle radical
dissent, even formulating casuistic doctrines like "clear and
present danger" to help convince us that the First Amendment
does not mean what it says. When the Southern states imposed
the tyranny of racial segregation on Black people and other
non-Whites after Emancipation, the Court, in *Plessy* v. *Ferguson*,
obligingly formulated the doctrine of "separate but equal" to
give constitutional justification to segregation.[33] And when the
government decided to uproot 112,000 law-abiding Japanese

33. 163 U.S. 537 (1896).

Americans from the West Coast at the onset of World War II, forcing them to relinquish their homes, businesses, farms and other possessions and herding them into concentration camps for the duration of the war on the incredible notion that they might harbor sympathies for the Japanese Imperial government and thus pose a threat to our West Coast defenses, the Supreme Court found that, given the exigencies of war, the government was acting within the limits of the Constitution.[34]

The Court Today

The Supreme Court's record in the area of personal liberties is gravely wanting, yet it is not totally devoid of merit. "Let us give the Court its due; it is little enough," Robert Dahl reminds us.[35] Over the years the Court has extended the protections of the First Amendment and other portions of the Bill of Rights to cover not only the federal government but state governments (via the Fourteenth Amendment). Attempts by the states to censor publications,[36] deny individuals the right to peaceful assembly[37] and weaken the separation between church and state[38] were occasionally overturned. During the 1960s, the Court under Chief Justice Earl Warren took some important steps to strengthen the defendant's rights in criminal justice proceedings. In a 1963 decision the Court held that "the right of an indigent defendant in a [state] criminal trial to have the assistance of counsel is a fundamental right essential to a fair trial and . . . conviction without the assistance of counsel violated the Four-

34. *Hirabayashi* v. *United States*, 320 U.S. 81 (1943), *Korematshu* v. *United States*, 323 U.S. 214 (1944) and *Ex parte Endo*, 323 U.S. 283 (1944). These decisions were rendered by the "liberal" Stone Court. As with many other shady aspects of American history, students are taught little about this. Implicit in the Japanese relocation was the assumption that the *race* likeness between Japanese here and in Japan would lead to treachery and disloyalty. The same racist reasoning was not, of course, applied to White "enemy ethnics" like the German-Americans and Italian-Americans, who were not treated as a fifth column or sent to concentration camps although some of them were quite sympathetic to the exploits of Hitler and Mussolini. For a long time the Japanese-Americans had been an object of resentment because of their successful farming and social mobility on the West Coast. The relocation left many of them destitute, and almost all their land was grabbed by Whites.

35. Robert A. Dahl, "Decision-Making in a Democracy: The Role of the Supreme Court as a National Policy-Maker," *Journal of Public Law*, 6, no. 2, 1958, p. 292.

36. *Near* v. *Minnesota*, 283 U.S. 697 (1931).

37. *DeJonge* v. *Oregon*, 299 U.S. 353 (1937).

38. *McCollum* v. *Board of Education*, 333 U.S. 203 (1948).

teenth Amendment."[39] In the *Escobedo* and *Miranda* cases the defendant's right to counsel was extended to include the onset of interrogation, one purpose being to diminish the likelihood of forced confessions of dubious validity.[40]

The malapportionment and "rotten boroughs" of many state and congressional legislative districts were struck down when the Warren Court ruled that district lines had to be redrawn in accordance with population distribution. In some states less than a third of the population elected more than half the legislators. Voters in the overpopulated districts, the Court reasoned, were being denied equal protection under the law and, in effect, losing their right to suffrage because of the "debasement" and "dilution" of their votes.[41] The Court also gave every indication of taking the disestablishment clause in the First Amendment seriously by ruling that prayers in the public school were a violation of separation of church and state.[42]

The Warren Court handed down a number of decisions aimed at abolishing segregation in public facilities, transportation and education. The most widely celebrated was that in *Brown* v. *Board of Education*,[43] which unanimously ruled that "separate educational facilities are inherently unequal" because of the inescapable imputation of inferiority cast upon the segregated minority group, an imputation that is all the greater when it has the sanction of law. This decision overruled the "separate but equal" doctrine enunciated in 1896 in the *Plessy* case.[44]

The direction the Court takes depends in part on the political composition of its majority. By 1973, refortified with four Nixon-appointed Justices, the Court under Chief Justice

39. See *Gideon* v. *Wainwright*, 372 U.S. 335 (1963).

40. *Escobedo* v. *Illinois*, 378 U.S. 478 (1964) and *Miranda* v. *Arizona*, 384 U.S. 436 (1966).

41. See *Baker* v. *Carr*, 369 U.S. 186 (1962) and *Reynolds* v. *Sims*, 377 U.S. 533 (1964). A similar decision was made in regard to congressional districts in *Wesberry* v. *Sanders*, 376 U.S. 1 (1964). It was anticipated that reapportionment would have all sorts of liberalizing effects on both state legislatures and Congress by shifting power from the overrepresented conservative rural areas to the supposedly more progressive and now more numerous urban and suburban districts. However, in the decade since the reapportionment decisions, there seems to have been no discernible change in the conservative, business-oriented propensities of state and national legislatures and their susceptibilities to large corporate interests. See *supra*, Chapters 12 and 13.

42. See *Engels* v. *Vitale*, 370 U.S. 421 (1962), and *School District of Abington* v. *Schempp*, 374 U.S. 203 (1963). The First Amendment reads: "Congress shall make no law respecting an establishment of religion, or prohibiting the free exercise thereof."

43. 347 U.S. 483 (1954).

44. *Plessy* v. *Ferguson* 163 U.S. 537 (1896).

Burger took a decidedly conservative turn. In the area of criminal justice, for instance, the Burger Court decided that it was no longer necessary to have a unanimous jury verdict for conviction—a decision that, in effect, abolished the need for having a jury agree that the prosecution has proven guilt beyond a reasonable doubt.[45] In another decision the Burger Court ruled that police may stop and frisk people almost at their own discretion, thus making it easier for them to intimidate dissenters, demonstrators, Blacks and other "troublesome" elements.[46] The Court has handed down decisions weakening the right against self-incrimination and denying reporters a right to confidential news sources.[47] In *Laird* v. *Tatum*,[48] the Burger Court was asked to rule on the constitutionality of Army surveillance of lawful civilian political activities and to oversee the destruction of derogatory files and dossiers on civilians who were guilty of no crime other than being politically active. The Court dismissed the case by a 5–4 vote, refusing to impose any limitation on government surveillance. The passionate dissent by Justice Douglas in the *Laird* case is worth quoting in part:

This case is a cancer in our body politic. . . . Army surveillance, like Army regimentation, is at war with the principles of the First Amendment. Those who already walk submissively will say there is no cause for alarm. But submissiveness is not our heritage. . . . The Bill of Rights was designed to keep agents of Government and official eavesdroppers away from assemblies of people. The aim was to allow men to be free and independent and to assert their rights against Government.

The Burger Court's dedication to inequality was manifested with exceptional clarity in its decision to prevent school districts with low property values from having as much money spent on education as those with higher property values. In many instances districts with high local expenditures receive high matching funds from the state governments, and poor districts receive proportionately less, thus *increasing* rather than diminishing inequalities. The Court decided, with Justice Powell writing the decision, that "a state may constitutionally vary the quality of education which it offers its children in accordance

45. *Johnson* v. *Louisiana*, 32 L. Ed. 2d 152 (1972) and *Apodaca* v. *Oregon*, 32 L. Ed. 2d 184 (1972).
46. In this instance, *Adams* v. *Williams*, the Burger Court was adhering to a policy already accepted by the Warren Court in *Terry* v. *Ohio*, 392 U.S. 1 (1968).
47. *United States* v. *Caldwell*, 33 L. Ed. 2d 626 (1972).
48. 408 U.S. 1 (1972).

with the amount of taxable wealth located within the school districts within which they reside.[49] The equal-protection clause of the Constitution did not require "absolute equality or precisely equal advantages." In fact, the Court seemed to be saying, there could be any degree of inequality short of absolute deprivation; as long as the Chicano children had *some* kind of school to go to, this would satisfy the Court's remarkably permissive reading of the equal-protection clause of the Fourteenth Amendment. The decision hardly lived up to the principles enunciated in the 1954 *Brown* case, as Justice Marshall pointed out in a dissent.

Also in keeping with its support of social inequality and its defense of privilege, the Burger Court decided that the principle of "one-man, one-vote" need not be observed in elections for special-purpose governmental bodies like water districts. Since the expenses of the water district are met by the landowners, the majority reasoned, it was not "unfair or inequitable to repose the franchise in landowners but not residents."[50] In his dissent Justice Douglas pointed out that four corporations owned nearly 85 percent of the 193,000 acres in the district while 189 landowners had less than 3 percent. Under weighted voting, "the corporate voter is put in the saddle." Small owners, tenant farmers and sharecroppers all should have a say, he insisted, because irrigation, water storage, water usage and flood control "implicate the entire community." The ballot, he pointed out in a companion case, is restricted to the wealthy few who can violate "our environmental ethics" and in other ways do their will.[51] In its own way, the Burger Court seemed to be holding true to the spirit of the Founding Fathers: those who own the land shall govern it.

In two other cases, the Court held, in 5–4 decisions, that indigents who could not afford court fees had no right to their day in court.[52] While not directly overruling certain Warren Court decisions, the Burger Court sometimes did its best to erode them. Finding no way to contravene the constitutionality of the earlier reapportionment cases, for instance, the Burger Court

49. *San Antonio Independent School District* v. *Rodriguez*, 36 L. Ed. 2d 16 (1973).

50. *Salyer Land Co.* v. *Tulare Lake Basin Water Storage District*, 35 L. Ed. 2d 659 (1973).

51. *Associated Enterprise, Inc.* v. *Toltec Watershed Improvement District*, 35 L. Ed. 2d 675 (1973).

52. *Ortwein* v. *Schwab*, 35 L. Ed. 2d 572 (1973). Also *United States* v. *Kraus*, 34 L. Ed. 2d 626 (1973).

decided that the "one-man, one-vote" rule should be applied less rigorously to the state legislative districts than to congressional districts. In allowing for a population deviation as wide as 16.4 percent, the Court reasoned that state districts have indigenous qualities that ought sometimes to be preserved.[53]

More recently the Burger Court reintroduced censorship of pornography in theaters and movies and in magazines and other publications, defining pornography as anything that (a) appeals as a whole to the "prurient interests" of the average person, (b) portrays "sexual conduct in a patently offensive way" while lacking "serious literary, artistic, political or scientific value," and (c) offends the "contemporary community standards" of various locales.[54] As with so many Supreme Court decisions, the explicit criteria offered by the Justices for the purpose of interpreting the Constitution raised more questions than they answered. For instance, what element of the community represents "community standards"—the blue-nosed Puritan or the blue-movie buff? How do we know when "prurient interests" are aroused and in what "average" person? If average people are so pleasantly aroused, who are the exceptional people left to judge the movie or book as "patently offensive"? And what determines whether the literary or artistic value of a work is "serious" or not? What the Court may have succeeded in doing in the pornography case is keep itself busy with a flood of new litigation for the next ten years. As Michigan's Attorney General Frank Kelley complained: "[The Court's decision] sets us back in the dark ages. Now prosecuting attorneys in every county and state will be grandstanding and every jury in every little community will have a crack at each new book, play and movie."[55]

Influence of the Court

It is easier to describe the blatantly political role played by the Court than to measure its actual political influence. But a few rough generalizations can be drawn. First, as a nonelective branch staffed by men of elitist legal, corporate and political background, the Court has exercised a generally conservative influence. On matters of social welfare legislation, the Court wielded a strategic minority veto for about seventy years. Laws

53. *Mahan* v. *Howell*, 35 L. Ed. 2d 320 (1973).
54. *New York Times*, June 23, 1973.
55. *Ibid*.

on workmen's compensation, child labor, unionization and other reform legislation of a kind that had been enacted in European countries a generation before were delayed for from ten to twenty-five years by the High Court. It prevented Congress from instituting income taxes, a decision that took eighteen years and a constitutional amendment to circumvent.[56]

But whatever our complaints about the "nine old men," we should remember that the Court's ability to impose its will on the nation is far from boundless. Presidents usually get the opportunity to appoint two or more members to the Court and thus exert an influence over its makeup.[57] Furthermore, the Court cannot make rulings at will but must wait until a case is brought to it either on appeal from a lower court or, far less frequently, as a case of original jurisdiction. And the Court agrees to hear only a small portion of the cases on its docket, thus leaving the final word to the lower courts in most instances.

Political currents and changing climates of opinion do not leave the Justices untouched. Members of the Court have been aware that the efficacy of their decisions depends on the willingness of other agencies of government to carry them out. A Court that runs too glaringly against the tide risks being attacked, as was the Warren Court by conservatives in Congress and among the public. Its appellate jurisdiction might be circumscribed by Congress, its decisions ignored, and the Court as an institution subjected to ridicule and hostility. Some members of the Court such as Justices Harlan and Frankfurter have been so impressed by the limitations of the Court's power and its vulnerability to the other branches as to counsel a doctrine of "judicial restraint," especially when the Court has tried to move innovatively.[58]

The Court is always operating in a·climate of opinion shaped by political forces larger than itself. Its willingness to depart from the casuistry of *Plessy* v. *Ferguson* and take the Fourteenth Amendment seriously in *Brown* v. *Board of Education* depended in part on the changing climate of opinion concerning race relations and segregation between 1896 and 1954. At the same time the Court is not purely a dependent variable. That it had to accept segregation for more than half a century before upholding the Constitution is not certain. The arguments used

56. *Pollock* v. *Farmers' Loan & Trust Co.*, 157 U.S. H29 (1895).
57. Dahl, "Decision-Making in a Democracy," p. 285.
58. For instance, see the dissents by Frankfurter and Harlan respectively in the apportionment cases: *Baker* v. *Carr*, 369 U.S. 186 (1962) and *Reynolds* v. *Sims*, 377 U.S. 533 (1964).

on the eve of the *Brown* decision—that the Court should not push people, that hearts and minds had to change first, that you can't legislate morality, and that there would be vehement and violent opposition—were the same arguments used during the days of the *Plessy* case. In fact there was vehement and often violent opposition to the *Brown* decision. But there also was an acceleration of opinion in support of the Court's ruling, in part activated by that very ruling. (Just as there was an increase in *segregationist* practices after the *Plessy* case, from 1896 to 1914, probably in part encouraged by *Plessy* and decisions like it.) Hence, some of the Court's decisions have an important feedback effect. By playing a crucial role in defining what is legitimate and constitutional, the Court gives encouraging cues to large sectors of the public. Unable to pass a civil rights act for seventy years, the Congress enacted three in the decade after the *Brown* case. And Blacks throughout the nation pressed harder in an attempt to make desegregation a reality. Organizing efforts for civil rights increased in both the North and the South, along with "Freedom Riders," sit-ins and mass demonstrations. The political consciousness of a generation was joined, and who is to say that the Warren Court did not play a part in that?

The Supreme Court, then, probably has a real effect on political consciousness and public policy, albeit in limited ways and for limited durations. It is debatable whether the Supreme Court has deserved the kind of calumny heaped upon it, but it certainly has rarely deserved the adulation that some give it. The Court, like the very laws and Constitution it interprets, is limited to a frame of reference that not only accepts the existing class and property relations as given but defends them as a fundamental right ("life, liberty, and property"). To the extent that the Court has promoted social change, it has been within the limits of the existing politico-economic class structure.

Democracy
for the Few

17 THE UNITED STATES IS SAID TO BE A
pluralistic society, and indeed a glance at
the social map of this country reveals a vast
agglomeration of regional, occupational and
ethnic groups and state, local and national
governing agencies. If by pluralism we mean
this multiplicity of private and public groups,
then the United States is pluralistic. But then
so is any modern society of size and complexity, including allegedly "totalitarian" ones like
the Soviet Union with its multiplicity of regional, occupational and ethnic groups and its
party, administrative, industrial and military
factions and interests all jostling for position
and power.[1]

But the proponents of pluralism, when
applying the concept to the United States,
presume to be saying something about how
power is distributed and how *democracy*
works. Specifically, pluralism means that (a)
power is shared among representative sectors
of the population; (b) the shaping of public
policy involves inputs from a wide range of
competing social groups; (c) no one group
enjoys permanent dominance or suffers permanent defeat; and (d) the distribution of ben-

1. See, for instance, Donald R. Kelley, "Interest Groups
in the USSR: The Impact of Political Sensitivity on Group
Influence," *Journal of Politics*, 34, August 1972, pp.
860–888; also H. Gordon Skilling and Franklyn Griffiths
(eds.), *Interest Groups in Soviet Politics* (Princeton, N.J.:
Princeton University Press, 1971). By the simple definition of pluralism offered above, even Nazi Germany might
qualify as pluralistic. The Nazi state was a loose, often
chaotic composite of fiercely competing groups. See
Heinz Höne, *The Order of the Death's Head* (New York:
Coward, McCann, and Geoghegan, 1970).

efits is roughly equitable or certainly not consistently exploitative. Thus Ralf Dahrendorf writes: "Instead of a battlefield, the scene of group conflict has become a kind of market in which relatively autonomous forces contend according to certain rules of the game, by virtue of which nobody is a permanent winner or loser."[2] If there are elites in our society, the pluralists say, they are numerous and specialized, and they are checked in their demands by other elites. No group can press its advantages "too far" and any group that is interested in an issue can find a way within the political system to make its influence felt.[3] Business elites have the capacity to utilize the services of the government to further their own interests, but, the pluralists argue, such interests are themselves varied and often conflicting. The government does many different things for many different people; it is not controlled by a monolithic corporate elite that gets what it wants on every question. Government stands above any one particular influence but responds to many.[4]

Pluralism for the Few

The evidence offered in the preceding chapters leaves us little reason to conclude that the United States is a "pluralistic democracy," as conceived by the pluralists. To summarize and expand upon some of the points previously made:

(1) Public policies, whether formulated by conservatives or by liberals, Republicans or Democrats, fairly consistently favor the large corporate interests at a substantial cost to many millions of workers, small farmers, small producers, consumers, taxpayers, low-income people, urban slum dwellers, indigent el-

2. Ralf Dahrendorf, *Class and Class Conflict in Industrial Society* (Stanford, Calif.: Stanford University Press, 1959), p. 67.

3. One of the earliest pluralist statements is in Earl Latham, *The Group Basis of Politics* (Ithaca: Cornell University Press, 1952). See also Arnold M. Rose, *The Power Structure* (New York: Oxford University Press, 1967); Robert Dahl, *Who Governs?* (New Haven: Yale University Press, 1961); Edward Banfield, *Political Influence* (New York: Free Press, 1961); Nelson Polsby, *Community Power and Political Theory* (New Haven: Yale University Press, 1963). The criticisms of pluralism are many: the best collection of critiques can be found in Charles A. McCoy and John Playford (eds.), *Apolitical Politics* (New York: Crowell, 1967); see also Marvin Surkin and Alan Wolfe (eds.), *An End to Political Science: The Caucus Papers* (New York: Basic Books, 1970).

4. Much of the literature in political science treats the President as someone who grapples with everyone else's interests but has none of his own: e.g., Richard E. Neustadt, *Presidential Power* (New York: John Wiley and Sons, 1960).

derly and rural poor. Those few benefits distributed to lower-income groups have proven gravely inadequate to their needs and have failed to reach millions who might qualify for assistance. Government efforts in crucial areas of social need have rarely fulfilled even the minimal expectations of reform-minded advocates. There are more people living in poverty today than there were ten years ago, more substandard housing, more environmental pollution and devastation, more deficiencies in our schools, hospitals and systems of public transportation, more military dictatorships throughout the world feeding on the largesse and power of the Pentagon, more people—from Iran to Greece to the Philippines to Brazil to Mississippi—suffering the social oppression of an American-backed status quo, more unearned and corrupt profits going to the giant corporations, more glut in the private commodity market and more scarcity and want in public services.

(2) To think of government as nothing more than a broker or referee amidst a vast array of competing groups (these groups presumably representing all the important and "countervailing" interests of the populace) is to forget that government best serves those who can best serve themselves. That is not to say that political leaders are indifferent to popular sentiments. When those sentiments are aroused to a certain intensity, leaders will respond, either by making minor concessions or by evoking images of change and democratic responsiveness that are vivid in appearance though usually lacking in substance. Leaders are always "responding" to the public, but so often it is with distracting irrelevancies, dilatory and discouraging tactics, facile reassurances, unfulfilled promises, outright lies or token programs that offer nothing more than a cosmetic application to a deep social problem. The overall performance of our political system even in times of so-called social reform might best be characterized as giving *symbolic* allocations to public sentiment and *substantive* allocations to powerful private interests.

Indeed, one might better think of ours as a dual political system. First, there is the symbolic political system centering around electoral and representative activities including party conflicts, voter turnout, political personalities, public pronouncements, official role-playing and certain ambiguous presentations of some of the public issues which bestir Presidents, governors, mayors and their respective legislatures. Then there is the substantive political system, involving multibillion-dollar contracts, tax write-offs, protections, rebates, grants, loss compensations, subsidies, leases, giveaways and the whole vast process of budgeting, legislating, advising, regulating, protecting and servicing major producer interests, now bending or ignoring the law on behalf of the powerful, now applying it with full punitive vigor against heretics and "troublemakers." The symbolic system is highly visible, taught in the schools, dissected by academicians, gossiped about by newsmen. The substantive system is seldom heard of or accounted for.

(3) Far from the fluid interplay envisioned by the pluralists, the political efficacy of groups and individuals is largely determined by the resources of power available to them, of which wealth is the most crucial. Not everyone with money chooses to use it for the purpose of exerting political influence, and not everyone with money need bother to do so. But when they so desire, those who control the wealth of society enjoy a persistent and pervasive political advantage. Instead of being just another of many interests in the influence system, corporate business occupies a particularly strategic position. Because business controls the very economy of the nation, government perforce enters into a unique and intimate relationship with it. The health of the capitalist economy is treated by policy-makers as a necessary condition for the health of the nation, and since it happens that the economy is in the hands of big companies, then presumably government's service to the public is best accomplished by service to these companies. The goals of business (rapid growth, high profits and secure markets) become the goals of government, and the "national interest" becomes identified with the dominant propertied interests. Since policy-makers must operate in, through, and with the private economy, it is not long before they are operating *for* it.

(4) The pluralists make much of the fact that wealthy interests do not always operate with clear and deliberate purpose.[5] To be sure, elites, like everyone else, make mistakes and suffer confusions as to what might be the most advantageous tactics in any particular situation. But if they are not omniscient and infallible, neither are they habitual laggards and imbeciles. If they do not always calculate rationally in the pursuit of their class interests, they do so often and successfully enough.

It is also true that the business community is not monolithic and unanimous on all issues. The socialist economist Paul

5. Dahl, *Who Governs?*, p. 272. Also see Robert A. Dahl, *Modern Political Analysis* (Englewood Cliffs, N.J.: Prentice-Hall, 1970).

Sweezy has pointed out some of the fissures within the business world: there are regional differences (Eastern versus Southwestern capital), ideological ones (reactionary versus liberal capitalism) and corporate ones (Ford versus General Motors)—all of which add an element of conflict and indeterminacy to economic and political policies. But these are the conflicts of haves versus haves and they seldom include the interests of the unorganized public. Nor, as Sweezy reminds us, should we exaggerate the depths of these divisions:

Capitalists can and do fight among themselves to further individual or group interests, and they differ over the best way of coping with the problems which arise from their class position; but overshadowing all these divisions is their common interest in preserving and strengthening a system which guarantees their wealth and privileges. In the event of a real threat to the system, there are no longer class differences—only class traitors, and they are few and far between.[6]

(5) If American government is not ruled by one cohesive, conspiratorial elite, there is ample evidence of continual collusion between various corporate and governmental elites in every area of the political economy. Though there is no one grand power elite, there are many fairly large ones. And these elites do not often restrain each other by competition. A look at the politico-economic system shows that many of the stronger ones tend to predominate in their particular spheres of activity more or less unmolested by other elites and unchecked by government.[7] The Republican political scientist Andrew Hacker notes:

Our ideology permits us to rest happy in the thought that the Anti-Trust Division of the Justice Department could, if it so desired, "break up" General Dynamics or International Business Machines into congeries of separate companies. The fact of power, however, is that this has not, cannot, and will not be done because government is weaker than the corporate institutions purportedly subordinate to it. This is the politics of capitalism. It is not at all expressive of a conspiracy but rather a harmony of political forms and economic interests on a plane determined by the ongoing needs of corporate institutions.[8]

6. Paul Sweezy, *The Present as History* (New York: Monthly Review Press, 1970). p. 138.
7. See Peter Bachrach, *The Theory of Democratic Elitism* (Boston: Little, Brown, 1967), p. 37.
8. Andrew Hacker (ed.), *The Corporation Take-Over* (New York: 1965), pp. 10–11.

As we have seen, corporations are not merely beyond the reach of government; they incorporate public authority in their own undertakings. Government does play a crucial role in restraining and redirecting sectors of the corporate economy that tend to become disruptive of the system as a whole: hence Teddy Roosevelt's occasional trust-busting, Franklin Roosevelt's opposition to holding companies, and John Kennedy's attempt to force steel companies to hold back their prices. But such actions are usually limited in their range and are induced by a desire to protect the business economy *in toto*. Only in appearance is government a neutral mediator or defender of the public interest.

Most elitist conflicts, we noted, are resolved not by compromise but by log rolling and involve more *collusion* than competition. These mutually satisfying arrangements among "competitors" rather consistently leave out the interests of broad, unorganized sectors of the public. The demands of have-nots may be heard occasionally as a clamor outside the gate, and now and then some scant morsels may be tossed to the unfortunates—especially if private suppliers can make money on it. But generally speaking, whether in times of conservative retrenchment or "progressive change," pluralist interest-group politics engages the interests of extremely limited portions of the population and operates within a field of political consensus that is largely shaped by the overall interests of corporate capitalism.

In addition, it is worth repeating: *the diffusion of power does not necessarily mean the democratization of power.* When decision-making power is parceled out, it goes to special public-private interest groups—quasi-autonomous, entrenched minorities that use public authority for unaccountable private purposes of low visibility. The fragmentation of power is the pocketing of power, a way of insulating portions of the political process from the tides of popular sentiments. This purpose was embodied in the constitutional structure by the Founding Fathers and has been perpetuated by government decision-making arrangements ever since 1787.

The Myth of the Mixed Economy

The continued growth of government activity in the economy has led some observers to the mistaken notion that we are gradually moving toward a "post-capitalist" society, one that is neither capitalist nor socialist but a "mixed economy."[9] This notion avoids any precise consideration of what government does and whom it benefits when mixing itself with the economy. Gabriel Kolko takes critical note of those who cannot differentiate between federal regulation *of* business and federal regulation *for* business:

The fetish of government regulation of the economy as a positive social good was one that sidetracked a substantial portion of European socialism ... and was not unique to the American experience. Such axiomatic and simplistic assumptions of what federal regulation would bring did not take into account problems of democratic control and participation, and in effect assumed that the power of government was neutral and socially beneficent. [10]

Both liberal and conservative theorists have treated the increasingly socialized *costs* of the public sector as evidence of increasingly socialized benefits, with the liberals generally approving and some conservatives disapproving of this trend.[11] In reality, government involvement in the economy represents not a growth in socialism (as that term is normally understood by socialists) but a growth in state-supported capitalism, *not the communization of private wealth but the privatization of the commonwealth.* This development has brought a great deal of government planning, but it is not of the kind intended by socialism, which emphasizes the subordination of private profit and the reallocation of resources for new social priorities. As several English socialists have pointed out, in criticism of the policies of the British Labour party:

Planning now means better forecasting, better coordination of investment and expansion decisions, a more purposeful control over demand. This enables the more technologically equipped and organized units in

9. See, for instance, Dahrendorf, *Class and Class Conflict in Industrial Society.*
10. Gabriel Kolko, *The Triumph of Conservatism* (Chicago: Quadrangle Books, 1967), p. 286.
11. For one among many examples of this, note the exchange between conservative Louis Hacker and liberals Charles Lindblom and Max Lerner on the desirability of the "welfare state": all three assume that the growth in government has been the result of social services to the needy and increased regulation of business. Hacker finds this "welfare state" undesirable while Lindblom and Lerner think it is good. None of them questions whether it is really happening. See their comments in the *American Scholar*, 19, Autumn 1950, pp. 481–491, reprinted in Hillman Bishop and Samuel Hendel (eds.), *Basic Issues of American Democracy*, 5th ed. (New York: Appleton-Century-Crofts, 1965).

the private sector to pursue their goals more efficiently, more "rationally." It also means more control over unions and over labor's power to bargain freely about wages. This involves another important transition. For in the course of this rationalization of capitalism, the gap between private industry and the State is narrowed.[12]

The gap narrows not only because of government's service to business but because of business' inescapable "service" to government. *Given the near monopoly they enjoy over society's productive capacity, the giant corporations remain the sole conduit for most public expenditures.* Whether it be for schools or school lunches, sewers or space ships, submarines or airplanes, harbors or highways, government relies almost exclusively on private contractors and suppliers.

These suppliers may be heavily subsidized or entirely funded from the public treasure, as seems true of some aeronautics firms, but they remain "private" in that they are privately incorporated and a profit—usually a most generous risk-free one —accrues to them for whatever services they perform. The government is not a *producer* in competition with business, such rivalry not being appreciated in a capitalist economy, but a titanic *purchaser* or *consumer* of business products. Bound by this consumer role, government, as it becomes more active, tends to become more dependent on business. This can be seen clearly during wars and cold wars, when intensified public spending brings greater governmental reliance on the organized centers of private industry. While some people bemoan the growth of government "interference" in business affairs, the reality is that big-business management has moved more deeply into public affairs with each new national mobilization, keeping public spending closely in line with industry's own profit interests.[13]

The commitment by government to mobilizing its industrial efforts primarily through private conduits in ways that do not compete with, and only serve to bolster, the private profit system

12. Stuart Hall, Raymond Williams and Edward Thompson, "The May Day Manifesto," excerpted in Carl Oglesby (ed.), *The New Left Reader* (New York: Grove Press, 1969), p. 115.

13. See Walter LaFeber, *The New Empire: An Interpretation of American Expansion, 1860–1898* (Ithaca, N.Y.: Cornell University Press, 1963) for evidence of the growing interdependence of government and business as each expanded its activities. Also see Paul Koistinen, "The 'Industrial-Military Complex' in Historical Perspective: The Inter War Years," in Irwin Unger (ed.), *Beyond Liberalism: The New Left Views American History* (Waltham, Mass.: Xerox College Publishing, 1971), pp. 227–239; and David Horowitz (ed.), *Corporations and the Cold War* (New York: Monthly Review Press, 1969).

marks one of the key differences between socialism and state-supported capitalism. Whether the difference is thought to be desirable or not, it first should be understood. The "mixed economy" as found in the United States has very little to do with socialism. Increases in spending may represent a growth in the public sector of the economy but not in the *publicly owned* sector. The distinction between the "public" and "private," then, is a misleading one, since *the growth of the public sector represents little more than an increase in the risk-free, high-profit market of the private sector.* Sometimes the government will exercise direct ownership of a particular service, either to assist private industry—as with certain port facilities and technological research and training institutions—or to perform services which private capital no longer finds it profitable to provide—as with nationalized coal mines in Great Britain or the bus and subway lines in many American cities. Private capital relinquishes its franchise and moves on to greener fields while the ownership and the losses are both passed on to the public.

There is the anticipation, common among some radical theorists, that as the problems of the economy deepen, modern capitalism will succumb to its own internal contradictions; as the economic "substructure" gives way, the "superstructure" of the capitalist state will be carried down with it and the opportunity for a humane, anti-imperialist, democratic, socialist society will be at hand. One difficulty with this position is that it underestimates the extent to which the political system can act with independent effect to preserve the capitalist class. The political system is more than a front for the economic interests it serves; it is the single most important force that corporate America has at its command. The power to use the police and the military, the power of eminent domain, the power to tax, spend and legislate, to use public funds for private profit, the power of limitless credit, the power to mobilize highly emotive symbols of loyalty and legitimacy—such resources of the state give corporate America a durability it could never provide for itself through the economy alone. The resilience of capitalism cannot be measured in isolated economic terms. Behind the corporation there stands the organized power of the state; "the stability and future of the economy is grounded, in the last analysis, on the power of the state to act to preserve it."[14] To maintain themselves, the corporations can call on the resources of the state to rationalize and

14. Kolko, *The Triumph of Conservatism*, p. 302.

subsidize their performance, maintain their profit levels, socialize costs by taxing the many and keep the malcontents under control through the generous application of official violence.

In sum, the merging of the public and private sectors is not merely a result of the growing complexity of technological society or a transition toward socialism; it is in large part the outcome of the realities of power and capitalist class interest.

Why Things Do Not Change Much

It is not quite accurate to presume that nonelites never win victories. The last century of intensive struggle between labor and management, continuing to this day and involving such groups as farm workers, hospital workers, teachers and white-collar employees, brought notable advances in the working conditions of millions.[15] But change, if not impossible within state-supported capitalism, is always limited by the overall imperatives of that system. Hence the lion's share of most domestic spending programs, even of those supposedly intended for the have-nots, goes to corporate enterprise.

At first, elites may oppose changes, not realizing the gains available to them. Thus the auto industry opposed safety features in automobiles until it realized that they could be installed as high-priced accessories which, under the new laws, the customer had to buy. And doctors vigorously opposed Medicare and Medicaid as steps toward "socialism" until they discovered gold in those programs. For with public funding available, the doctors

15. These advances have been exaggerated in the popular mind. Thus one hears complaints about plumbers and construction workers who make more than doctors, and sanitation workers who make more than college professors. Such complaints are unfounded. First, I am not sure why sanitation workers should not make more than college professors, since they work harder and at more unpleasant tasks. Second, as a matter of fact, they make substantially less. Even the well-paid "aristocracy of labor" in the construction field, given seasonal layoffs and assuming they can find work at all, earn about $10,000 in a good year. The average auto worker, backed by one of the stronger unions and operating in one of the better-paying labor markets, takes home less after years on the assembly line than the young college graduate who enters a management trainee program for the telephone company or the same auto industry. And income differences between managerial and professional occupations and working-class ones are widening rather than narrowing (see the *New York Times*, December 27, 1972). Furthermore, discussions on "how good labor has it" always focus on these better-paying jobs and ignore the forty million or more workers who earn subsistence or poverty-level wages, like the farm workers who make $2200 a year, and who face high injury rates, job insecurity, and chronic indebtedness as common conditions of life.

and the hospitals now were able to double and triple their fees, charging their patients amounts they would not have dared impose had the patient been the sole payer. The result is that medical expenses zoomed upward without a commensurate improvement in medical care—although certainly some elderly people now have assistance they would not have had earlier. *To pour more money into a service without a change in the market relations enjoyed by the suppliers is merely to make more public funds available to the suppliers without guaranteeing an improvement in the service.* It is somewhat ironic to credit capitalism with the ability to reform itself through gradual improvements when most of the reforms have been vehemently resisted by capitalist elites, and most of the problems needing reform have been caused or intensified by capitalism, and most of the actual programs end up primarily benefiting the capitalist producers.

Mr. Nixon was correct when he complained in late 1972 that we have thrown billions at our social problems with no results. But we can part company with him when he concludes, as do other conservatives, that since little can be done about social problems in the *present* system, then they are insoluble. For the elites who own this country, if wiping out widespread poverty and starvation entails changing the entire system and jeopardizing elite class positions, then better to have poverty and starvation.

Some of the more liberal elites believe our problems can be solved within the present system of state-supported capitalism, it being principally a matter of changing our "warped priorities." To be sure the priorities are warped: by the end of the 1960s, upper-income Americans were spending $2 billion a year on jewelry—more than was spent on housing for the poor—and no less than $3 billion on pleasure boating—a half billion more than what the fifty states spend on welfare. Over the years greater sums have been budgeted by the government for the development of the Navy's submarine-rescue vehicle than for occupational safety, public libraries and day-care centers combined.

The total expenses of the entire legislative branch and the judiciary branch and all the regulatory commissions combined constitute a little more than one half of 1 percent of the Pentagon's budget. More public monies are given away every year to the creditor class, the top one half of 1 percent of the population, in interest payments on public bonds, than are spent in five years on services to the bottom 20 percent. The "Tax

Reform Bill" of 1973, while abolishing a few of the less important tax shelters for wealthy individuals, provides new tax credits for the upper-income groups, including property-tax relief, and additional tax breaks for the oil industry that more than offset the minor reforms and will actually cost the Treasury about $600 million a year in lost revenues—a sum to be made up by cutting aid to the poor and embarking on still more regressive deficit spending.[16]

The government has any number of policy options which might be pursued: it could end its costly overseas military interventions, drastically cut its military expenditures, cease its underground nuclear testing, phase out its expensive space programs, eliminate the multibillion-dollar tax loopholes for corporations and rich individuals, increase taxes on industrial profits, cut taxes for lower- and middle-income groups, prosecute industries for pollution and for widespread monopolistic practices, end multibillion-dollar giveaways and legislate a guaranteed minimum income well above the poverty level. Government also could distribute to almost two million poor farmers the billions now received by rich agricultural producers, and it could engage in a concerted effort at conservation and enter directly into nonprofit production and ownership in the areas of health, housing, education and mass transportation.

Such moves have been urged, but in almost every instance government has pursued policies that have moved in an opposite direction. It is not enough to scold those who resist change as if they did so out of obstinance, perversity or ill-will; it is necessary to understand the dynamics of power and interest that make these policies persist in the face of all appeals and human needs to the contrary. Those who bemoan the "warped priorities" of our society assume that the present politico-economic system could produce a whole different set of effects. But the question is, *Why* have new and more humane priorities not been pursued? And the answer is twofold: first, because the realities of power do not allow for fundamental reform, and second, because the present politico-economic system could not sustain itself if such reforms were initiated. Let us take each of these in turn:

(1) Quite simply, those who have the interest in fundamental change have not the power, while those who have the power have not the interest. It is not that decision-makers have been unable to figure out the technical steps for change; it is that they

16. *New York Times* editorial, May 7, 1973.

oppose the things that change entails. The first intent of most politicians is not to fight for social change but to survive and prosper. Given this, they are inclined to respond positively not to group *needs* but to group *demands,* to those who have the resources to command their attention. In political life as in economic life, needs do not become marketable demands until they are backed by "buying power" or "exchange power" for only then is it in the "producer's" interest to respond. The problem for many unorganized citizens and workers is that they have few political resources of their own to exchange. For the politician, as for most people, the compelling quality of any argument is determined less by its logic and evidence than by the strength of its advocates. And the advocate is strong if the resources he controls are desired and needed by the politician. The wants of the unorganized public seldom become demands—that is, they seldom become imperatives to which political officials find it in their own interest to respond, especially if the changes needed would put the official on a collision course with those who own and control the resources of the society and who see little wrong with the world as it is.

(2) Most of the demands for fundamental change in our priorities are impossible to effect within the present system if that system is to maintain itself. The reason our labor, skills, technology and natural resources are not used for social need and egalitarian redistribution is that they are used for corporate gain. The corporations cannot build low-rent houses and feed the poor because their interest is not in social reconstruction but in private profit. For the state to maintain whatever "prosperity" it can, it must do so within the ongoing system of corporate investments. To maintain investments, it must guarantee high-profit yields. To make fundamental changes in our priorities, the state would have to effect major redistributions in income and taxation, cut business subsidies, end deficit spending and interest payments to the rich, redirect capital investments toward nonprofit or low-profit goals and impose severe and sometimes crippling penalties for pollution and monopolistic practices. But if the state did all this, the investment incentives would be greatly diminished, the risks for private capital would be too high, many companies could not survive and unemployment would reach disastrous heights. State-supported capitalism cannot exist without state support, without passing its immense costs and inefficiencies on to the public. The only way the state could

redirect the wealth of society toward egalitarian goals would be to exercise total control over capital investments and capital return, but that would mean, in effect, public ownership of the means of production—or *socialism*.

It is understandable then why appeals to fair play and exhortations for change do not bring the fundamental reallocations needed: quite simply, the problem of change is no easier for the haves than for the have-nots. Contrary to the admonitions of liberal critics, it is neither stupidity nor opaqueness which prevents those who own and control the property and the institutions of this society from satisfying the demand for change. To be sure, the established elites suffer their share of self-righteous stubbornness, but more often than not, meaningful changes are not embarked upon because they would literally threaten the survival of privileged interests; like most other social groups the elites show little inclination to commit class suicide.

What is being argued here is that, contrary to the view of liberal critics like Ralph Nader, the nation's immense social problems are not aberrant offshoots of a basically good and maybe even great society but endemic, inherent manifestations of the prevailing forms of class privilege, power and property.[17] As long as liberals proceed with an incorrect diagnosis, they will never come up with solutions. As long as we look for solutions within the very system that causes the problems, then we will continue to produce cosmetic, band-aid programs. The end result is shameful public poverty and shameless private wealth.

What the People Want

During the 1960s and early 1970s large numbers of women, poor people, middle-class professionals, Blacks, Chicanos, Native Americans and other racial minorities began voicing their opposition to many of the ongoing beliefs and practices of American society.

17. It is not that state-supported capitalism is the cause of every social ill in modern society but that capitalism and the capitalist state have no fundamental commitment to remedying social ills, despite their command over vast resources that might be directed toward such ends. And, from the evidence of past chapters, it might be argued that state-supported capitalism has been doing much to create, sustain and intensify the very conditions which breed social ills both at home and abroad.

BLACK PROTEST

It was probably no accident that in the postwar era the first challenges to the established ideology and to the image of "America, the beautiful" came from Black people. Forcibly brought to this country centuries ago as chattels for the sole purpose of economic exploitation, Blacks, after the Emancipation and over the generations, continued to suffer every exploitation, discrimination, terrorization and violence to body and spirit that White America was capable of inflicting. By the 1960s Blacks were saying publicly what many of them had always felt privately: that there is no justice for Black people in White America, that Blacks do not share equally in the progress our country is allegedly enjoying and that they must develop their own identities and consciousness and mobilize against White bosses, unions, landlords, merchants, police, government officials and the White power system in general.

As the Black protest grew, other groups began getting the message, and by the early 1970s Chicano, Native American, Puerto Rican and women's liberation groups were voicing similar indictments about the social roles and social conditions imposed upon them. And just as the Black protest started with demands for integration into the established system only to develop serious questions about the desirability of that goal ("Who wants to integrate into a burning house?"), so did the other protest groups begin to wonder whether piecemeal entry into the established structure would bring them any closer to a resolution of widespread social ills. When a Black becomes a corporation vice-president or a woman becomes a Navy pilot it is a net loss for all oppressed people, they argued, since corporate executives and Navy officers, whether White males or Black females, serve the interests of those in power and not those in need.

Today many Black leaders reject total integration as an unrealistic and even undesirable goal. Integration, they point out, usually means the selective absorption of talented Blacks into White-dominated institutions, with little substantive return to the Black masses. No ethnic group in the United States ever wanted total integration, Nathan Wright, Jr., notes: "All have asked simply for desegregation. Desegregation involves some integration as a means to an end but not as an end in itself."[18]

18. Nathan Wright, Jr., "The Crises Which Bred Black Power," in Floyd D. Barbow (ed.), *The Black Power Revolt* (Boston: Sargent, Porter, 1968), p. 117.

Desegregation is an important step forward, leading to the removal of legal and de facto barriers that loom as instruments of racial insult and oppression. Ultimately, though, the betterment of the Black people will come, radical Blacks say, not through piecemeal absorption into the White establishment but through a sweeping upheaval of the entire exploitative politico-economic system and the deliverance of the resources of power into the hands of the poor and the working people of all races—what we call social revolution.[19]

THE COUNTERCULTURE

By the late 1960s substantial numbers of middle-class youth began turning away from the elitist, authoritarian values of the dominant society and developing life styles of their own. Some have sought to "return to the earth," settling in rural places and eschewing the worst aspects of consumerism. They have shown a concern for ecology and an interest in people's arts and crafts, and an interest in cultural exotica, including Eastern religions, astrology, witchcraft, various occult phenomena and, of course, psychedelic drugs. The hip culture has experimented with "alternative institutions" such as cooperative day-care centers, free schools, people's stores, people's clinics, people's theaters, food cooperatives, underground newspapers, communal farms and urban collectives. Such endeavors often have been short-lived because somewhere along the line the hippy undertaking has had to contend with the high-profit, high-cost supplier, landlord or dealer.

Counterculture youth are highly critical of what they see as the older generation's life-styles: the preoccupation with personal advancement and material accumulation, the conformity of tastes and intolerance for deviant styles, the concern with appearances, formalities and middle-class niceties and the addiction to alcohol, suburbia, mortgages and medical drugs.[20] But

19. Julius Lester, "The Current State of Black America," *New Politics*, 10, June 1973, pp. 4–13. For an earlier statement see my "Assimilation and Counter-Assimilation: From Civil Rights to Black Radicalism," in Philip Green and Sanford Levinson (eds.), *Power and Community* (New York: Pantheon, 1969), pp. 173–194.

20. The real "drug problem," some counterculture people contend, is not among those who use pot and acid but among the millions of middle-aged Americans, mostly women, who consume large quantities of, and are often addicted to, amphetamines, barbiturates, and other stimulants and tranquillizers. The pushers are doctors; the profits for the drug industry are stupendous.

there is a real question whether the older generation is as stodgy and "up tight" and the youth as tolerant and "liberated" as the latter say. Perhaps too much has been made of the social significance of this cultural revolution; certainly it is not clear that changes in life-styles bring changes in the organization of the society. The hippy propensity to go "do your own thing" carries something of the same self-indulgent and privatized approach to life that is characteristic of middle-class "straights" and "squares." The unwillingness of some youths to fulfill the conventional work roles of the present society is understandable, since, as the youth say, most of our labor is for the benefit of exploiters and "rip-off artists." But even in the most decent society, some work is necessary, including that needed to produce food, shelter, clothing and medical care. Those in the drug culture who make a point of not working, having "tuned in, turned on, and dropped out," are directly or indirectly living off the labor of other people who cannot afford such exotic life choices. The resentment expressed by ordinary working people toward the hip culture, then, is not without some justification.[21]

Generally the counterculture attitude toward politics is one of withdrawal and cynicism. Since politics in all its manifestations, including radical politics, is deemed tainted, then the idea is to place a great distance between oneself and political issues. But in doing so one places a great distance between oneself and one's responsibility to others. As Michael P. Lerner observes:

If the goal of life is simply good vibes and pleasant experiences, serious struggle will inevitably be avoided. Why become involved in hassles? Struggle, we are told, is a bummer. It is true that as long as the rulers have the immense power of the police and the military at their disposal, those who struggle will face unpleasant consequences. Grooving on trees and flowers is less likely to lead one into trouble than demonstrating against the murder of Black Panthers. . . . Why not let everyone "do their own thing"? "Different strokes for different folks." This position very often leads to a political quietism that is hard to disturb.[22]

Yet the counterculture is not populated exclusively by mindless hedonists and escapists. Within its ranks are many who hold thoughtful and criticial views of the world and whose approach to things has a potentially subverting impact on the status quo.

21. See Michael P. Lerner, *The New Socialist Revolution: An Introduction to Its Theory and Strategy* (New York: Delta, 1973), pp. 151 ff., for a critical discussion of the counterculture.
22. *Ibid.*, p. 158.

Many are critical of the profiteering practices of this society. They question the prevailing concepts of ownership, expertise, exclusivity, success and institutional elitism. They are interested not only in what is to be done but the way it is done. They have called into question some of the basic images and values of capitalist culture and have offered a vision that competes with the world as we know it and as we believed it had to be.

THE NEW LEFT

Along with the growth of the counterculture and in reaction to the Vietnam war, there came a profound change in political consciousness among many concerned people on and off the campus. While some Americans accept U.S. military involvement overseas as necessary and good or are prone to swallow their doubts and place faith in their leaders ("My country, right or wrong"), the antiwar demonstrators reacted with growing anger and militancy against U.S. intervention in Vietnam and elsewhere. On campuses and in the streets, at draft boards and recruiting places, "the Movement confronted the war machine," using such tactics as teach-ins, mass demonstrations, sit-ins, draft resistance, disrupting traffic, blocking troop trains, trashing windows, taking over buildings and—on rare occasions—fire bombing and dynamiting defense and corporate establishments. Confronted with a government that violated the law of the land at will by conducting illegal and secretive wars in Indochina and infringing on the constitutional rights of dissenters at home, a government that committed heinous war crimes in Vietnam and elsewhere, the radical activists decided that civil disobedience was a justifiable course of action against such enormities.

The forms of direct and sometimes violent confrontation used by the protestors were the same ones used by working people in America for more than a century, and by other underdog people who have found established political channels hostile to their demands. Those in power seldom respond out of the goodness of their hearts, and when they make concessions, be it to workers, Blacks or student protestors, it is only because they feel they have to—that is, only when the concession serves as a means of taking the impetus out of the rebellion and avoiding still more serious confrontations. Lacking the kind of resources the wealthy and powerful use with such telling effect to influence public officeholders, underdog groups have had to resort to street actions that dramatize their wants, mobilize their ranks, increase their nuisance value and create an impetus toward change. The choice has been, as Marcuse notes, either to surrender to the power of the status quo or violate its law and order. To obey the law, in this context, is to submit to the prevailing order.[23]

Just as significantly, dissent has escalated not only in tactics but in the scope of its indictment. The Movement's attack against U.S. overseas interventions has expanded into an attack against the entire capitalist system, which radical protestors see as fostering poverty and repression at home and abroad.[24] Faith in "the American Way" is now seen as an invitation to hypocrisy. If we are so dedicated to peace, they ask, why are we so violent? If we are so prosperous, why is there such poverty? If we are so happy, why is there so much anxiety and discontent? If we are so free, why is there so much political repression? If we are so helpful toward other peoples, why are we so hated throughout the world? Serious doubts are raised about the whole quality of life in capitalist America: the adulation of "free enterprise," the glorification of military power, the mindless flag waving and the ruthless pursuit of success and money. Like the counterculture people, the New Leftists reject much of what conventional Americans cherish. By the early 1970s most of those who called themselves radicals were advocating the installation of an "anti-imperialist, anti-racist, anti-sexist, democratic socialism."

Whether or not this message won a wide currency, it did noticeably broaden the spectrum of American political opinion. If a few years ago most campus protestors thought of Vietnam as a "mistake," today that war is considered by many to be a manifestation of corporate and military imperialism. Not long ago pollution was considered "everybody's problem"; today ecologically minded students and other citizens are concluding that our politico-economic elites prefer to leave it that way. People, on campus and off, are concluding that America's problems result not from oversight and neglect but from the way power and property are organized.

23. Herbert Marcuse, *Essay on Liberation* (Boston: Beacon Press, 1969), pp. 69–70.
24. For an excellent statement on the theory and practice of the New Left, see Lerner, *The New Socialist Revolution*. One of the best collections of New Left writings and documents is Massimo Teodori, *The New Left: A Documentary History* (Indianapolis: Bobbs-Merrill, 1969).

WORKERS

Middle-class liberals emphasize that no one is more jingoistic, conservative, bourgeois, and racist than the American worker.[25] It follows that anyone who imagines that workers will become a force for revolutionary change is indulging in ideological reveries. But, in fact, a great many workers do not fit the Archie Bunker stereotype that middle-class people have of them. For the few hard hats who beat up peace demonstrators, there were many more workers, including teamsters, auto workers, hospital workers and farm laborers, who by 1970 were giving open support to campus strikes and other antiwar activities. Even as early as 1964, as a Gallup poll showed, working-class people were much less willing to escalate the war than college-graduate, upper-income people. Furthermore, most workers are not in well-paying craft unions. The many millions, including many women and Blacks, who do the dirtiest, lowest paid and sometimes most unhealthy work of the society have no illusions about having achieved middle-class affluence. While American workers have been portrayed as content and complacent, in reality the history of the struggle between labor and management in this country has often been grim and violent.[26] Today the struggle involves elements in the work force previously untouched by unionism—such as farm, hospital and clerical workers, teachers and other government employees. Rank and file rebellions against conservative union leadership have broken out among steel workers, auto workers and most successfully among coal miners—to the increasing discomfiture of both union bureaucrats and corporate managers. Struggles between labor and management now encompass not only the traditional issue of wages and hours but also questions of work safety, benefits, job security and managerial authority.

Young workers want less forced overtime and more time to live their own lives. They often wear their hair long, smoke pot and feel more common identity with the youth culture and with demonstrators than do older workers, and many of them are increasingly less awed and more critical of management and union leaders. Racist attitudes are still found among many White

25. These liberals ought to try talking to the average businessman.
26. For an excellent study of radicalism and militancy in the American labor movement see Jeremy Brecher, *Strike* (New York: Quick Fox, 1972); also Richard O. Boyer and Herbert M. Morais, *Labor's Untold Story* (New York: United Electrical, Radio and Machine Workers, 1972).

workers, beset as they are by fears that what little they have may be taken away by those who are not far behind, or not far enough behind. Yet the workers' attitudes on race are not much worse and are often better than those found among conservative middle-class people—certainly better than the attitudes shown by a number of prominent members of Congress. In many of the newer union movements there has been an integration of Black and White efforts seldom found in most areas of American life.

The struggles and protests of workers are usually reported unsympathetically if at all in the business-owned media, and their opinions and grievances are seldom recorded. But one thing seems certain: it is a grossly misleading stereotype to portray workers as bourgeois, conservative, racist flag-wavers who have neither the will nor the capacity to move against the injustices of this society—including the injustices they suffer themselves.

QUESTIONING THE STATUS QUO

Even within those most authoritarian of institutions, the Army and the prisons, one detects a growing restiveness. The Army desertion rate rose dramatically during the Vietnam war years. Overt expressions of opposition to the war, along with acts of insubordination and violence against superiors, became commonplace enough to cause a serious breakdown of discipline in Vietnam, a situation that was resolved only with the withdrawal of ground troops. More recently, among enlisted ranks within the Navy and the Air Force, the signs of protest and resistance are becoming difficult to overlook, and the "new volunteer army" is having trouble recruiting volunteers. Prison rebellions, hardly a new phenomenon in our history, are manifesting a political content not previously known, as radical and militant prisoners find increasingly sympathetic audiences among their fellow inmates.

Even among "the elite professionals," those whose first concern has been to make as much money as possible, one finds a shift in values and commitments. Among some younger members of the medical profession, for instance, there is a new inclination to rise above the plundering entrepreneurial impulses that characterize so many doctors and move toward more socially dedicated uses of medicine. Similar developments can be found within the law profession with the emergence of radical law collectives and the complaints of law school students about the conservative, property-oriented curricula imposed on them. And even among sedulous college professors one detects a little more willingness to question the high-handed measures of trustees and administrators, to democratize decision making at the department level and to entertain heretical ideas in the classroom.

The protestors and rebels are a minority, some people have argued, and they do not represent what the great bulk of average Americans want. These latter are against drastic change—as evidenced by the overwhelming mandate given to the conservative candidate in the 1972 presidential election. But how overwhelming was that mandate, and what actually is the state of opinion in the United States today? Richard Nixon was re-elected in 1972 without too much love or enthusiasm by less than 33 percent of those eligible to vote. Another 21 percent or so voted for McGovern, while 45 percent, representing a disproportionate number of the socially deprived and alienated, stayed home. Nixon chose to interpret his victory as an endorsement of his conservative policies. But most of the pre-election polls showed strong public disapproval of his handling of inflation, unemployment, pollution and other domestic problems.[27] A post-election Harris poll in January 1973 and a subsequent Harris poll in April indicated that, by majorities of more than two to one, citizens favored increased spending to (a) curb air and water pollution, (b) aid education and (c) help the poor. At the same time, they were *against* increased spending for highways, the military and the space program. By 72 to 20 percent they judged that "too much money is going into wars and defense." By 80 to 13 percent they felt the tax system was set up to favor the rich at the expense of the average person. As of 1973, *on every major policy issue, the electorate seemed to be in favor of moving in a direction quite opposite to the one taken by the Nixon administration.*[28]

27. Support for Nixon was strongest on the issue of "ending" the Vietnam war and the rapprochement with China and the Soviet Union. Nixon did appeal to that conventional middle-class segment of Whites who were anxious about Black demands and who hated the counterculture and the student demonstrators. Also many voters saw McGovern as someone who was too weak and indecisive to be President. See Michael Parenti and Catherine MacKinnon, "The Nixon Victory and Beyond," *New Politics*, 10, Winter 1973, pp. 4–8.

28. As reported in the *New York Post*, January 8, 1973, and the *Burlington Free Press*, April 12, 1973. The large majority willing to "help the poor" were thinking of programs other than welfare. Increased spending for welfare, seen by many as being nothing but "handouts," was rejected by two to one. Public opinion in the

How can we speak of most government policies as being products of the democratic will? What democratic will demanded that Washington be honeycombed with high-paid lobbyists and corporate lawyers who would spend their time raiding the public treasury on behalf of rich clients? When was the public consulted on tideland oil leases, Alaskan oil leases, bloated defense contracts, agribusiness subsidies and tax write-offs? When did the American people insist on having unsafe, overpriced drugs and foods circulate unrestricted and an FDA that protects rather than punishes the companies that market such products? When did they urge the government to help the gas, electric and telephone companies to overcharge the public? When did the voice of the people clamor for a multibillion-dollar space program that fattened corporate contractors and satisfied the curiosity of some astronomers and scientists while leaving the rest of us still more burdened by taxes and deprived of necessary services here on earth? What democratic will decreed that we destroy the Cambodian countryside between 1969 and 1971 in a bombing campaign that was conducted without the consent or even the knowledge of Congress and the public? And what large sector of public opinion demanded that the government intervene secretly in Laos with U.S. Marines in 1969 or financially sustain a war of Portuguese colonial oppression in Africa?

Far from giving their assent, ordinary people have had to struggle to find out what is going on. And to the extent that a popular will has been registered, it has been demonstrably in the opposite direction, against the worst abuses and most blatant privileges of plutocracy, against the spoilage of the environment and the plunder of the treasury, against the use of government power to serve corporate conglomerates, and against military intervention in other countries.

Millions of Americans, of course, are still committed to the acquisitive, competitive values discussed in Chapter Three. Millions still live with a fear of equality and a scarcity psychology that pits each against the other. Much of this sentiment is reenforced by the simple fact that the system obliges us to compete against each other in order to survive and in order to live with any modicum of comfort and security. But despite these powerful conditioning forces, despite the secret actions and

aftermath of the Watergate scandal showed a great deal of public disillusionment with our political leadership and institutions. See *New York Times*, August 13, 1973.

manipulations used by the state to maintain the status quo and despite elitist control over most of the resources of power and over the institutions and information of this society, the American people are becoming increasingly aware of the exploitative and unjust imperatives of the ongoing system. Opinion surveys throughout 1972 and 1973 noted the marked decline in "faith" that the public, including many middle Americans, felt for its political and economic institutions, a development troublesome enough to evoke alarmed comments from business leaders and their counterparts in government. Ordinary Americans are not as oblivious to their own needs as are their leaders. They suspect that they are being victimized as wage earners, tenants, home owners, taxpayers, commuters and consumers. And there is a spirit of protest growing among them even as they feel uncomfortable about the more radical protestors.

Although most college campuses quieted down by 1973, the new political consciousness has not been put to rest. In 1973, for the first time in American history, a nationwide consumer boycott took place against inflationary meat prices. In that same year strikes occurred in many major industries; 200,000 people marched on Washington on Inauguration Day to demand Nixon's impeachment; sit-ins and demonstrations occurred on numerous campuses—although few of these were reported by a business-owned media that kept telling us we wanted to return to the 1950s. Today, more than ever, people are questioning the status quo.

Upward from Capitalism

More than half a century ago the great sociologist Max Weber wrote: "The question is: How are freedom and democracy in the long run at all possible under the domination of highly developed capitalism?"[29] That question is still with us. And the answer suggested in this book is that freedom and democracy have at best a highly tenuous and marginal existence in capitalist society. The political system will belong to the people only when the resources of power belong to them, enabling them to effect their democratic will at all levels of private and public institutional life. This will entail a struggle of momentous scope against the corporate elites that now control our labor and our politics.

29. *From Max Weber: Essays in Sociology* (New York: Oxford University Press, 1958), ed. H. H. Gerth and C. Wright Mills.

The purpose will be not to replace those at the top with others but to demonstrate that we do not need anyone *on top,* that there are no immutable sociological imperatives that necessitate the growth of gargantuan government and stratified, bureaucratized, authoritarian institutions and that those who are involved in the life activities of an institution should have command of its resources. In a democratic socialist social system, the factories, mills, mines, offices, educational institutions, newspapers, hospitals, etc., will not be privately owned for private gain but will be controlled by and for their clients and workers. That is the goal toward which our efforts should be directed.

What is important under socialism is not only whether something is publicly owned and financed but the *purpose* or goals toward which production is directed and the way priorities are set and decisions made. The commitment is, or should be, to communal, collective and responsible decision making and toward the elimination of poverty and pollution, the end of imperialism, the equalization of life chances, the bettering of the lives of millions of needy working people.[30] Once the creative energies of people are liberated from the irrational social purposes of a capitalist system, the potentialities for human advancement and individual initiative will be greatly increased, as has happened in a number of Third World countries that have liberated themselves from imperialism. Under the present system we are taught passivity, consumerism, spectatorism, isolation and incompetence. Our energies often are directed into specialized and mindless tasks for the production of a glut of gadgets and gimmicks that no one really asked for. We are taught that the controlling decisions over our lives must remain in the hands of those "above" us, those who claim to know better—or else "there would be chaos." There are people who insist that worker control of factories is "impracticable," yet worker-control systems have been set up in China, Sweden and even in a few factories in the United States (although in the latter two nations the profits remain in the hands of the corporate owners), with

30. In the view of many socialists, especially those identified with the radical movement in America, public ownership of the means of production for the purpose of building an authoritarian, hierarchical society with substantial income inequalities, dominated by a bureaucratic elite as in the USSR, is not socialism, or, at best, it is a tragically misshaped form of socialism, one that might provide a fairly decent minimum standard of social services for all its citizens, including free education and good medical care, but that denies them the opportunities for personal initiative and cooperative control over the conditions of work, study, community and environment and over the products of their minds and their labor and over the larger policies of their nation.

workers devising their own job assignments, teaching each other new skills, setting their own work paces, making managerial decisions, controlling budgets and production schedules, etc. The results have been remarkable for worker morale and production efficiency, but in capitalist nations such innovations are potentially dangerous to the owning class, for once workers realize they do not need management to command them, they may begin to question why the profits must go to the corporate owners, who contribute nothing to production.

There are people who cannot imagine an alternative university system and are frightened at the prospect of changing the present structure, which gives nearly total power to successful businessmen who serve as oligarchic trustees while the rest of us remain powerless dependents. Yet there already exist more rationally and democratically organized institutions of learning. There are people who cannot imagine that hospitals can be organized in any way that would diminish the elitist, authoritarian, money-making role of the head doctors and allow staff and patients to play a real part in decision making, openly criticizing mistakes and collectively working for improvements. Yet such hospitals, and quite good ones, exist in other parts of the world.[31] What a pathetic failure of the political imagination that some of our professional people cannot, or dare not, imagine more sensible, efficient and democratic ways of organizing our social, political and economic institutions. Out of a fear that their class and professional privileges might be challenged, some people resist all equalizing changes and commit themselves to living unexamined lives.

But those of us who have some feeling for social justice and liberation must educate ourselves about the nature of the politico-economic system we live in (hopefully this book has been a step in that direction). We must liberate our political imaginations and learn about alternative forms of social organization and alternative social values. We must confront and engage our peers in the kind of dialogue that heightens our awareness and helps us free ourselves and each other from the elitist, hierarchical values that imprison us, including the bigotry toward working-class people and the sexism, racism and fear of equality we have all been taught. We must in our places of work and community organize politically, learn to work cooperatively, engage in direct action, demonstrations, strikes, boycotts and

31. See Joshua Horne, *Away With All Pests* (New York: Monthly Review Press, 1971).

picketing when issues of social justice are involved; and we should continue to raise troublesome questions about why un-answerable executive power must be exercised over us on behalf of the few.

Finally we must educate others, through the use of what limited political resources we have, to the unjust and undemo-cratic features of state-supported capitalism. People who insist on being presented with a blueprint for change before they move an inch are probably not very interested in change. There is no finished blueprint for the new society. The forms of challenge and change and the alternative community will arise from the actions of the people—as is already happening. With time and with struggle, as the possibility of a better social life grows stronger, people will become increasingly intolerant of the monumental abuses and injustices of the present socioeconomic system. The day will come, as it came in social orders of the past, when those who seem invincible will be shaken from their pinnacles and a new, humane and truly democratic society will begin to emerge.

Index

Bayley, David H., 114
Bazelon, David, 247
Beard, Charles A., 46, 49–50, 60
Beard, Mary R., 60
Becker, Theodore, 115, 122, 129, 131
Bendiner, Robert, 204
Bennett, Fay, 103
Benson, Robert S., 99
Berg, Ivar, 95
Berle, A. A., Jr., 15
Bigart, Homar, 94
Bishop, Hillman, 278
Black, Hugo, 260
Blackburn, Sara, 131
Black protest, 122–24, 286–87
Blakkan, Renee, 100, 108
Bloomberg, Ray, 117
Blumenfeld, Ralph, 115, 118
Boland, Edward, 98
Bolling, Richard, 194
Boyer, Richard O., 291
Branch, Taylor, 88, 92, 107
Brazil, 82
Brecher, Jeremy, 291
Brookings Institution, 78
Brown, Clarence, 199
Brown, Robert E., 46
Browning, Frank, 123
Brown v. *Board of Education*, 264, 268–69
Buckley, James, 182
Budget Bureau, 243
Bureaucracy, 227–48. *See also* Government
Bureau of the Mines, 102, 239–40
Burger, Warren, 264–65, 266
Burkhalter, Everett, 194
Burnett, Carol, 171
Burnham, Walter Dean, 157, 158, 161
Burns, James McGregor, 63
Business Advisory Council, 243

Caldwell, Earl, 174
Cambodia, 228, 294
Campbell, Angus, 163
Campbell, Joseph, 238
Campbell, Philip, 217
Capitalism, 9, 28, 295–98; and government, 279–81; concerns of, 17, 19, 285; laissez-faire, 41
Caplovitz, David, 14, 101
Carter v. *Carter Coal Co.*, 254
Cassidy, Joseph, 82
Cater, Douglass, 147, 189, 196, 238
Caudill, Harry M., 102

Central Intelligence Agency, 125, 228, 231
Chevigny, Paul, 114
Chile, 228, 245–46
Cirino, Robert, 167, 168, 169, 170, 171
Civil Aeronautics Board, 70, 240
Civilian Conservation Corps, 64. *See also* New Deal
Civil rights, 53, 67, 269; acts, 269
Clark, F. G., 16
Clark, Joseph C., 194, 195, 203, 204
Clark, Joseph S., 194, 204
Clark, Kenneth B., 91–92
Clark, Tom, 259
Cleaver, Eldridge, 126
Clines, Francis X., 94
Cloward, Richard A., 63, 64, 65
Clune, William H., 97
Cochran, Bert, 76, 77, 79, 80
Coffin, Tristram, 80
Cohen, Jerry S., 69, 183, 236
Coleman, John, 150
Coles, Nick, 116
Coles, Robert, 12
Colfax, J. David, 128
Colson, Charles, 215
Commerce Department, 242
Committee to Re-elect the President, 177
Communist party, 259, 260
Congo, 228
Congress, 151, 153, 154, 182, 193; and conflicts of interest, 199–200; and foreign policy, 220–21; and government agencies, 234–39; and special interests, 202–03, 222–23, 228, 231, 232, 233; and the Supreme Court, 253–54, 255, 256; committees of, 4, 194, 195–96; creation of, 48, 49; secrecy in, 197–98; seniority system of, 194–95; workings of, 200, 202–07
Conkin, Paul K., 63, 65, 67
Conservatives, 36, 169–70. *See also* Political parties
Constitution, 1, 249, 250, 252–56; and civil liberties, 53–54; framers of the, 49–53; framing of the, 43–47, 48, 52–53, 193
Consumerism, 30
Consumer protection, 100–01
Conte, Silvio, 70
Cook, Fred C., 231
Coolidge, Calvin, 57–58
Coons, John E., 97

Copeland, Lammot duPont, 247
Corporations: and research, 20, 71; and the military, 76–79; control of, 15–17, 25–29; criminality of, 111–12; influence of, 22–23, 219, 228, 244–46, 266, 277, 280–81; overseas investments of, 80–83, 86; productivity of, 19–21; profits of, 17, 19, 21–23, 74–75, 80–81, 284–85; taxation of, 73, 89
Corruption, 190–91, 206
Corwin, R. D., 75
Counterculture, 287–89
Courts, 120–21, 129–30. *See also* Law; Supreme Court
Cowen, Peter, 190
Crime, 110–11, 123–25
Cronkite, Walter, 174
Cuba, 211, 228
Curtis, Thomas, 176

Dahl, Robert A., 142, 263, 268, 272, 275
Dahrendorf, Ralf, 272, 278
Daley, Richard, 142
Daum, Susan M., 103
Davidson, Carl, 94
Davis, Benjamin, 148
Dean, John W., 215
Debs v. *United States*, 257
Defense Department, 202, 241; spending, 78, 80, 83–84. *See also* Military
Delgado, José M., 135
Democracy, 38–39, 271–72
Democratic National Committee, 170
Democratic party, 143–44, 195. *See also* Political parties
Dennis et al. v. *United States*, 259
Der Stern, 178
Dickson, Paul, 221
Dietsch, Robert W., 243
Dillon, Douglas, 73
Di Palma, Giuseppe, 158
Dissenters, 289–90; in office, 151–52; repression of, 122–37, 149, 256–62
Doctors, 104–05, 281–82, 292
Dolbeare, Kenneth M., 234, 235
Domhoff, G. William, 16, 103, 180, 183
Dominican Republic, 180–81, 228
Donner, Frank, 123
Donovan, John C., 180, 221
Douglas, Paul, 99, 195

Douglas, William O., 241, 250–51, 260, 265, 266
Downie, Leonard, Jr., 112
Drugs, 119–20, 287–88
Duverger, Maurice, 148

Eastland, James, 199
Economic Development Administration, 96
Economy: regulation of the, 70–72, 74–76. *See also* Government
Ecuador, 246
Edelman, Murray J., 234, 235
Edsall, Thomas B., 190
Education: federal funds for, 96–97
Edwards, Richard C., 25
Ehrenreich, John, 104
Eisenhower, Dwight D., 76, 86, 220, 227
Elections, 38, 141, 149–50, 154–55, 185; participation in, 157, 160–61, 162–65. *See also* Political campaigns; Voting
Elites, 32–35, 53, 272. *See also* Special interest groups
Ellsberg, Daniel, 125, 174
Emerson, Thomas I., 258
Employment, 13–14, 95
Ennis, Bruce J., 138
Environment. *See* Pollution
Epstein, Benjamin, 170
Epstein, Jason, 128
Ervin, Frank, 136
Escobedo v. *Illinois*, 264
Espionage Act, 257
Eszterhas, Joe, 131
Eulau, Heinz, 161

Fallows, James M., 72, 153, 184, 194, 217, 238
Farkas, Ruth, 215
Farmers Home Administration, 95–96
Farrand, Max, 44, 45, 49, 249
Federal Aviation Administration, 228, 241
Federal Bureau of Investigation, 122, 123, 124, 125, 132
Federal Communications Commission, 71, 241
Federalist papers, 47
Federal Power Commission, 241
Federal Register, 232
Federal Reserve: Act, 62; Board, 241

Lewis, Anthony, 241
Lewis, John L., 66
Liberals, 35, 36–37, 86, 170. *See also* Political parties
Lindblom, Charles, 278
Lippmann, Walter, 143
Lipset, Seymour M., 161
Lipsitz, Lewis, 162
Lobbyists, 216, 217, 231, 232; and congressmen, 198–99, 202–03; influence of, 186–90, 196–97, 231. *See also* Special interest groups
Lochner v. *New York*, 252
Lockard, Duane, 217, 233
Locker, Michael, 181
Long, Russell, 72, 182, 185, 199
Louisiana State College, 132
Lowi, Theodore, 242
Lundberg, Ferdinand, 14, 87
Lynd, Staughton, 52
Lyons, Richards D., 106

Maass, Arthur, 241
McAffee, Cathy, 79
McAteer, J. David, 102
McCarthy, Eugene, 83
McConnell, Grant, 69, 188, 196, 234, 235, 242, 244, 247
McCormack, John, 198
McCoy, Charles A., 272
McDonald, Forrest, 46
Macdonald, Ross, 105, 241
McGinnis, Joe, 146
McGovern, George, 150–51, 293
McGuire, James, 123
MacKinnon, Catherine, 293
McLaughlin, Andrew C., 44
McMahan, Ian, 213
McMaster, John Bach, 45
McNamara, Robert, 16
Madden, Richard, 204
Madison, James, 42, 44, 47, 49
Magdoff, Harry, 81, 82, 86
Marcuse, Herbert, 290
Marine, Gene, 131
Mark, Vernon, 136
Marshall, Thurgood, 266
Marx, Karl, 5, 7
Mason, George, 49, 53
Mayer, Jean, 95
Mayes, Harvey, 129
Means, Gardner C., 15
Media: entertainment, 171–73; news, 167–71; ownership of the, 178; repression of the, 173–74, 176–77. *See also* Press

Medical care, 104–05, 281–82
Meiklejohn, Alexander, 261
Mendeloff, John, 87
Mendelsohn, Harold, 114
Mercer, John, 48
Mermelstein, David, 73, 211, 213, 247
Merriam, Charles E., 160
Metcalf, Lee, 71, 217, 232
Meyers, Joel, 137
Miles, Michael, 128
Miliband, Ralph, 16, 181, 182
Military, 122, 230–31, 289, 292; aid abroad, 83–86; contracts, 78; spending, 76–80, 91, 107, 231. *See also* Defense Department
Mill, John Stuart, 261
Miller, Herman P., 87
Miller, John C., 44
Miller, S. M., 87
Miller, Samuel F., 251
Millins, Rita, 103
Mills, C. Wright, 17, 180, 295
Mills, Wilbur, 196
Minority groups. *See* Special interest groups
Minority parties. *See* Third parties
Minor v. *Happersett*, 254
Mintz, Morton, 69, 103, 183, 236
Miranda v. *Arizona*, 264
Mitchell, Broadus, 51
Mitchell, John, 132, 173
Mitchell, Louise Pearson, 51
Mitford, Jessica, 128, 258
Mitgang, Herbert, 120
Morais, Herbert M., 291
Morehead v. *New York*, 254
Morris, Gouverneur, 48–49
Movement. *See* New Left
Murray, Vernon, 115, 122, 129, 131

Nabach, Joseph, 28
Nader, Ralph, 97, 110, 111, 205, 241, 285
Nagel, Stuart, 115, 117
National Association of Manufacturers, 189
National Industrial Recovery Act, 63. *See also* New Deal
National Petroleum Council, 243
National Security Agency, 231
Nelson, Garrison, 197, 204
Neuro-Research Foundation, 136
Neustadt, Richard E., 272
Nevins, Allan, 59
New Deal, 63–68

Thompson, Edward, 279
Thurow, Lester, 87
Time, Inc. v. *Hill,* 256
Tocqueville, Alexis de, 179
Torgoff, Stephen, 94, 174
Transportation: Department, 241;
 funds for, 99–100
Truman, Harry, 211
Trussel, Douglas, 217
Tugwell, Rexford, 67

Udall, Stewart, 239
Unger, Irwin, 52, 62, 66, 279
United Fruit Company, 83
U.S. Army. *See* Military
U.S. Government. *See* Government
U.S. Steel Corporation, 21, 106
United States v. *Butler,* 250
United States v. *Caldwell,* 265
Universities, 26; and defense
 research, 78–79
Urban renewal, 98–99
Utilities, 71, 188, 232

Vanik, Charles, 150
Veblen, Thorstein, 22, 85
Verba, Sidney, 164
Vietnam War, 197, 211, 228, 230, 289,
 290, 292
Vinson, Fred M., 259
VISTA program, 95
Voloshen, Nathan, 198
Vonnegut, Kurt, Jr., 35
Voting, 49, 157–62; as an irrational
 response, 162–65. *See also* Elections

Wage-price freeze, 74–75. *See also*
 Economy; Government
Waldron, Martin, 187, 190
Walton, Mary, 190
Warren, Earl, 263–64

Watergate, 124–25, 191, 294
Watkins, Robert, 199
Watson, Arthur K., 215
Watson, Thomas, 16
Wealth, 14–16, 25, 180, 182
Weber, Max, 227, 295
Weinstein, James, 61
Weisberg, Barry, 72, 107
Weisbord, Burton A., 97
Weisskopf, Thomas E., 25
Welfare, 91, 92, 94
Welles, Gideon, 58
Wertheimer, Alan, 164
White, Orion F., Jr., 233
Whitehead, Clay, 176
Whitten, Leslie, 174
Wickard v. *Filburn,* 255
Wiener, Frederick B., 261
Wiesner, Jerome, 77
Wiley, Brad, 63
Williams, John J., 70, 82
Williams, Raymond, 279
Williams, William Appleman, 7, 28
Wilson, Charles, 16
Wilson, Woodrow, 62, 186, 211
Winter-Berger, Robert, 114, 186, 190,
 198
Wise, David, 174, 177, 231
Wiseman, Frederic, 139
Wolfe, Alan, 122, 272
Wolman, Harold, 99
Workers. *See* Labor
Worker safety, 101–04
World Bank, 81
Wright, Frank, 184
Wright, Nathan, Jr., 286

Yates et al. v. *United States,* 260

Ziegler, Ron, 177
Zwick, David R., 153, 184, 194, 217,
 238